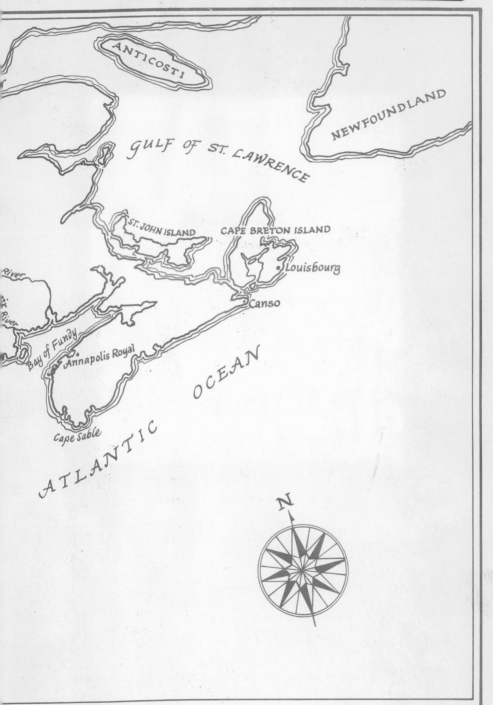

ANTICOSTI

NEWFOUNDLAND

GULF OF ST. LAWRENCE

ST. JOHN ISLAND

CAPE BRETON ISLAND

•Louisbourg

River

River

Canso

Bay of Fundy

•Annapolis Royal

ATLANTIC OCEAN

Cape Sable

ATLANTIC

N

WILLIAM SHIRLEY

*King's Governor
of
Massachusetts*

The Institute of Early American History and Culture is sponsored jointly by the College of William and Mary and Colonial Williamsburg, Incorporated. Publication of this book has been assisted by a grant from the Lilly Endowment, Inc.

WILLIAM SHIRLEY

Portrait by Thomas Hudson. Courtesy of Mrs. Norman J. Marsh. On loan
to the Wadsworth Athenaeum, Hartford, Connecticut.

WILLIAM SHIRLEY

King's Governor
of
Massachusetts

By
JOHN A. SCHUTZ

PUBLISHED FOR THE
Institute of Early American History and Culture
AT WILLIAMSBURG, VIRGINIA

BY

The University of North Carolina Press · Chapel Hill

Manufactured in the United States of America

PRINTED BY THE SEEMAN PRINTERY, DURHAM, N. C.

Preface

In 1729, just two years before William Shirley arrived at Boston, politics in Massachusetts were inflamed by a desperate contest between the Governor and legislature. Their dispute became so bitter that it was taken to London where Jonathan Belcher, an outspoken critic of the Governor, presented the legislature's case to the ministry. Before the issue was settled, the Governor died, and Belcher was named his successor.

The pattern was familiar. In other years, succession to the governorship resulted from political battles in Boston which were settled by appeals to the London authorities. Customarily, a new governor was chosen by London politicians who consulted their supporters in commerce and agriculture with a hope of satisfying the business community. Political leaders in Massachusetts had only an indirect influence upon the selection of their chief executive; hence they were quick to test each new governor's ability to serve their interests and exert appropriate pressure upon him whenever their wishes were denied. Sooner or later sufficient opposition built up to force his recall.

Since political feuding with the governor was commonplace, that official's tenure of office was as short as his life was unhappy; Shute, Dummer, Burnet, and Belcher left the governorship after bitter crises. But with Shirley's accession something happened. For fifteen years, 1741-56, his system of political alliances brought an era of relative good feeling. Legislative business during some years was so placid that outwardly, at least, little seems to have disturbed the internal unity of the colony, and when Shirley was recalled in 1756, his departure was generally regretted. What kind of man accomplished this phenomenon of stable government in the history of colonial Massachusetts? What preparation had he for the governorship? The present study will attempt to answer these questions, but it is primarily an analysis of Shirley's career as an Anglo-American politician. It will investigate the sources of his power and his methods for preserving authority.

In order to avoid disturbing the reader by oddities of eighteenth-century usage, I have modernized spelling and punctuation in the quotations whenever it was possible to do this without altering the meaning of the material.

This book could hardly have been completed without the generous assistance of the California Institute of Technology, Whittier College, the Henry E. Huntington Library, and the Danforth Foundation. They made it possible for me to undertake the enormous task of bringing the Shirley documents together.

To the staffs of the Massachusetts State Archives and the Massachusetts Historical Society and, most particularly, the Huntington Library in San Marino, I am indebted for invaluable service. My thanks go also to the librarians of the Boston Public Library, the New-York Historical Society, the New York Public Library, the Library of Congress, the Connecticut Historical Society, the Connecticut State Library, the Rhode Island State Archives, the William L. Clements Library, the University of California at Los Angeles, the Public Archives of Canada; and in England, the Public Record Office, the British Museum, and the Royal Archives at Windsor.

In writing this biography, I have leaned so heavily upon my friends—both personal and historical—that I would like to think of them as coauthors. To the late George Arthur Wood, whose incomplete biography of Shirley appeared many years ago and who died before the second volume could be finished, I am deeply grateful for listing many manuscript sources. To Walter Lewis, Maud O'Neil, Rosemary Di Salvo, and Beach

Langston, I owe a debt of appreciation for stimulation and encouragement. To Professors Frank J. Klingberg, William Warren Sweet, Malcolm Freiberg, and Douglass Adair, I must express my thanks for their advice in solving many points of research. And to Margaret Hesketh-Williams, Marion Chevalier, Norma Cuthbert, Mary Isabel Fry, and Benjamin Whitten, who were always ready to order books and films, I offer my special thanks. Near the completion of my study I was fortunate to locate living members of the Shirley-Erving family. James G. King, Erving Pruyn, Cornelia King Marsh (Mrs. Norman J.), and John Erving Cooper have generously permitted me to examine family portraits and manuscripts of great importance to my study. Lastly, I wish to express my appreciation to James M. Smith, Frederick A. Hetzel, and E. James Ferguson of the Institute of Early American History and Culture for their help in the various steps of preparing the manuscript. Their assistance again impressed upon me what a great historian once said of an editor: "He is a man of virtue and devotion who rarely gets the praise he deserves from the author or public." My sincere thanks to these three editors.

JOHN A. SCHUTZ
Los Angeles, California

Contents

Illustrations

WILLIAM SHIRLEY

King's Governor
of
Massachusetts

I

Newcastle's Friend

THE SHIRLEYS were an old Sussex family that was related to other English families more distinguished than themselves. Their cousins were Onslows, Essexes, and Walsinghams; their nieces and nephews were Godmans, Westerns, and Stapleys. They owned estates of various sizes in the county, but due to the custom of primogeniture the eldest sons of the Shirley lines possessed the landed wealth as well as the accompanying titles. The William Shirleys, descendents of Thomas Shirley and Elizabeth Stapley Shirley, were a younger branch that had little more than the family name and connections.

Upon the restoration of the monarchy in 1660, the first William Shirley moved to London to engage in trade. His judgment soon proved itself, and in less than three decades he owned a thriving business in textiles and promoted his eldest son, William II, to a marriage with their distant cousin, Elizabeth Godman, heiress of a Sussex gentleman.

On December 2, 1694, Elizabeth gave birth to an heir to the William Shirley name and fortune.[1] Even before the youngster was old enough to attend the Merchant Taylors' School, the family decided that William III would be prepared for college and a profession.[2] Their plans were so carefully formed that

1. The Bible notations of the family's vital statistics are reprinted in the Colonial Society of Massachusetts, *Publications,* 8 (Boston, 1895-in progress), 243-44. Other data on the family are contained in Evelyn Shirley, *Stemmata Shirleiana* (Westminster, 1873), 305, 317-22. The eighth child, Elizabeth, followed them to Boston in 1733. The children were born in the following succession: Frances (1720-1745), William (1721-1755), Elizabeth (1722-1790), Judith (1723-1754), Harriet (1724-1802), John (1725-1755), Thomas (1727-1800), Maria (1729-1816), Ralph (1734-1737).

2. John and J. A. Venn, eds., *Alumni Cantabrigienses* (Cambridge, Eng., 1922-in progress), IV, pt. 1, 67; William Shirley II (1667-1701) will, Somerset House, dated Mar. 15, 1699; William C. Farr, ed., *Merchant Taylors' School* (Oxford, 1929), 42, 51.

not even the deaths of his paternal grandfather and father interrupted his education; he studied successively at Pembroke College, Cambridge, and Inner Temple. Upon the death of his grandfather Godman in 1717, William inherited the Sussex estate of Ote Hall and a sum of money. He used part of the bequest to purchase a clerkship in the London government, and not long afterward he was admitted to the bar.[3]

About this time, he married a London heiress, Frances Barker, whom he made the lady of Ote Hall. His inheritance now included a rambling country mansion and almost ten thousand pounds—he signed his name "William Shirley, Esquire." His resources of family and wealth enabled him to gain influence in both city and county affairs, but he had cultivated expensive tastes during his college days, speculated heavily, and with the depression of 1721, disaster upon disaster wiped out his inheritance. The meager rents of Ote Hall were barely sufficient to meet his mounting expenses. By 1731 his wife had given birth to three sons, William, John, and Thomas, and five daughters, Elizabeth, Frances, Harriet, Judith, and Maria. Worry over their welfare and his inability to improve the income he derived from his rent rolls and law practice pressed him harder each year until he and Frances began searching for a better way to solve their problems.[4]

Relatives advised Shirley to try his luck in America, both as a lawyer and a public official, and recommended that his best approach was to seek the patronage of the Duke of Newcastle, a dispenser of colonial offices and a county aristocrat of Sussex. Through friends in Newcastle's household, Shirley secured an audience with the Duke, with whom he had been acquainted since youth. They were nearly the same age, and Newcastle, aware of Shirley's political and personal merits, readily promised him a colonial appointment whenever there was a suit-

3. Shirley was admitted to Inner Temple Oct. 23, 1713, and called to the bar July 3, 1720, Inner Temple Records; Shirley held a clerkship in the city of London from Mar. 11, 1717, until Nov. 24, 1719, MSS of the Corporation of London.

4. Percy S. Godman, *Some Account of the Family of Godman* (London, 1897), 29, 49-50; *Sussex Archaeological Collections relating to the History and Antiquities of the County* (Oxford and Sussex, 1848-1934), XIX, 61-70 and XXXVI, 24, 43-44.

able vacancy. But he warned Shirley that patronage depended upon British politics and that months might pass before he would be favored. In the meantime, it would be well for him to practice law in Boston and manage the local business of his London friends. Newcastle offered to write a strong letter soliciting the favor of the governor of Massachusetts, Jonathan Belcher. Newcastle's endorsement, itself a substantial accomplishment, enabled Shirley to secure numerous letters of introduction from merchants, visiting Americans, and members of Parliament. When all was ready in the mid-summer of 1731, the Shirleys took the stage to the coast and embarked on their voyage to Boston.

I

On the evening of the family's arrival Boston was crowded with people. Smoke from the wood fires of an October afternoon hung in the cool air, and tradesmen were closing shop for the night. The hurry of the last-minute business swirled around the carriages which took the Shirleys up the hill to an inn. Leaving Frances and a servant in charge of the children, Shirley hastened to the Governor's mansion and presented his letters to the tall, red-complexioned Belcher: one from Belcher's son Jonathan, whom Shirley had befriended in London, and another from the Duke of Newcastle. The Duke's letter introduced "Mr. William Shirley, a very sensible man, and a friend and neighbor of mine in Sussex, who was bred to the law, in which he is very well skilled, going to New England to settle and to follow his profession there. I . . . recommend him to your protection . . . which I shall acknowledge as a particular obligation."[5] Belcher was sufficiently impressed to invite the newcomer to dinner.

As the two men sat in the Governor's beautiful mansion the next evening, Shirley sensed that Belcher was taking his measure, testing the strength of his ties with Newcastle and the London merchants and lawyers. At one point, purposely

5. Newcastle to Belcher, Aug. 17, 1731, Colonial Office Papers, Ser. 325, XXXVI, 307, Public Record Office; *Belcher Papers* (Massachusetts Historical Society, *Collections*, 6th Ser., vols. 6-7 [Boston, 1893-1894]), I, 20-21, 25, 40, 44, 60. Hereafter cited as *Belcher Papers*.

exaggerating his political connections, he pretended to divulge confidentially his expectations for patronage and a law practice —probably with just enough truth to arouse the Governor's curiosity without revealing his plans.[6] The deception had good reason behind it.

Shirley knew that the Governor was preoccupied with politics. His patron, Charles, Viscount Townshend, brother-in-law of Sir Robert Walpole, had been recently forced from the ministry. The loss of this support was particularly distasteful to Belcher because he was obliged, in the meantime, to battle the Massachusetts legislature. The home government had instructed him to force through the legislature certain financial measures that would relieve him of dependence on the whims of the colony for his annual salary appropriation. Americans interpreted this move as a threat to local government, and a political deadlock ensued. In this critical juncture, Belcher was admittedly looking for additional English support, for he needed the assistance of a strong patron to rally the full power of the British government to his side and ward off the attacks traditionally made in London upon colonial officials.[7] Nevertheless, Shirley deemed it wise to seek an alliance with Belcher. In his estimation, the Governor was only temporarily embarrassed; although his powers of office were diminished, he was still the chief dispenser of patronage in the colony, the King's representative, and a great merchant and landowner. When he overcame his difficulties with the legislature he could be most helpful. For the present, with Belcher seeking firmer support in London, Shirley would exploit his own friendship with Newcastle to win assistance from the Governor.

By accident Shirley struck upon something else that Belcher valued, perhaps more than the security of the governorship. Belcher's son was a student at Middle Temple, and he had grandiose plans for the youth; he envisioned Jonathan as lord chancellor of England or, at the very least, a famous jurist and

6. *Belcher Papers*, I, 32, 88; Shirley to Waldo, Apr. 15, 1739, Henry Knox MSS, L, 45, Mass. Hist. Soc.
7. Belcher to Wilmington, Jan. 5, 1732, and Nov. 13, 1733, Belcher MSS, Boston Pub. Lib.

member of Parliament. There was more here than a father's
wishful thinking. As a native of New England, Belcher had
used wealth and family to rise to a place of influence in the
colony; he now hoped that Jonathan could employ the same
means to establish their family in the British aristocracy. Understanding the earnestness of the Governor about his son's
career, Shirley volunteered advice and offered to write letters
of introduction to leading members of the London bar and to
send a letter to Newcastle.

The evening was important for Shirley. Before it was over,
Belcher assured him of help in finding legal work until Newcastle could arrange an appointment. Later, when the Governor had an opportunity to think over their conversation, he
wrote friends that Shirley was a man of ability, poise, and
political connections. He praised him as an "ingenuous, sober,
and modest gentleman"—generous words from Belcher, who
often used the vocabulary of abuse. One of his letters
went to the Superior Court of Massachusetts, recommending
Shirley's admission to the bar.[8]

II

Although it was fall and the trees were bare and the roads
muddy, Shirley was delighted with Boston. "If I might form
a judgment from the short experience, which I have yet made
of Boston and my countrymen there, I should pronounce it,
next to London, the most agreeable town I ever lived in."
Visiting Harvard College, he was escorted by the distinguished
secretary of the colony, Josiah Willard, and was deeply impressed. "I could not forbear imagining that the college bears
a resemblance to what Oxford and Cambridge colleges were in
old Chaucer's days, and that Mr. [Henry] Flynt's apartment
and manner of life was like those of a master of a college in
Harry the Second's reign. . . . But doubt not in half a century
to see the buildings of Harvard College . . . rival those of the
Mother Country."[9]

8. *Belcher Papers*, I, 21, 44. Shirley was admitted to the Massachusetts
bar on Nov. 17, 1731, Superior Court Minute Books, XIX, Suffolk County
Court Records, Boston.
9. Shirley to Clarke, Nov. 22, 1731, Dolbeare MSS, Mass. Hist. Soc.

Little escaped his inquiring eyes during these weeks of investigation. He saw that Massachusetts was experiencing momentous changes. The port of Boston was crowded with vessels; and on its wharves the best manufactures of Europe were being unloaded. Up in the town heavy wagons rattled along streets lined with shops and warehouses, and merchants, Indians, and settlers conducted an unending stream of business.[10] These signs of progress pleased Shirley. Boston was a business community that he understood, a place where he could make a home for his family. His many references, together with the personal aid of the Governor, opened doors to him, and he soon welcomed as clients such distinguished residents as John Boydell, Samuel Waldo, Charles Apthorp, and Nathaniel Byfield.

Old Judge Byfield had need of a good lawyer. He was judge of the local vice-admiralty court, and the scarred veteran of countless disputes with Boston seamen. His duties required him to penalize smugglers, settle wage disputes between seamen and shipowners, and handle many matters connected with navigation and the enforcement of the trade laws. From time to time smugglers were able to circumvent the court's jurisdiction by bringing actions against him, personally, in the civil courts. A particularly bitter legal dispute developed from a suit brought in 1732 by the popular Elisha Cooke, self-appointed champion of the Boston smugglers. Cooke secured several crippling judgments, and the harassed Byfield, at the suggestion of his relative the Governor, engaged Shirley's services.[11] Shirley gained immediate prominence by daring to fight Cooke in a number of court battles which included an unprecedented appeal to the Privy Council in London.[12]

Though the Council's ruling was inconclusive, Shirley handled himself well during the trial and appeals of the case. His legal skill impressed John Boydell, another official of the

10. Carl Bridenbaugh, *Cities in the Wilderness* (New York, 1938), 257-60, 265-73, 277, 289-94; H. B. Parkes, "New England in the Seventeen-Thirties," *New England Quarterly*, 3 (1930), 397-419.

11. Swasey *v.* Byfield, Apr. 1, 1732, C. O. 5/874, 68.

12. Shirley to Newcastle, July 1, 1733, Additional MSS, 32688, British Museum. Hereafter cited as Add. MSS.

admiralty jurisdiction, who advised his English friends to engage Shirley when they had difficult cases.[13]   But it was the
Governor who paid Shirley the greatest tribute by instructing
young Jonathan to write him for advice and by commissioning
him to draw up a will and transact other legal business.
Belcher's sponsorship reflected his trouble with Shirley's ad-
versary, Elisha Cooke, who was also the Governor's opponent
in the House of Representatives and was principally responsible
for the current legislative deadlock.   Shirley's fight against
Cooke had strengthened the Governor's hand, and he was
eventually able to remove Cooke from appointive offices.   In
the meantime, Belcher found other legal work for Shirley.

One of the most interesting and pitiful cases Shirley gained
through Belcher concerned the starvation of a group of Palatine
immigrants.   A company of 140, they had taken passage on the
ship *Loving Unity* in the summer of 1731, about the time the
Shirleys were embarking for Boston.   They soon fell victim to
hunger and disease; eventually "extreme distress for want of
provisions" brought death to almost one hundred.   Lack of
supplies was only partly responsible; cruelties inflicted by the
captain contributed to the death of many passengers.   After
the ship docked at Plymouth, the misery of her passengers
caused members of the Massachusetts legislature to commission Shirley to bring legal charges into court.[14]   Shirley in-
terrogated the survivors and inspected the ship, then appeared
before Judge Byfield and accused the captain of brutality,
theft, and violation of contract.

As was customary when a case aroused great public interest,
the trial was held in the council chamber of the Court House.
People filled the seats and crowded the doorways to catch sight
of the witnesses.   The Palatines told appalling stories.   One
young man, Philip Webber, described the blows upon his face
"to the effusion of blood, at a time when he was endeavouring
to obtain butter out of his own chest in order to support his
sick mother."[15]   Other passengers wept as they described the

13. Boydell to Yeamans, Jan. 15, 1733, Greenough MSS, Mass. Hist. Soc.
14. Webber *v.* Tresaker, Feb. 17, 1732, Admiralty Court Records, Mass.
(transcripts), III, 107-8, Lib. Cong.
15. Palatines *v.* Lobb, Feb. 17, 1732, *ibid.*, 106-7.

death and burial of friends. The evidence piled up, but the brutality of ship captains was nothing new, and Shirley's charges of willful negligence were not acceptable to the court. When the captain was released with a light fine, Shirley saw the possibility of a civil action and commenced prosecution in the Suffolk County courts. Proceedings dragged on during the better part of 1732. Although his efforts to win justice for the Palatines were fruitless, he was rewarded generously by the House of Representatives.[16]

This public recognition of his legal ability led to other cases in a town bustling with commercial enterprise. Boston had more than an ordinary amount of legal business for the size of its population; its townsmen loved court battles—perhaps they were encouraged by the low fees of court and lawyer. Shirley had the usual run of common-law litigation: actions in trespass, case, covenant, replein, and detinue. He drafted many wills, collected rents, and selected suitable tenants for London clients. By November 1732 he had undertaken the prosecution of four cases for Charles Apthorp, the great Boston merchant who was a fellow Anglican parishioner of King's Chapel, and two or three cases for Samuel Waldo, another Boston merchant, who had lands and businesses scattered from Rhode Island to Maine.[17] Both merchants soon made him responsible for collecting their accounts, and his successes in the Sussex County courts took him in their interests to Essex and York counties. For a time in 1733 and 1734 he traveled on circuit with the Superior Court justices as he argued briefs for his clients in the county courts. His association with prominent men brought other clients—farmers, fishermen, shopkeepers, and churchmen. On one occasion, at least, he dared criticize the Governor by joining John Read, William Bollan,

16. *Journals of the House of Representatives of Massachusetts* (Boston, 1919-in progress), XI, 368. Hereafter cited as *Mass. House Journals.*

17. Shirley represented Waldo and Apthorp in the Suffolk County courts beginning in Nov. 1732. Examples of the litigation: Apthorp v. Bentley, Nov. 15, 1732, 34529, fol. 54, Suffolk County Court Records, Boston, a suit to collect £10, court granted £20, Shirley's fee was 10 shillings; Apthorp v. Calder, Dec. 19, 1732, 34530, fol. 55, *ibid.,* a suit to collect £14, court granted £25, Shirley's fee was 10 shillings. Wendell Garrett, *Apthorp House 1760-1960* (Cambridge, Mass., 1960), 3-7.

and Robert Auchmuty in defending the rights and privileges of the Church of England in Massachusetts.

Shirley's ambition, however, was not satisfied. His law practice was extensive and consultations filled his daily life, but fees were small. A deed, a will, or legal advice brought ten to fourteen shillings, paid often in vegetables, poultry, and merchandise. He found that his income did not allow him to give his family the comforts and prestige he felt they deserved after coming to this distant land.[18]

What he really desired was not more legal business, but political preferment. With the promised position from Newcastle still not a reality, he became restless. He wrote Newcastle, and the Duke again interceded with Belcher. The Governor was fully aware of Newcastle's power, but he was too involved with local problems to aid Shirley, and he evaded a direct reply.[19] His bitter quarrel with the Massachusetts House of Representatives was entering its third year. The House had neglected to vote his salary, and he had little money to run the government. Although he ruthlessly used the prerogatives of his office to support his administration, the available patronage was not sufficient to establish his authority. Contributing to his difficulties was his lack of favor in London and his inability to foresee the consequences of his appointments. Friends of known opposition to British authority, such as Elisha Cooke, were given public office and then dismissed when the inevitable clash of interests occurred. Others were held in office by allowing them minor infractions of the law or

18. A rough estimate of Shirley's relative position in the legal profession of Boston can be made from the number of cases he prosecuted. The Minute Books of the Suffolk Superior Court, 1734-1738, list 254 cases for the 1734-1735 session:

Shirley	22 cases	Overing	10
Auchmuty	34	Marion	12
Read	48	Law	15
Gridley	8	Hiller	11
Bollan	37	Undetermined	66

This list does not reveal the relative importance of the cases, the extent of the fees, etc., nor does it show the extent of his practice in the other county courts. He complained to David Dunbar, Oct. 8, 1733, that he was very busy at Worcester, C. O. 5/877, 230-31.

19. Belcher to Wilmington, Jan. 5, 1733, Belcher MSS, Boston Pub. Lib.

by giving them support in disputes with law officers. His erratic behavior unsettled politics and compromised him before his superiors. He also alienated many people by his fierce temper and indiscreet statements, and although he befriended Shirley, he bypassed him many times in filling offices and recommending candidates for posts in the admiralty jurisdiction. His unpredictable behavior made Shirley uncertain whether Belcher would ever favor him.[20]

His experience with the Governor probably confirmed Shirley's notion as to what offices he would accept. He had set his mind against a purely local position, for he did not want to be considered a colonial and did not want to be entirely dependent on Belcher for favors. Ideally, he would have chosen the British administrative post of postmaster or collector of the port of Boston, but within the scope of the British bureaucracy he knew that his opportunities were restricted and that he might have to take whatever was available.[21]

A vacancy in the admiralty court occurred in the spring of 1733, when old Judge Byfield died. Belcher bowed to the Duke's pressure and appointed Shirley interim judge, pending a formal commission from London. A few weeks on the bench, however, revealed some aspects of the job that Shirley did not like. In addition to requiring far more technical knowledge than he possessed, it paid very little and interfered with his growing law practice. He explained his predicament to the advocate general of the court, Robert Auchmuty, an English trained barrister. They agreed to exchange commissions. Auchmuty had served fifteen years as advocate and assistant advocate, and in 1728 he temporarily filled the judgeship. He was an expert in admiralty law and should have been appointed judge in preference to Shirley; but he had weak political connections in London. He appreciated advancement through Shirley's good offices.[22]

20. It would be difficult to list all of Belcher's enemies in 1733. He had alienated the Dudley family, William and Paul, Elisha Cooke, Benning Wentworth, Theodore Atkinson, Samuel Waldo, David Dunbar, and Charles Apthorp.

21. Shirley to Newcastle, July 1, 1733, Add. MSS, 32688, 17-18; Boydell to Yeamans, Jan. 15, 1733, Greenough MSS, Mass. Hist. Soc.

22. Burchett to Belcher, Aug. 3, 1733, Admiralty Records, II, 1053, 209, P.R.O.; Burchett to Penrice, July 27, 1733, *ibid.*, 208.

When they notified Belcher of their wishes, he agreed to the exchange of commissions and applied for Newcastle's approval. There was little else he could have done. As it was, he had delayed too long in favoring Shirley with a post, and his own political fortunes suffered as a result. By an unprecedented action of the home government, his son Andrew, the naval officer of Boston harbor, was replaced by a spoilsman sponsored by the Duke.[23]

Though Shirley's appointment was speedily confirmed, he was bold enough, even while expressing appreciation for the position, to tell his patron that it was not altogether satisfactory. He was, he said, ready to go anywhere in America for something better. Privately, he was delighted with his new appointment; it offered him the opportunity to serve his merchant allies in London and made new comforts possible for his family. He leased a large brick house on Queen Street that had more room for his eight children and the luxury of a yard and trees.

III

As advocate general Shirley was plunged into the maritime life of New England. His duties, though primarily judicial in character, were concerned with the welfare of seamen, partnership disputes, smuggling and trade regulations, supervision of port business, and, most important of all, the presentation of cases before civil and admiralty judges. Working in consort with a large number of officials—collectors, surveyors, marshals, registers, naval officers, and assistant advocates—Shirley prepared many briefs monthly; this task included obtaining depositions, gathering evidence, and securing witnesses. He then argued his cases before the courts, calling witnesses, cross-examining, and making pleas to the judges.[24]

Sometimes patience and wisdom were essential in handling unruly sailors. In Camell v. Turney, a seaman complained of

23. Belcher to Jonathan Belcher, Jr., Jan. 6, 1735, *Belcher Papers*, II, 180-81; Instructions to the Governors of Massachusetts, 1732-1743, p. 1309, Mass. Hist. Soc.
24. Admiralty Court Records, Mass., III, V, Lib. Cong.; Shirley to Dunbar, Oct. 8, 1733, C. O. 5/877, 230-31.

incapacity because of illness and demanded to be released from his contract and given terminal pay. Shirley ascertained the facts, then put his recommendations before Judge Auchmuty, who ruled that "the distemper . . . was contracted by the proponent's sin and folly and that truly by his own act he has disabled himself from performing his contract. I can't in justice give the proponent the full of his wages."[25]

Other sailors were less easily disciplined. In October 1736, a special court of admiralty was held for John Barnes, a hard-bitten slaver whose salty language and evil deeds were notorious. Barnes had beaten a Negro lad to death and thrown the body into the ocean. Though he put forth a stout defense, he was found guilty and condemned to be hanged. While awaiting British review of the death sentence, Shirley discovered that it was easier to convict Barnes than it was to hang him. Twice he mysteriously broke confinement and twice he was caught after wild chases along the water front. It is not known whether he was finally hanged.[26]

Other cases in a day's work might grow out of customs investigations by port officials. Over the decades since 1660 England had enacted a considerable number of trade regulations. In a world of bitter rivalries she had attempted to increase her state power by confining shipping more and more to the empire, developing a merchant marine, and funneling outside trade through English ports. The dependencies of the state, the colonies, were expected to make sacrifices for the enhancement of national power, because colonies were considered to be contributory to the strength of the mother country. While the colonies accepted the premises of the imperial system, their merchants were not willing to confine all commerce to imperial sources. They traded with French, Dutch, and Spanish merchants and used various ruses to disguise their business. The profits from this commerce, however, were usually spent in paying British accounts, for the colonies ordinarily purchased more from the home country than they sold

25. Admiralty Court Records, Mass., V, 6a, 9, Lib. Cong.
26. *The Boston Weekly News-Letter*, Oct. 14, 1736, Mar. 3, Sept. 1, 1737; Fitch Edward Oliver, ed., *The Diaries of Benjamin Lynde and of Benjamin Lynde, Jr.* (Boston, 1880), 89.

to it. British merchants who were concerned with colonial trade were caught in a dilemma. They wanted the trade laws, but they also enjoyed the greater commerce that arose from violations of those laws. Shirley's job as an official of the empire was to discourage the excesses of this smuggling by prosecuting offenders in the admiralty courts. Spot checks of cargoes often turned up quantities of merchandise that were not listed in the ship's papers. Though minor amounts of smuggled goods were carried on most vessels and were usually allowed to pass through the customs, officials were particularly hard upon the captains who smuggled and broke other regulations. On October 4, 1733, for example, Shirley "exhibited an information against the ship Eagle for importing three hogsheads of wine, the same being the growth and production of Europe and not having been laden and shipped in England, Wales, or the town of Berwick upon [the] Tweed."[27] Condemnation proceedings were underway.

Shirley had to keep busy because his compensation depended upon fees and commissions. While he did not like the arrangement and persuaded Belcher to apply for a fixed salary, he made a fairly good living. When a vessel was caught smuggling, he shared in the profits from the sale of ship and cargo, which often amounted to hundreds of pounds. His gain was the merchants' loss, and it was reflected in his relations with them. He knew that most merchants carried on petty smuggling, and he tried to moderate his seizures, choosing only the worst offenders for prosecution. He did this with the approval of the Admiralty and succeeded thus in avoiding threats to his life and property, as well as his job.

Shirley was often away from home, performing his duties in Rhode Island, Massachusetts, New Hampshire, and the district of Maine. In distant ports admiralty officials took care of routine matters, but Shirley had to be on hand for the more serious cases. For his Boston office he engaged the services of William Bollan, English born like himself, an active member of the local bar, and a fellow parishioner of King's Chapel. About

27. Admiralty Court Records, Mass., III, 115, Lib. Cong.

ten years younger than Shirley, Bollan was competent and merited the trust Shirley soon bestowed upon him.[28]

IV

With Bollan on his staff, Shirley could give more time to the enterprises of that fierce Scot David Dunbar, whose services as surveyor general of the King's woods and lieutenant governor of New Hampshire kept New England in turmoil. Unpredictable and tactless, this former British colonel defied the landed interests of New Hampshire and Maine by claiming the largest white pines in these colonies as the property of the royal navy. Mast-timber was a valuable natural resource. Though willing to sell timber to the highest bidder, the people of the region rejected any right of the crown to sequester their property for the navy. They considered Dunbar an intruder and his contractors parasites. But Surveyor Dunbar, who seemed to have the law on his side, wanted the timber to be given to the navy free of all charges, even if he had to enforce his will by using the army. His threats angered Governor Belcher who, as the governor of New Hampshire, refused Dunbar the use of law enforcing authorities and favored some of the very people Dunbar was accusing. Their disagreements were repeatedly argued before the Board of Trade in London, and Belcher was even provoked to demand Dunbar's removal from office. Shirley had witnessed this struggle long before he became advocate general and was sympathetic to Belcher's side of the dispute. But he now was responsible for helping the surveyor enforce the forest laws.

Shirley discovered immediately that he was hindered by the ambiguities of the law, which had never been satisfactorily interpreted, despite the agitation of the surveyors since 1691. Under the Massachusetts charter, pine trees of twenty-four inches in diameter were reserved if standing on lands not owned by private individuals; an act of 1722 reserved pines growing outside the townships; and an act of 1729 prohibited the felling of pines on public lands without a license. More

28. Malcolm Freiberg, "William Bollan, Agent of Massachusetts," *More Books*, 23 (1948).

important was a provision in this last act which prohibited the unlicensed cutting of any pines over twenty-four inches standing on private lands, unless the lands had been private property before 1690.

The forest laws may have been clear to their sponsors, but enforcement of them raised acute difficulties. Did the charter mean only those pines twenty-four inches in diameter in 1691, or all pines twenty-four inches in diameter? Did it give the surveyor power to safeguard the trees until they could grow to the required size? Did he have the right to enter private property and select pines for the royal navy? Did he have the power to inspect the logging operations of the private landowners? Nobody knew. A further legal complexity arose from the fact that to evade the law, new townships had been created in unoccupied areas of Maine; title to these lands was also in dispute. The uncertainty of the law increased the difficulty of detecting crime, and the trial of offenders was often a complicated process. British law provided for prosecution of culprits in admiralty courts, but there was no provision to prevent countersuits against the surveyor in the civil courts before New England judges and juries, which were notoriously antagonistic to the forest laws. These civil decisions were customarily appealed by the crown, but the higher courts were no more sympathetic than the lower ones. Sometimes there were so many court orders pending against the surveyor that he was forced to seek cover.[29]

Shirley soon realized that Belcher had a different role in forest law enforcement than he had believed. Belcher had refused to use the powers of government to insure proper hearings before the civil courts, and he had permitted interested justices of the peace to hear cases. He had encouraged the hostility of the Council and had withheld the usual honors of office from Dunbar. Belcher's behavior was often criticized, but Shirley did not divulge it to the home government, confining his reports to matters of law enforcement. He merely advised a transfer of all litigation to the admiralty courts, which

29. Armstrong to Dunbar, Nov. 24, 1728, C. O. 5/10, 63-64; Jere Dunbar to David Dunbar, Dec. 4, 1728, *ibid.*, 49-50.

were presided over by a judge and unencumbered by juries. Shirley's deliberative approach to the problem of Belcher's conduct contrasted with Dunbar's explosive reactions.[30] For years Dunbar had been harassed by writs from defendents of his timber prosecutions. He struck back wildly at his opposition, excoriating the local officials and singling out Governor Belcher for his bitterest complaints. Ultimately, he took the law into his own hands by destroying the timber and tools of the loggers.[31]

Even though Shirley accepted the controversy as an inevitable consequence of conflicting interests, he was unprepared for the riot that occurred in 1734. While marking white pines in the forests near Exeter, Dunbar and his workmen discovered and seized a huge amount of illegally cut timber. The seizure infuriated the bootlegging woodsmen. In the encounter which followed, hand-to-hand fighting endangered Dunbar's life. His men were beaten; several were thrown from stacks of timber into mud pits, and others had their clothes torn off.[32] Dunbar promptly applied to the New Hampshire Council for military aid, but the Council rejected his plea, advising him to communicate with Belcher, who was then at Boston.

Dunbar, after notifying Belcher of the riot, begged Shirley to prosecute the offenders and impress upon the Governor the seriousness of the disorder. The violence troubled Shirley too, principally because the contempt shown the surveyor seemed to be directed against British authority—indeed, to be rebellious. He visited the Governor. "I waited upon his Excellency," he informed Dunbar, "with the design to have acquainted him with my sentiments upon this affair. But he prevented me by reading your letters and a proclamation that he was preparing to send down to you. I observed to him upon it, that there was no reward proposed in it. But his answer was that there was no money in the treasury. He had, I perceived, been writ-

30. Shirley to Dunbar, May 6, 1734, C. O. 5/876, 105.
31. *Ibid.;* Dunbar to Belcher, Apr. 29, 1734, C. O. 5/10, 161-63.
32. Shirley to Admiralty, Nov. 9, 1734, C. O. 5/878, 1; Charles H. Bell, *History of the Town of Exeter, New Hampshire* (Exeter, 1888), 72-75.

ing a long answer to some of your letters, that had so warmed
him as to stop his ears against any who gave advice, for which
reason I desisted." Shirley concluded his letter with a char-
acteristic comment about the American reaction to crown procedure: "I am extremely glad that every step which you have
taken in this affair has been legal, and under a decree of the
Court of Admiralty, otherwise those proceedings would have
been termed arbitrary, misrepresented at home, and exclaimed
against here."[33]

Soon after writing this letter he visited the scene of the riot
with his assistants. The evidence they found supported Dunbar's accusations. Shirley, however, needed a way of exposing
the offenders. He eventually chose a complicated line of attack by way of prosecuting a case unconnected with the riot.
The merit of this case, from his point of view, was that it would
raise for legal judgment the question of Dunbar's right to enter
private property to mark the royal pines. It had the further
advantage of bringing to his support the influence of a powerful New Englander. The case had originated in the act of an
employee of the naval sub-contractor, who had cut marked
timber on private land and had been arrested for trespassing.
The justices of the peace fined the employee and Belcher refused to intervene. At this point the sub-contractor, Samuel
Waldo, himself well connected in London through the naval
contracting firm of Ralph Gulston and Company, appealed to
Shirley for help and agreed to meet any extraordinary expenses
in fighting his employee's case. Shirley took the case (Frost v.
Leighton) speedily through the York County Courts, to Boston
on appeal, and then to the Privy Council in England, where a
favorable decision was rendered in April 1736.[34]

While this appeal was pending, Shirley secured a review
of law enforcement by the Board of Trade. The Board ac-

33. Shirley to Dunbar, May 6, 1734, C. O. 5/876, 105-6; Dunbar to
Belcher, Apr. 26, 1734, C. O. 5/10, 155-59; Shirley to Admiralty, May 6,
1739, Admiralty Records, I, 3817, 107-28.
34. Shirley to Admiralty, Nov. 9, 1734, C. O. 5/878, 1; Arthur Meier
Schlesinger, "Colonial Appeals to the Privy Council, II," Political Science
Quarterly, 28 (1913), 434-36; Andrew McFarland Davis, "The Case of Frost
vs. Leighton," American Historical Review, 2 (1896-97), 229-40. Davis is
inaccurate in many statements.

cepted his complaints and sent Belcher a strongly worded letter which criticized the attitude of local justices of the peace. Anticipating the Board's support, Shirley had already sent a statement to the Admiralty that assailed judges who were swayed by partisan politics—judges who were Belcher's appointees.[35] The Governor, however, could not be prevailed upon to enforce the law.[36] The issue was fundamental to powerful interest groups in the colony. Belcher and his friends, even when confronted by orders from the Privy Council and Board of Trade, used every device at their disposal to fight back. Because many of them were landowners, timber merchants, and shippers of timber, they considered the decision an attack upon their rightful means of making a living.[37]

Shirley tried to avoid a personal dispute with the Governor, but he associated with Belcher's bitter enemies, Dunbar and Waldo, and was frequently seen with their friends, Benning Wentworth and Theodore Atkinson of New Hampshire. The prospects of a break with the Governor disturbed him, for his increasing law business involved the good will of the merchants, many of whom supported the administration.[38] Thus far he had managed to remain on fair terms with Belcher.[39] He was often a guest in the Governor's mansion, and he received gifts of books from Belcher and his son, to whom Shirley continued to write.[40] But their relations were very strained.[41]

35. Board of Trade to Belcher, Sept. 10, 1735, Instructions to the Governors of Massachusetts, 1732-1743, Mass. Hist. Soc.; Shirley to Admiralty, Mar. 22, 1738, C. O. 5/95, 137-42; Belcher to Waldron, May 9, 1734, Photostat coll., Mass. Hist. Soc.

36. Board of Trade to Belcher, Jan. 18, 1737, C. O. 5/917, 186-87. The Board actually accused Belcher in the case of Samuel Graves of interfering with the judicial process.

37. Shirley to Burchett, May 8, 1739, Admiralty Records, I, 3817, 145-53; Shirley to Superior Court Judges, Oct. 17, 1743, Shirley MSS, Mass. Hist. Soc.

38. Minute Books, 1735-1738, Suffolk Superior Court. Shirley was the fifth most active lawyer in the court during the sessions of 1737-1738.

39. Belcher to Frances Shirley, Nov. 30, 1736, Belcher Letter Book, 1735-1738, 71-75, Mass. Hist. Soc.; Belcher to Oxenden, Nov. 30, 1736, ibid., 75-77.

40. Belcher to Jonathan Belcher, Jr., Dec. 12, 1737, ibid., 476. No catalog of Shirley's Library seems to exist. He owned William Lambarde's The Duties of Constables . . . ; Edward Leigh's A Philosophical Commentary . . . ; John Cowell's A Law Dictionary. . . .

41. Lawsuits challenging Shirley's authority were permitted by Belcher's judges: Breed v. Shirley, July 1736, Suffolk Superior Court, 41967, fol. 128; and June 1737, 44466, fol. 86. Shirley won a judgment of £3.

The perils of fence straddling were dramatized one evening while Shirley was sitting with Waldo in a Boston tavern. Unexpectedly they were joined by Elisha Cooke, who shouted out a drunken toast in which he named Dunbar the Governor's successor. Shirley and Waldo left the tavern and later apologized to Belcher.[42] During that meeting with the Governor, Shirley referred to the reluctance of local judges and juries to convict anyone of breaking the forest laws. Belcher replied by blaming Dunbar's blundering raids for the recent violence. Although he promised to protect the white pines growing on unincorporated lands and to investigate certain infractions of the law, he failed to clarify his position otherwise. Shirley advised Dunbar to refrain from opposing the Governor until another appeal was entertained by the London authorities. To support this appeal, he obtained depositions from Auchmuty and Waldo and assisted Dunbar in preparing his reports. But he had little confidence in the result. With so many colonial officials, from lowly officers to the Governor himself, conspiring to evade the law, both he and Dunbar were convinced that no amount of exertion in America would be effective without a change in the forest law and a change of governors.[43]

V

Shirley and his wife frequently discussed these problems of patronage politics when they planned their future. The consequences of a disagreement with Belcher were formidable, for his power in New England, despite his multiplying enemies, seemed to be growing stronger.[44] Yet the Shirleys saw some gains in their personal life. By 1736 their eldest child, Frances, was nearly sixteen, and their eldest son, William, was a year younger. Ralph, the only child born in America, was two years old. They lived comfortably on Queen Street, and the three-story brick house was filled with children's laughter and chatter. They had gained good friends. The Samuel Waldos, the

---

42. Their apology was dated May 7, 1734, C. O. 5/876, 214.
43. Shirley to the Superior Court Judges, Oct. 17, 1743, Shirley MSS.
44. *The Boston Weekly News-Letter,* May 29, 1735; Shirley to Dunbar, May 6, 1734, C. O. 5/876, 105-6; Shirley to Waldo, Apr. 15, 1739, Shirley MSS.

Boydells, the Apthorps, and the Auchmutys were their intimates. Waldo and Shirley, drawn together as they fought Belcher's supporters, were in regular consultation as Shirley handled Waldo's law cases and joined him in several land transactions. Auchmuty's son Samuel was about the same age as young William, and the boys were often together.

These friendships were genuine, but the Shirleys still had no roots in native society. Their associations were mostly confined to the British spoilsmen of Boston, people of the admiralty court, Americans relying for a living upon British contracts, and members of King's Chapel. Although Shirley loved books and respected academic training, his sons were not being prepared for Harvard College. He feared the influence of Congregationalism upon them and their contamination by colonial ideas. It is not surprising, then, that Frances Shirley spoke of Boston as a "Foreign Country" and that William Shirley after five years was willing to leave Massachusetts if something better was offered in another part of America.[45]

Finally, in 1736, this general dissatisfaction with life at Boston drove the Shirleys to another important decision, reached with the same hard-minded deliberation that characterized their decision to come to America. Frances would leave her husband and children in America and travel to England, where she would press the Duke of Newcastle for more favors. Her ambitions for William's future were almost boundless, and she willingly assumed the burden of petitioning for preferment. Whether she anticipated in 1736 the intense struggle over patronage that would keep her in London for many years is not known from her letters. But desperation often overlooks the sacrifice.

45. Frances Shirley to the Board of Trade, 1736, C. O. 5/876.

II

Newcastle's Promises

THE SIXTEEN months following Frances's departure were a
period of anxiety for Shirley. He received frequent letters from
his wife describing the obstacles she experienced trying to
interview the Duke of Newcastle, and he himself appealed to
the Duke—sometimes by letter and often through the interven-
tion of friends.[1] Newcastle's attitude bewildered them, and in
their uneasiness they even solicited the help of Newcastle's
brother, Henry Pelham, who promised to speak with the Duke.
These persistent inquiries finally stirred the Duke into repeat-
ing his pledge of assistance whenever there was a propitious
turn of politics.[2] His present inability to favor them was no
doubt genuine, as the Shirleys soon realized, but Newcastle was
notoriously careless, even about his personal affairs, and needed
to be reminded of his promises. During 1738 and 1739, each
time they heard of a vacancy in the colonial service they sent
him a petition.[3]

As their petitioning continued month by month, Shirley was
drawn more closely into Massachusetts politics. The issues of
taxation and salary, which perennially disturbed relations between the Governor and the legislature, had given way to fac-
tional strife over appointments and the distribution of other

1. Frances Shirley was accompanied by her eldest son, William, and by
the wife of the New York governor, Col. Soc. Mass., *Publications*, 8 (1906),
243-44; Charles Henry Lincoln, ed., *Correspondence of William Shirley, Governor of Massachusetts and Military Commander in America, 1731-1760* (New
York, 1912), I, 9. Hereafter cited as *Shirley Correspondence.*

2. Frances Shirley to Newcastle, June 1738, State Papers Office, 35, 65,
fol. 11, P.R.O.

3. *Shirley Correspondence*, I, 12. The Shirleys even solicited supporting
letters from Governor Belcher: Belcher to Frances Shirley, Nov. 30, 1736,
Belcher Letter Book, 1735-1738, 71-75, Mass. Hist. Soc.

favors.[4] Tension was again increasing between Belcher and his enemies, and Shirley found his own position more and more trying. He had pacified Dunbar while Frost v. Leighton was on appeal to the Privy Council, but matters came to a head when the local authorities deliberately flouted the decision.

This time the dispute was infinitely more serious, for Dunbar was determined to put his grievances personally before the home government. News of his decision emboldened Belcher's other enemies, particularly the Allen brothers, James and Jeremiah. "Full of wrath and fury at the Governor," they were fighting to regain their former share of official patronage.[5] The Allens were not men to be antagonized; their willingness to espouse popular causes had won them a large following in Boston. Benning and Mark Wentworth of New Hampshire, also foes of the administration because Belcher had deprived their family of office, welcomed Dunbar's opposition. Always ready to embarrass the Governor, the Wentworths had managed to gain control of the New Hampshire Assembly, using local issues of absentee government, boundary difficulties with Massachusetts, and patronage disposal to discredit Belcher's policies. They exerted their influence to have John Thomlinson, the wealthy London merchant, chosen colonial agent and enlisted his aid in opposing the Governor in the home country. When Dunbar renewed hostilities against Belcher, they also redoubled their efforts, and Benning Wentworth eventually went to London to join forces with Thomlinson in the attack.[6]

By this time Samuel Waldo was also in London. A most dangerous enemy, Waldo was ruthless in his search for ways to expose the Governor's derelictions. Acting with his employers, the Gulston firm of naval contractors, he lodged strong protests with the Admiralty and the Board of Trade. His motive was in

---

4. Belcher to Jonathan Belcher, Jr., Dec. 12, 1737, *ibid.*, 476-77.

5. Belcher to Partridge, Jan. 25, 1737, *ibid.*, 137; Clifford K. Shipton, "James Allen," *Biographical Sketches of Those who attended Harvard College in the Classes 1713-1721, with Bibliographical and other Notes: Sibley's Harvard Graduates*, VI (Boston, 1942), 159-64. By 1740 the Allens were again on good terms with Belcher.

6. Belcher to Jonathan Belcher, Jr., June 25, 1737, Belcher Letter Book, 1735-1738, 264-66. "I suppose Dunbar may be arrived by this time; he is full of the Devil and will leave no stone unturned to do me hurt."

part revenge, in part the desire to conserve the profits of timber procurement which were menaced by the Governor's policies. In addition to his timber interests, his dispute with Belcher involved land claims in Maine. It seems that Belcher had used the uncertainty of Waldo's titles as the basis for a kind of blackmail to keep him friendly to the administration; but his threats had served only to aggravate relations and make reconciliation impossible.[7]

I

Belcher was obviously frightened by the stream of enemies leaving Massachusetts and New Hampshire; their protests were flooding the London government. British officials, in turn, pressed the colonial agents for explanations of New England politics. The Governor, who had no great patron to handle his affairs, begged his friends and relatives in London to assist him. In exchange for kind letters to Newcastle, Sir Robert Walpole, and Lord Wilmington, he remitted hogsheads of fish, barrels of pickels, and other items of New England produce.[8]

Though his friends kept Belcher informed of the activities against him, their letters were no more illuminating than those which Shirley received from his wife. Frances was a vigilant reporter of London politics whose letters set forth in detail the struggles for control of Massachusetts. By making her information available to Waldo and his associates in London, she checkmated the actions of Belcher's friends. Gradually she wove the aspirations of these men into her husband's quest for patronage, and she became less interested in locating elsewhere in America as she realized the opportunities opening to her husband in Massachusetts.

Her services in London were augmented by Shirley's efforts in Boston. He was Waldo's attorney, Dunbar's political agent, and Wentworth's advisor on strategy in New Hampshire politics. In these matters, as in most others, he still tried to avoid actions that would antagonize the Governor. Ostensibly

7. Belcher to Waldron, May 13, 1734, *Belcher Papers*, II, 64; Shirley to Waldo, Apr. 15, 1739, Knox MSS, L, 45; Shirley to Admiralty, May 6, 1739, Admiralty Records, I, 3817, 107-28.

8. Belcher to Partridge, Nov. 26, 1739, *Belcher Papers*, II, 250.

their association was as cordial as ever.[9]   Shirley was inherently tactful, to be sure, but his success in retaining Belcher's confidence was probably due to his oblique approach to the Governor's dealing with the timber smugglers.   Although he witnessed the efforts of Waldo, Dunbar, Wentworth, and their friends to oppose the Governor, he himself moved cautiously, and Belcher's enemies received no apparent help from him. By this time he aspired to be a governor himself, but supplanting Belcher seemed for the moment to be out of reach.   Belcher could be removed only by an act of the ministry, and Shirley had been informed that Sir Robert Walpole favored keeping him in office.   Therefore, rather than criticize Belcher directly in his dispatches, Shirley enlarged upon the advisability of splitting Maine and parts of New Hampshire from Massachusetts, thus creating a government in the northeast which would be strong enough to cope with forest law enforcement. By inference, at least, he put himself forward as the man who could bring law and order to the area.[10]

Nevertheless, when it seemed worthwhile, he did not hesitate to risk conflict with Belcher.   In 1737 he vied for the position of Boston naval officer, a patronage post worth £500 a year.   Although the office was customarily at the disposal of the Governor, Newcastle had intervened to secure the appointment of Benjamin Pemberton four years earlier.   The Duke's action had been doubly distasteful to the Governor because his younger son, Andrew, and his son-in-law, Byfield Lyde, had been ejected from the office.   Belcher vowed revenge against Pemberton and complained repeatedly about this violation of his vested rights.[11]   His protests made little headway until 1737, when the Admiralty officials of Boston became annoyed with Pemberton's conduct of his office and sent an account of their grievances to London.   Using the services of

9. Belcher to Jonathan Belcher, Jr., May 7, 1737, Belcher Letter Book, 1735-1738, 190-99.   Unlike Shirley, Auchmuty did not retain Belcher's friendship (p. 192): Belcher observed that he "is an Irish Rascal, [who] behaves with ingratitude and indecency."

10. *Shirley Correspondence*, I, 6-8.

11. Belcher to Jonathan Belcher, Jr., Nov. 25, 1737, Belcher Letter Book, 1735-1738, 442-45; Belcher to Holden, Nov. 25, 1737, *ibid.*, 445-47.

Shirley's friend John Yeamans, the London merchant, they insisted upon Pemberton's immediate removal. Shirley stepped into this situation in an effort to secure the office for himself. Although he knew that the Governor was mobilizing support for Lyde's reappointment to Pemberton's naval office, he wrote Yeamans putting his own name forward.[12] Even after he realized the Governor had full knowledge of his desires, he persisted in his efforts to gain the post. He did not know, however, that Belcher was ready to defend Pemberton if there was a chance that Shirley would receive the post; nor was he aware that Belcher had secretly sent Lyde over to London to manage their family interests in the affair. The Governor instructed his friends to withhold news of Lyde's arrival until the young man had presented his petition. The Governor's warning is revealing: "Perhaps Mrs. Shirley may hear of it."[13]

It was natural for Shirley and Belcher to contend for the naval office because it was closely connected with their own affairs. However, neither man wanted their rivalry to go further; each had a healthy respect for the other's position in local and English politics. Belcher, moreover, was impressed with Shirley's talent as a lawyer, as well as his command of patronage, and wished to cultivate their friendship further. His own political position in London had been steadily deteriorating, and Shirley's good relations with Newcastle seemed to offer an avenue for him to approach the home government. Belcher and his son gave Shirley even more expensive presents. The Governor underscored their tactics when he told Jonathan that Shirley's friendship "will rebound into your own pocket."[14]

Shirley's reputation was growing. An increasing number of people believed he possessed the necessary qualifications for the governorship. They valued his accomplishments as advocate general and his friendship with Newcastle.[15] They ad-

12. Shirley to Yeamans, July 4, 1737, Greenough MSS. Yeamans was related to Samuel Shute, former governor of Massachusetts and friend of Sir Robert Walpole.
13. Belcher to Jonathan Belcher, Jr., Nov. 25, 1737, Belcher Letter Book, 1735-1738, 444.
14. Belcher to Jonathan Belcher, Jr., Sept. 23 and Dec. 12, 1737, ibid., 355, 476.
15. Belcher to Frances Shirley, Nov. 30, 1736, ibid., 71-75.

mired his ability to associate with both the Governor and the Governor's enemies. When his daughter Elizabeth married Eliakim Hutchinson, a wealthy merchant and prominent member of King's Chapel, Shirley gained prestige in socially sensitive Boston.[16] The son of a distinguished father, Eliakim was related to the Shrimpton family and was a nephew of Lieutenant Governor Spencer Phips.

The Shirleys were gaining position in the Boston community in other ways. Their youngest son, Thomas, was enrolled in the Boston Latin School, and the older boys were serving apprenticeships in local mercantile establishments.[17] Despite his initial hesitation in acquiring property in America, Shirley had invested money in land. Some properties he accepted in lieu of payment for legal services performed for Waldo; others he purchased outright. His business dealings brought him into close association with such wealthy merchants as Peter Faneuil.[18]

With his increased stature in the community, Shirley was less satisfied to wait for Newcastle's political favors. As advocate general he had opportunities to enlarge his earnings if he dared irritate the Governor's friends by enforcing the customs laws. He could easily ensnare merchants who produced faulty registration papers, smuggled minor items in an otherwise legal cargo, or failed to document their full cargoes. Law violations increased in the years after 1736, when the pressures of an acute depression tempted some merchants to cut corners, and Shirley initiated a thorough inspection of ships entering Massachusetts ports.[19] He uncovered quantities of smuggled molasses, wine, cloth, and timber and trapped such merchants as Thomas Hancock. For every successful prosecution, he received one-third of the receipts of the condemnation sale.[20]

16. Shipton, "Eliakim Hutchinson," *Sibley's Harvard Graduates,* VIII (Boston, 1951), 726-29.

17. *Catalogue of the Masters and Scholars who have belonged to the Public Latin School* (Boston, 1878), 13; Shirley to Yeamans, July 4, 1737, Photostat coll., Mass.. Hist. Soc.

18. Deeds for land, July 4, 1737, Photostat coll. and July 30, 1738, Knox MSS, L, 35; Apthorp *v.* Frank, July 1738, Suffolk Superior Court, 46999; *Boston Evening Transcript,* Feb. 23, 1921.

19. W. T. Baxter, *The House of Hancock* (Cambridge, Mass., 1945), 66.

20. *Ibid.,* 72-73; Admiralty Court Records, Mass., V, Box 3, 119.

These fees quickly doubled his annual income, but the swift raids angered the merchants of Boston, who took their grievances to the Governor.

Belcher, in a private meeting with Shirley, outlined the consequences of these seizures for his administration. The offenders were leaders of the legislature and the business community, valuable political allies. When Shirley cited the law and reminded the Governor of his duties as a royal executive, Belcher responded with an explosion of temper.[21] He knew that his position was untenable. His political friends were lawbreakers, and he could not appeal on their behalf to the British ministry. On the other hand, he lacked the power to discipline Shirley, Auchmuty, and the port authorities, whose tenure of office depended upon the home government.

Belcher also had to face the consequences of a serious economic depression. In the debtor economy of Massachusetts, money was always scarce because an excess of imports over exports drew hard coin to Britain in payment of balances. Without any banks or fiscal institutions to extend the money supply, the colony had issued paper money to provide a circulating medium and allow normal monetary transactions to continue. This currency was especially popular with debtors because its value depreciated and steadily reduced the burden of debt. Merchant creditors understandably opposed increasing the amount of paper money unless they could be certain of controlling its value, for they themselves owed debts to British merchants that could not be settled in paper money. In opposing currency inflation, they had the authority of the royal governor on their side.

A growing trade depression, however, had intensified the monetary crisis. When local merchants were required to make payments, both at home and abroad, they called in loans and restricted credit. The resulting economic pressure aroused legislators and set off debates in the General Court, but the lower house was powerless to do anything when the Governor

21. Shirley to Waldo, Apr. 15, 1739, Knox MSS, L, 45; Dorothy S. Towle, "Smuggling Canary Wine in 1740," *New England Quarterly*, 6 (1933), 144-54.

and Council refused to sanction additions to the currency. Belcher's stand did nothing to enhance his popular support; it also alienated a number of merchants who preferred to meet the emergency by issuing their personal commercial paper or who proposed the more drastic measure of forming banks and printing paper money. These modes of surmounting the restrictions on monetary issues angered Belcher and his supporters.[22]

II

Uneasy about the extent of opposition, Belcher tried again to rebuild his political fences in London, where he knew his enemies were hard at work. In letters to his son and several merchants and friends, including the influential Richard Partridge and Eliakim Palmer, he described the knavery of his opponents. Waldo, that "restless, malicious mortal . . . [who] had been under a fit of rheumatism and piles," was relentless; Belcher correctly suspected him of collecting evidence against the Massachusetts government. Belcher's patron, Lord Townshend, had just died, but the Governor begged Townshend's sons to help him out of respect for their father's memory.[23] He also asked Partridge to remind the Quakers of London of his past services to their brethren in New England, and he sent over quantities of American products for distribution as gifts to anyone in high place who would give him sympathy.

In this struggle for political survival, Belcher possessed some important advantages. His aggressive personality was scarcely an asset, but he was still the royal governor, still the dispenser of patronage in two colonies, still the friend of merchants and smugglers. As a demonstration of strength, he chose to discipline a few enemies. Robert Auchmuty was threatened with suspension from office because he owed money to English creditors and was facing law suits in the local courts. The King, Belcher wrote the Admiralty, should not be served

22. Belcher to Royal, Nov. 16, 1736, Belcher Letter Book, 1735-1738, 39-42. The bills of credit, said Belcher, "are become no better than a public fraud." *Mass. House Journals*, XVII, x-xi.

23. Belcher to Waldron, June 12, 1738, Sedgwick Papers, II, Mass. Hist. Soc. and Sept. 24, 1739, *Belcher Papers*, II, 201-3; Belcher to Partridge, Oct. 16, Oct. 22, and Oct. 30, 1739, *ibid.*, 208-10, 217-21, 235-39.

by insolvents. Another foe, Paul Dudley, son of the former governor and a popular legislator, was ejected from the Council. Even Dudley's non-political brother William apparently lost his place on the bench.[24] And Samuel Waldo, whose property titles in Maine were still involved in technical difficulties, was confronted with new legal writs that, according to Belcher, would "make him clap his tail between his legs and leer home like a dog."[25]

When Shirley defended Waldo before the Governor, he received some distinct hints that their friendship was deteriorating. Belcher "talked to me so impertinently about your affairs," he informed Waldo, that "if you had heard him, it would have galled you to the heart as it did me. However, I believe what I said to him did not leave him very easy. He threatens you very much. And in short he must be got out, or, I don't see how you can return with any comfort for the rest of your days."[26]

Several weeks after this scene, a mysterious letter addressed to the Duke of Newcastle was widely circulated in Boston. Its author, probably Samuel Waldo or David Dunbar, writing under a pseudonym, argued the necessity of removing Belcher and named Shirley as his best successor. When Newcastle wrote Shirley for an explanation, he informed his patron that he was regarded by some people as a suitable successor for Belcher. The opportunity needed to be deftly handled, however, because it was a serious attack on a fellow spoilsman who had once favored him. Shirley outlined the situation in a carefully considered letter that involved Belcher only by implication:

I am also persuaded that this letter did not come from any friend of mine, but from some person, who designed to discredit me in your Grace's opinion. For if the writer of it had really designed to serve me, and prejudice Governor Belcher, he would, I doubt not,

24. Belcher to Horace Walpole, Jan. 21, 1740, *ibid.*, II, 264-68. Belcher had been quarreling with Paul Dudley since 1716. The Dudleys had the patronage support of Walpole, and Belcher was removing them from office at the same time that he was soliciting Walpole's help against Dunbar and Waldo.
25. Belcher to Coram, Nov. 20, 1739, *ibid.*, II, 246.
26. Shirley to Waldo, May 9, 1739, Knox MSS, L, 45.

have consulted me as to the propriety of framing it, and sending it. And I hope I am not fallen so low in your Grace's opinion as your Grace can think me guilty of offering so very weak, and silly an abuse of your Grace's goodness as to encourage so pitiful a contrivance.

There is indeed one gentleman in the province, whose jealousy I can't forbear mistrusting in this affair, and who, I know, would now be glad by any contrivance to hurt me in your Grace's opinion. It may seem hard and groundless to impute so mean and improbable an artifice to a gentleman in the highest station among us, but as I am thoroughly acquainted with his politics, and am knowing to other instances of the like kind of treachery from him toward another gentleman now in England . . . I dare almost risque my credit upon the truth of my suspicion.[27]

He concluded these insinuations by reminding Newcastle that he was still in the market for a better position.

Shirley may not have known the author of the pseudonymous letter, but he welcomed its results. Many prominent colonials came privately to his office—Benjamin and Peter Faneuil, Charles Apthorp, Paul Dudley, Theodore Atkinson, and Christopher Kilby. Kilby, the new agent of the House of Representatives, was on his way to London, and he would carry the reports of Belcher's foes to the home government. Shirley's growing support in Massachusetts encouraged him to ponder whether he should pay the price of actively seeking the governorship: joining battle against Belcher.

In patronage matters Shirley did not move fast or lightly. Considerations of the governorship required a long view into the future, with calculations of his probable success and estimates of his future political life. If there was a chance of succeeding Belcher in Massachusetts, he wanted to be available.[28] But much depended on Newcastle's opinion. Could he depend upon the loyalty of the Duke in a contest between spoilsmen? As an intensely practical man, he knew that Newcastle's reaction was most important: "What gives me the greatest uneasiness in the matter is that the Duke of Newcastle seems by his

---

27. *Shirley Correspondence*, I, 14; William Stevens Perry, ed., *Papers Relating to the History of the Church in Massachusetts* (Privately printed, 1873), 318-19. Hereafter cited as Perry, *Papers of Mass. Church.*
28. Shirley to Waldo, Apr. 15, 1739, Knox MSS, L, 45.

answers to Mrs. Shirley unwilling to turn Jonathan Belcher out; and that he [Belcher] has some access to his Grace by an underhand friend; and though I doubt not of his promise, in case Belcher is out, yet I am afraid he [Newcastle] is not very willing he should go out."[29]

Since Newcastle's favor was essential, Shirley set about to obtain the Duke's backing for an attack on Belcher. His strategy was to embarrass Belcher on policy levels, and then evaluate the results for Newcastle and the Walpole administration. To that end, Shirley appointed Waldo his representative in London and pledged him the lieutenant governorship if a vacancy should occur while he was governor.[30] He needed money for these investigations and maneuvers; hence he insisted on Waldo's direct financial assistance and his aid in borrowing money from their friends. Loans were quickly arranged with Yeamans, Faneuil, Apthorp, Thomlinson, and, perhaps, even from Newcastle's brother Henry Pelham. He then instructed Waldo in the elaborate business of courting favor: "You must take care [to] . . . get at Sir Charles [Wager] properly: Mr. Midcott, a friend of mine, knows Mr. [Thomas] Winnington, one of the Lords of Admiralty, and I believe could introduce you to him. If you would by means of Dean Auchmuty [Robert's brother] spurr up my Lord Granard against him to speak to Sir Charles Wager about this affair, it might be of service. You know what an errant villain he [Belcher] has been to the King's interest in the woods."[31]

III

The most damaging attack on Belcher, as upon any opponent, was to undermine his London support. Shirley remembered that Belcher, to secure the backing for the governorship of some English bishops in 1730 had made certain promises that he had never fulfilled. If Frances and Waldo could find documents to prove Belcher's neglect of the Anglican interest, they were to use them "to wake up the Archbishop of

29. Shirley to Waldo, Apr. 21, 1739, *ibid.*
30. Shirley to Waldo, May 9, 1739, *ibid.*
31. Shirley to Waldo, Apr. 21, 1739, *ibid.*

Canterbury."[32]   Shirley's own record was excellent as a defender of suffering Anglicanism in Massachusetts; he was a vestryman and church warden.   Now his pastor, Roger Price, assured the London authorities that he was "a very worthy gentleman."[33]

So long as the Walpole ministry favored Belcher, it was impossible to remove him; but if his antagonism toward British politics could be established, success was certain.   Shirley revived, if it ever had died, the old case of Frost v. Leighton that involved the issue of enforcement of the forest laws.   With the help of William Bollan, he wrote briefs and solicited supporting statements from Auchmuty and Dunbar.   He rehashed the account of perverted justice, disloyalty of officials to the crown, theft of trees, and Belcher's lack of cooperation. Though most of the information had been used before, Shirley sought to attach blame to Belcher for the confusion and delay in adjudicating the case.

In the meantime, Dunbar reported to the Admiralty, dramatizing the seriousness of the offense in the light of the current war crisis between Britain and Spain, which increased the need for masts.   Employing the services of his patron, Martin Bladen of the Board of Trade, Dunbar had little trouble being heard, both as surveyor general and as lieutenant governor of New Hampshire.   "When his Majesty is pleased to give that country another governor," he prophesied, "I dare answer there will be no more complaints of the destruction of the woods."[34]

Another crisis further depleted the Governor's store of good will in London and almost destroyed him politically.   The affairs of New Hampshire, long inflamed by a variety of issues, had become critical because Belcher favored Massachusetts in a boundary line controversy.   Opposition to him in New Hampshire had weakened his control of the legislature, with the result that the colonial agent, John Thomlinson, risked

32. Dunbar reported to Newcastle on Belcher's hostility toward the Anglican Church, Dec. 5, 1735, C. O. 5/10, 173-75; Shirley to Waldo, May 7, 1740, Knox MSS, L, 48.

33. Price to Bishop of London, May 9, 1740, Perry, *Papers of Mass. Church*, 340-41.

34. Dunbar to Burchett, Aug. 8, 1739, Admiralty Records, I, 3817, 163-65.

blaming him for the boundary crisis. Thomlinson's attack in London led the Board of Trade to send an agent to investigate the charges; when the Board's representative reached Boston, Shirley entertained him and gave him evidence against Belcher that was later shown to Lord Chancellor Hardwicke.[35] The upshot of Thomlinson's attack was that the Privy Council recommended a more favorable boundary for New Hampshire and a separate governor.

Victory was almost within Shirley's grasp. Belcher, however, was rescued by circumstances. Before the Privy Council's recommendations were issued, war with Spain brought greater problems before the government. The lords of the Council, in the interest of harmony, instructed the colonial leaders to lay aside their grievances until the return of peace. This order virtually closed the matter of the New Hampshire boundary. Belcher cheerfully planned revenge against Waldo if he dared return to Boston. "The grand affair of a new governor is almost out of sight," he wrote; "Trinkalo [Waldo] will return a sort of a beheaded puppy, and if he should yelp, he'll not be able to bite. . . . We have a squadron of deaths, writs, arrests, and judgments waiting to alight him."[36]

Belcher was overly optimistic in his excitement. Having come so close to engineering his total defeat, Thomlinson and Shirley were not discouraged by the Privy Council's order. Thomlinson lent Shirley approximately one thousand pounds, and in return Shirley offered his assistance to Thomlinson's friend Benning Wentworth, who long aspired to be governor of New Hampshire.[37] He undoubtedly also pledged the aid of Waldo, Apthorp, Dunbar, and other dissenters of Belcher's regime then in London.

While these arrangements were being completed, Newcastle at last made his position clear. Despite his previous reluctance to interfere with a spoilsman of the Walpole administration, the Duke offered Mrs. Shirley a plan that put him directly behind the movement to recall Belcher. Why did

35. Shirley to Waldo, May 9, 1739, Knox MSS, L, 45.
36. Belcher to Waldron, Oct. 27, 1740, *Belcher Papers*, II, 336-37.
37. Belcher to Partridge, Jan. 26, 1741, *ibid.*, II, 362.

Newcastle change his tactics? Shirley decided that part of his reason was a desire to help the Shirley family, but he knew that the strongest cause of the Duke's support lay in the political realignments then taking place in England. Walpole's administration was weakening, and as head of a war faction, Newcastle was courting the merchant class of England in an attempt to mobilize energy to the task of victory; the promise to Shirley was the price of securing unity in Massachusetts.[38]

The War of Jenkins' Ear, almost completely a mercantilist venture to gain trade for British interests, had begun with assaults upon Spanish islands in the Caribbean and on the Spanish coast of the Gulf of Mexico. With extensive operations against Cartagena and Havana on the planning board, Newcastle wanted New England to be ready with men and provisions. He hoped to avoid a patronage issue in Massachusetts until the war was underway and, incidentally, until he had consolidated his power. He asked Shirley to aid Belcher in mobilizing the men and materiel, and for this help he promised Shirley the governorship as soon as it was practical to remove Belcher. For the time being, Shirley was instructed to "go to Mr. Belcher, and assure him, that you are ready and desirous to give him all the assistance in your power."[39] Shirley avoided a personal meeting with the Governor, but in a letter delivered by his son William, he offered his aid in raising the expeditionary force and promised to enlist the cooperation of his friends. After his extended campaign to unseat Belcher, Shirley's offer of assistance seemed audacious to the Governor. In his letters to London, Belcher searched his repertoire of epithets for the right words to describe his contempt for Shirley—that "ingrate . . . that meddler . . . that pettifogger . . . that quondam, impoverished lawyer."[40]

Belcher's volcanic temper forced Shirley, as he told Newcastle, to contribute "to the service of the expedition . . . with-

38. Basil Williams, *The Whig Supremacy, 1714-1760* (Oxford, 1939), 200-2, 220-55.

39. *Shirley Correspondence*, I, 18-19; Belcher to Shirley, July 12, 1740,. *Belcher Papers*, II, 310.

40. Belcher to Jonathan Belcher, Jr., May 19 and Dec. 1, 1740, to Partridge,. July 15, 1740, *ibid.*, II, 301, 352, 313.

out his Excellency's knowledge." He urged his New Hampshire friends to support the mobilization, and he won the backing of the authorities of Rhode Island. The response of New Englanders was almost universally favorable; the mobilization proved successful. Shirley assumed much of the credit in his letters to Newcastle.[41] His final report was placed personally in the Duke's hands by Frances Shirley, who found the Duke more and more easy to see. Faithful to his promise, the Duke sent the report to Martin Bladen. Bladen, already sympathetic with Shirley's ambitions through his association with Dunbar, considered the report a substantial testimonial of fitness for office. It established Shirley as Belcher's successor whenever the ministry decided to make the change.[42]

IV

Belcher was a tough warrior. Despite his many enemies, he was still in office and might have inflicted greater damage had not a gathering political hurricane caught him in its funnel. The tightening of credit had now become a crucial issue in Massachusetts, and the pressure for paper money was so great that two companies were organized in 1740 to relieve the financial disaster. The first, the Land Bank and Manufactury Scheme, was founded by John Colman and 395 supporters, including such influential men as Robert Auchmuty, Samuel Adams, John Choate, Thomas Cheever, and Robert Hale. They planned an emission of £150,000 in bills of credit to be secured by the good faith and property of the subscribers. In their haste to get the bank established, they paid little attention to such essentials as the circulation of the bills, reserves for their retirements, and the administration of the company. Their main objective was the relief of the credit crisis. The stockholders hastened to put the bills into circulation by accepting discounts that immediately made the bills of uncertain value. Frightened by the crudeness of the land bank operation, the Boston merchants offered a more conservative plan of their own, the Silver Scheme. Under the leadership of Edward

41. *Shirley Correspondence,* I, 25.
42. Bladen to Newcastle, Oct. 8, 1740, C. O. 5/899, 376.

Hutchinson, James Bowdoin, Joshua Winslow, Samuel Sewall, Edmund Quincy, and Andrew Oliver, more than one hundred merchants formed a company that proposed to issue £120,000 in silver notes that would be acceptable by them for merchandise and in business transactions.[43]

As the colonists took sides, Shirley used the excuse of impoverished finances (his wife was abroad) to avoid a subscription to the land bank, and he urged Eliakim Hutchinson and William Bollan to keep out of the controversy. While members of the land bank gained control of the House of Representatives, advocates of the silver bank won the sympathy of Governor and Council and pressed Belcher to intimidate the land bank's promoters and seek the help of the ministry. Belcher cooperated. From his wife's letters, Shirley learned of unfavorable official reaction, particularly in Parliament where such schemes had been considered dubious ventures since the South Sea Bubble of 1720. From the gossip of law court and tavern, Shirley heard the indignation of the Boston community to Belcher's purge. Men of the caliber of Samuel Adams, Samuel Watts, Robert Hale, John Choate, William Stoddard, all popular leaders, were ejected from their offices as justices of the peace because they would not bow to the threats of the Governor. Henry Lee, of Worcester, complained to Belcher: "I regard being punished for differences in my opinion from the Council to be a civil prosecution."[44] Threats and dismissals were useless against such bitterness. The land bank not only survived but grew in popularity. Outraged by Belcher's tactics, the House of Representatives instructed its special agent, Christopher Kilby, to deliver a protest to the British ministry.

During the spring of 1741 Shirley's correspondents described the rapid decline of the Governor's popularity in England, and Shirley hoped that the growing hostility in Massachusetts toward Belcher would be reflected in the May

43. Andrew McFarland Davis, "Provincial Banks: Land and Silver," Col. Soc. Mass., *Publications*, 3 (1900), 2-40; Robert J. Taylor, *Western Massachusetts in the Revolution* (Providence, 1954), 52-54.

44. Quoted in Davis, "Provincial Banks," 21; Robert E. Brown, *Middle-Class Democracy and the Revolution in Massachusetts, 1691-1780* (Ithaca, 1955), 128-32.

election of representatives. Belcher remained happily confident of success. Intoxicated by his own electioneering, he told an old friend that his destruction of the opposition in Massachusetts had laid the foundations for better royal government: "I really believe George the IId. will not only be King of Great Britain, but finally will be governor of Great Massachusetts." He gleefully noted that "Mrs. Gipsy [Mrs. Shirley] sighs and sometimes sobs" as she saw his friends go toward victory.[45]

The election results shocked the Governor. A majority of the new House revealed its defiance by choosing as its speaker, Samuel Watts, one of the leaders of the land bank party. Belcher rejected Watts and demanded a more suitable speaker; the House retaliated by purging the Council of nearly half of its previous members. Such men of wealth and influence as John Turner, Jonathan Remington, John Osborn, and Benjamin Lynde, Sr., were replaced by Samuel Adams, James Minot, Daniel Epes, and Thomas Norton. Belcher in turn rejected the new councilors and dissolved the House of Representatives.[46]

A session of the legislature, however, was absolutely necessary, for the treasury had no funds, and pressing matters of defense awaited legislative action. Worried about the reaction to the crisis in London if he did not act quickly, Belcher settled the dispute with the House on his own terms. Nonetheless, he was premature in calling for elections so soon after the recent clash, and the new House showed its belligerence from the opening day, choosing for its speaker John Choate, a land banker like Samuel Watts. Again the Governor disapproved, and again the House selected a speaker sympathetic to the land bank party.

At no time in its history had Massachusetts been embroiled in a more serious quarrel. Though Belcher relinquished his natural role of arbitrator for that of a partisan, the crisis was

45. Belcher to Waldron, May 25, 1741, Bixby coll., Mass. Hist. Soc.; Belcher to Admiralty, Jan. 27, 1741, Admiralty Papers, I, 3817, 199-200.
46. Andrew McFarland Davis, "Legislation and Litigation connected with the Land Bank of 1740," American Antiquarian Society, Proceedings, New Ser., 11 (1896-97), 86-90; George Athan Billias, The Massachusetts Land Bankers of 1740, University of Maine Studies, 2nd Ser., LXI, No. 17 (Orono, 1959), 8-16; Theodore Thayer, "The Land-Bank System in the American Colonies," Journal of Economic History, 13 (1953), 145-59.

only partly of his making. He had hoped to subdue the land
bankers by threats, wholesale removals from office, and
ejection from the House of Representatives through its dissolution, but the aroused emotions of the community got out of
hand. Towns turned on their delegates, held mass meetings,
and gave support to the land bankers. Instead of over-
whelming the opposition, Belcher was caught in the rising
flood of anger.

At this critical juncture, two pieces of important news arrived from London. By a clumsy application of the Bubble
Act, Parliament had outlawed the two banks and set the date
of September 29, 1741, for an end of their activities. Resistance
by the stockholders was punishable by economic penalties
tantamount to enforced bankruptcy. Before the Massachusetts
legislators could decide upon an appropriate course of action,
a messenger from the Governor's office handed the speaker an
official dispatch from the Board of Trade. Its colorless, legalistic language officialized what had been rumored for weeks:
The colony had a new governor, and he was "William Shirley,
Esquire."[47]

The Board's announcement came as a "terrible shock" to
Belcher. He could not believe that the ministry would
abandon him at a moment when he was fighting for a sound
currency in Massachusetts. He had expected Wentworth to
be made governor of New Hampshire, but Shirley's appointment was to him a personal disaster, representing the loss of
friendship, the collapse of patronage, and the submission of
Walpole, Wilmington, and Wager to political pressure.[48]
When Belcher recovered his breath, he wrote to a friend: "I
sincerely wish all feuds, animosities, and politics may vanish
and die, in the administration of my . . . successor, but this I
should not wish, were we not assured from the Sacred Pages
that with God all things are possible."[49]

Although some members of the House of Representatives

47. *Mass. House Journals*, XIX, 5-8, 15-16; *The Boston Weekly News-
Letter*, Jan. 8 and 22, Feb. 5, Apr. 16, May 7 and 21, 1741.
48. Belcher to Partridge, July 3, 1741, *Belcher Papers*, II, 402.
49. Belcher to Waldron, July 20, 1741, New Hampshire Misc., III, Lib.
Cong.

shared his bitterness, there was a general feeling of relief at the Governor's recall, not so much because Shirley was his successor, but because the political deadlock was broken. Massachusetts had approached a crisis over whether the land bank or the specie bank should prevail. Now, both banks were suppressed, and neither group could have its way. Shirley's friends were jubilant over his succession, but others, not personally attached to him, hesitated in pledging their cooperation until he should disclose his policies. They remembered his vigorous enforcement of the mercantile laws, his association with the naval contractors, and were not pleased with his connections. Belcher's friends were angry, and their attitude would be a factor in determining the success of the new administration. One of them was quoted as saying "damn it we can't have a worse [governor than Shirley]."[50] They had no other leader than Belcher, however, and he had lost his authority.

Shirley had already weighed the perils of succession politics and had a realistic attitude towards his new position: "I am not at all afraid of the danger of being turned out of the government," he wrote Waldo, "being sufficiently persuaded that [even if turned out] I shall be pretty strong by means of a family interest; my acquaintance with the Newcastle family; and several other friends in Parliament. . . . Besides I doubt not . . . of establishing a good interest in the [this] country upon the lasting principles of justice and honor. . . . If in three or four years' time I could leave to spend a few months at home, I doubt not, by the advantageous circumstances of my post, family, and large acquaintance . . . that I should increase . . . my interest very much—and these are the circumstances which induce me to accept this post."[51] Nevertheless, his appointment brought great happiness to Shirley. After ten years of waiting, he had gained a position which conferred prestige, power, and the opportunity to dispense a large patronage. He had won the kind of preferment he had solicited

50. Richard Waldron, Jr., to Richard Waldron, Sr., June 27, 1741, Mass. Papers, New York Historical Society.
51. Shirley to Waldo, Apr. 15, 1739, Knox MSS, L, 45.

from Newcastle at their first meeting in 1731. His pleasure was limited by the anticipated burdens of office, for he knew that the problems facing Massachusetts were complex—liquidation of the banks, reformation of the currency, balancing the budget. He also knew that the hostility of many years was not removed by a change of governor.

V

More than twenty enemies of Belcher were living in London in 1741 when he was recalled from the governorship of Massachusetts and New Hampshire. Most of their work was completed when his downfall was accomplished. Waldo left to take up his duties as Shirley's political advisor and to undo the damage which his contracting business had suffered under Belcher's administration.[52]   Kilby stayed on in hope of becoming the permanent agent of Massachusetts in the place of aging Francis Wilks. Wentworth left in the early summer of 1741, stopping in Boston to remind Shirley that he would need help in ridding New Hampshire of Belcher's friends. Almost the last to leave London was Charles Apthorp, who stayed into 1742 helping Kilby and Thomlinson mobilize merchant support for Shirley's administration.[53]

Shirley's staunchest ally was none of these, but rather his wife. His appointment as governor of Massachusetts brought to her the satisfaction of having accomplished a difficult mission. Her five-year absence was a high price for love to pay for patronage; but in spite of her desire to be with her family, she delayed her return to Boston still another year in order to conclude various matters of preferment. One task required especially diplomatic handling. The Shirleys wanted their son William to replace as Boston naval officer Benjamin Pemberton, the official whom they and Belcher had tried to unseat in 1737. The post had great importance in trade regulation, and it was considered the most valuable patronage gift of a

52. Thomlinson to Waldo, Apr. 7, 1742, Massachusetts Archives, LIII, 118; Gulston to Waldo, July 13, 1742, ibid., LIII, 119.

53. Shirley to Apthorp, Oct. 17, 1741, Shirley MSS; Shirley to Thomlinson, Feb. 27 and May 5, 1742, ibid.

Massachusetts governor. The Shirleys were determined to have it for their son. "I think it natural," Frances wrote to Newcastle, "to suppose that if Mr. Shirley must appoint a naval officer it will be his son. If that should be the case and I might presume to ask a favor in addition to your late goodness it should be that your Grace would not oblige him to turn his son out again, for, in that case, it will not only be this loss of a provision for our son, but would lessen Mr. Shirley very much in the eyes of the people."[54]

Before Newcastle could reply to Frances, Shirley had removed Pemberton and appointed William, Jr.[55] This abrupt action forced Newcastle's hand, but he readily approved the appointment and then advised Frances to strengthen the family's connections with the ministry by also cultivating the friendship of Lord Wilmington, lord president of the Council and one-time supporter of Belcher. Frances visited Wilmington, whom she found ready to become another patron of the family.[56] She sought also the patronage of Henry Pelham, the paymaster of British forces, and he agreed to look out for their interests.[57] Some weeks later when she petitioned in behalf of William Bollan's appointment as advocate general, these patrons granted her audiences and assured her of their assistance. By early spring, 1742, William, Jr., was confirmed by the Admiralty in his naval post. Mrs. Shirley, her mission accomplished, was free to return home. In a few months her ship entered Boston harbor amid the bursts of cannon at Castle William and clanging church bells.

54. *Shirley Correspondence*, I, 37-38.
55. *Ibid.*, I, 41-42.
56. Shirley to Wilmington, Apr. 30, 1742, Historical Manuscripts Commission, *Eleventh Report, Appendix, Part IV* (London, 1887): *The Manuscripts of the Marquess Townshend*, 292-94; Leonard Woods Labaree, *Royal Government in America* (New Haven, 1930), 104-5; *Belcher Papers*, I, 376-78 and II, 155-56, 167-70.
57. The correspondence for this period between Shirley and Pelham seems to be lost. Those letters that are available at a later period show the relationship of patron and client: Shirley to Pelham, July 27 and Sept. 27, 1745, Huntington Lib. MSS, 9706, 9707.

III

The New Governor

As SHIRLEY must shrewdly have guessed, the legislature put aside its heated debates on the banks until it could ascertain his opinions. Though he was personally known to most prominent politicians, he had refrained from participating in public affairs, except to enforce the trade laws and oppose Belcher. On issues of defense, taxes, and inflation, his opinions were a matter for speculation. Merchant Thomas Hancock observed, in a letter typical for the day, that Shirley was not going to have an easy administration; too much hatred kept men from compromising the issues. And there were the policies of the British ministry. Belcher, notwithstanding his dyspeptic temperament, was a victim of policies beyond his capacity to enforce; Shirley would inherit a like situation. Support of the new administration, cautioned Hancock, should be withheld until Shirley's opinions were known.[1]

For the month that Shirley had to await the arrival of his commissions he carefully avoided any public pronouncements. The quarrel over the banks continued to spread, inflaming most other colonial matters, and the essential budget bills to provide funds for salaries and defense were put aside in the legislature for routine business concerning appointments and plans for the approaching inauguration. In his home Shirley received leaders of both banks quietly and on the eve of his inauguration held a conference with Benjamin Lynde of Salem, the chief justice of the Superior Court and an associate of the Governor, who promised the support of his family and friends.[2]

1. Hancock to Kilby, Apr. 17, 1740, Hancock Papers, III, Baker Lib., Harvard Univ.: "Depend my Friend, few of Belcher's enemies will like a change for Sh——y, this I assure you."
2. The Boston Weekly News-Letter, Aug. 20, 1741; Oliver, The Diaries of Benjamin Lynde, 114-15; Mass. House Journals, XIX, 16-63.

On August 14—after a night of lightning and thunder—the regal procession assembled, and by forenoon Shirley, Belcher, Phips, and members of the legislature and town of Boston had gathered in the Court House. The day's ritual began with the reading of Shirley's commission; then the oaths were administered to the new governor; and Belcher gave the valedictory address, his great figure and powerful voice adding to the solemnity of the occasion.

At the conclusion of his speech, the throngs on the streets below the council chamber cheered the new governor, and church bells pealed throughout the town. Uniformed militiamen fired "three vollies," and batteries of cannon thundered from distant Castle William. Shirley and his associates paraded to Withered's Tavern, where toast after toast to king, governor, former governor, and legislature measurably relaxed the tensions of the past months.

Back at his home on Newbury Street, Shirley found a crowd of supporters. Their joy was perhaps a bit dampened by the financial crisis and political feuds, but Shirley received many wishes for a successful administration.[3] He accepted these salutations graciously, though formally, and made it a point to draw no political lines in greeting his guests. While he was never unduly austere, his height of nearly six feet added a pleasant dignity to his appearance. The lines of his face made him seem older than his forty-seven years and suggested concern over the critical problems that faced the province.

I

Because Province House was not ready for immediate occupancy, Shirley and his family continued to live at their Newberry Street home.[4] The parlor and adjoining rooms were turned into offices for the Governor. Shirley's first official act

3. Among those organizations saluting Shirley's accession to office were the Masons of Boston, Saint John's Lodge. Though Shirley readily accepted the best wishes of their officers, he was careful not to pledge his attendance at the meetings. Belcher had been a member and continued to attend their functions until his departure for England in 1745; *History of Saint John's Lodge of Boston* (Boston, 1917), 34-35.

4. Council Records, X, 533-36, Mass. Archives; Oliver, *The Diaries of Benjamin Lynde*, 114.

was to continue most officeholders in their jobs until he had time to review their conduct; however he discharged the controversial Benjamin Pemberton as naval officer and appointed William Shirley, Junior, to the post. He gathered his older sons and his son-in-law around him in the capacity of a personal staff and appointed William Bollan as advocate general, urging Newcastle to confirm the nomination.[5]

Early on the morning of August 15, 1741, he formally interviewed the colonial secretary, Josiah Willard. Thirteen years Shirley's elder, Willard had held the post since 1717 and was known for his efficiency and devotion to duty. He was easily the most experienced person to whom the Governor could turn.[6] With Willard's help, Shirley examined Belcher's Instructions from the Board of Trade, the Admiralty, and the secretaries of state. There were general instructions authorizing the Governor to maintain law and order, permit open and free debate in the legislature, choose men of character and ability for public office, and enforce the British laws of trade and navigation.[7] More specific instructions required him to support the war mobilization, terminate the banking crisis, and secure a permanent annual salary that would free him from yearly debates with the legislature.

The actions of the Governor were subject to review by the Board of Trade, the Treasury Board, and the Admiralty Board. His partner in ruling the colony was the legislature (General Court); his administrative policies and decisions were to be worked out in cooperation with the upper house, the Council, whose members were chosen by the lower house, the House of Representatives, and submitted to him for final approval.[8] The

5. *Shirley Correspondence*, I, 41-42; Burchett to Shirley, Apr. 19, 1742, Admiralty Records, II, 476, 138-39: "Their Lordships have appointed Mr. William Bollan, at your recommendation, to be advocate general of the vice-admiralty of the province of the Massachusetts Bay."

6. Shipton, "Josiah Willard," *Sibley's Harvard Graduates*, IV (1933), 425-32.

7. *Shirley Correspondence*, I, 43-76. The Instructions were received in 1742; until their arrival Shirley followed Belcher's.

8. Military appointments were entirely in the governor's hands. Most of the civilian appointments were subject to Council approval—like judgeships, coroners, sheriffs, and certain judicial posts. Shirley to Thomlinson, May 5, 1742, Apr. 6, May 2, and Sept. 20, 1743, Shirley MSS. The members of the

Council's consideration of most issues provided a check on his power and gave its members great prestige in Massachusetts. Although Shirley hoped that he might eventually control some nominations to the Council of twenty-eight by exerting influence in the House of Representatives, he knew that the disposition of the House was to re-elect incumbent members of the Council.

During the recent crisis nearly one-half the Council had been expelled by the House of Representatives, but under normal conditions the lower house was the more fluid body. Its members were chosen annually in May by the established towns, and sometimes as many as one-third were newly elected, though a relatively permanent group of legislators gave continuity to the proceedings. Men like John Choate, Robert Hale, James Allen, and Paul Dudley were as influential as the councilors in setting political patterns. The House had a notorious reputation for stubbornness and independence in financial matters, yet a harmonious relationship with the governor was essential to good government. Shirley had witnessed the three-year battle between Belcher and the House during the early 1730's, and the legislators' unpredictable behavior weighed heavily on his mind. He must have been heartened by the visits of thirteen of the more than one hundred members of the lower house.

On Sunday, August 16, Shirley and his children borrowed a coach and drove to King's Chapel. They were seated in pew four, vacated by the Governor's son-in-law so that the Shirleys could sit in a seat of appropriate distinction.[9] Church at-

---

1741 Council were (*Mass. House Journals*, XIX, 7-8): Francis Foxcroft, Anthony Stoddard, William Foye, Josiah Willard, John Greenleaf, John Cushing, Shubal Gorham, William Pepperrell, Richard Bill, Samuel Danforth, Jeremiah Moulton, Samuel Came, Jacob Wendell, John Read, and John Jeffries. There were thirteen vacancies due to Belcher's purge of the Council. These places were not filled until the 1742 elections.

9. Belcher to Jonathan Belcher, Jr., Dec. 6, 1731, *Belcher Papers*, I, 76-81; Barnard to Hancock, July 8, 1748, Hancock Papers, Mass. Hist. Soc. This first coach has an interesting history. It was purchased in the summer of 1741 and shipped by Sedgwick, Kilby and Company, but was seized by the Spanish enroute to Boston. Barnard's employees did not take out the agreed upon insurance, and Shirley refused not only to pay the transportation but held Barnard's Company liable for the loss of the coach. Their dispute continued for ten years.

tendance may have nourished Shirley spiritually, but it was also a politic activity, for the outspoken Anglican clergymen of Massachusetts had for years admonished Belcher for neglect of the church.

On this Sunday the family had many visitors. Representative Robert Hale of Beverly, a leading land banker and doctor of medicine, came to pledge his help, and Shirley promised to emphasize the colony's financial problems the next day in his first speech before the legislature.[10]   Several Congregational clergymen who were disturbed by the idleness of youths on the docks and streets arrived to urge his support of a bill "for a better observation and keeping of the Lord's Day." Shirley may have inquired about the revivals still in progress in Boston as the result of George Whitefield's preaching, but he was undoubtedly careful, as was his habit, to withhold comment.

Shortly after ten o'clock the next morning, Shirley spoke in the packed council chamber of the Court House, giving his first legislative pronouncement to an audience that would later scrutinize every word of the printed address for revelations of British policy.   In his introduction, Shirley expressed his personal identification with the colony: "It is no small satisfaction to me upon this occasion, to consider that I come to the administration no stranger to your laws, your liberties, or interests, that . . . from the reception I have met with here for several years, my affections are become naturalized to the country."[11]

He made brief statements on the defenses of Castle William, the urgency of stopping trade with the enemy, the desirability of settling the boundary line with Rhode Island (he had been serving on the boundary commission prior to his appointment as governor).   Discoursing on the evil effect of inflation on public credit, he recalled to his audience that paper currency had depreciated nearly 40 per cent in the last eleven years.   Supporting his arguments with statistical and analytical materials, he urged the legislature to study the problems of

10. Oliver, *The Diaries of Benjamin Lynde*, 114-15.
11. *Mass. House Journals*, XIX, 64-67.

credit and to place its findings before Parliament. He then stressed the need for funds to cover the operational expenses of the government and concluded his speech with a plea for cooperation and friendship.

His address disappointed many legislators, who had expected to find specific proposals for the liquidation of the banks. Shirley stated only that he had discussed the province's inflationary problems "with gentlemen of the first figure and credit in trade among us." On being pressed privately to extend his remarks, he surprised many when he refused to comment upon the right of the British government to outlaw the banks and offered only his services in concluding their business as fast as possible.[12] But Shirley probably went as far as he dared. Bound as he was by instructions from the Board of Trade, commitments to his supporters, and the realities of imperial politics, he could easily make enemies by showing his hand. His was now to be a policy of conciliation, middle of the road compromises, and balance of power politics.

II

Though Shirley's public utterances were purposely guarded, his letters to Newcastle reveal the seriousness of his problems. The twin issues of credit and defense demanded immediate attention: "The treasury is empty; Castle William, the chief fortress and key of the province, and all its other garrisons, forts, and fortifications are out of repair . . . and in danger of being deserted by the officers and soldiers, to whom arrears of wages are due as there is to all the civil offices of the government." His expectations of success, he reminded Newcastle, were small: "I am now entering upon the government of a province where Colonel Shute quitted the chair and Mr. Burnett broke his heart through the temper and opposition of the people; and Mr. Belcher in the midst of his countrymen failed of carrying any one of those points for the Crown which might have been expected from him; and . . . the House of Representatives tell me in their address that they are con-

12. *Ibid.*, 67.

cerned my accession to the chair should be attended with . . .
difficulties.[13] These problems of morale and credit required
a background of knowledge and the cooperation of the General Court. Until he had a loyal group of tested friends to run
the legislature, Shirley was compelled to rely upon the random
good will of the houses.

During August and September, while the members of the
houses liquidated the banks, business on the floor was generally routine. Shirley received without contest a salary allowance
of £650 in paper currency and funds for the repair of Province
House.[14] The salary was far less than he had expected, but he
chose to avoid making it an issue while the banking crisis was
unresolved. By mid-September the committees were occupied
with defense and budgetary problems. The British army,
after suffering a set-back in the Caribbean, had requested more
reinforcements, and Shirley pressed strongly for the appropriate legislation. He was gratified by a vote authorizing the dispatch of 500 men, although the legislature failed to provide the
necessary funds for recruiting and transporting the troops to
the Caribbean. After failing in two urgent appeals, he turned
to the Council for help and was advised to issue a proclamation
calling for enlistments and to put John Winslow, a popular
military leader, in charge of recruitment. But raising men required money, which only the lower house could supply. In
desperation, he appealed to the legislature: "I desire you would
consider how much His Majesty's service will be prejudiced by
our delay. . . , and what blame and dishonor will acrue to this
government, if . . . our present conduct should retard and have
a tendency to discourage His Majesty's service in the expedition, whilst the other neighboring governments are forwarding
it to the utmost of their power."[15] This, his third appeal, was
finally heard. The House of Representatives chose three of its
members—Thomas Cushing, Samuel Watts, and Ezekiel Cheever—to purchase necessary transports and to supervise the selec-

13. *Shirley Correspondence*, I, 76, 40; Jeffries to Savage, Dec. 11, 1741,
Savage Papers, I, 16, Mass. Hist. Soc.
14. *Mass. House Journals*, XIX, 68, 72-73, 80, 94.
15. *Ibid.*, XIX, 140.

tion of the recruits. Their work progressed speedily, much to the Governor's relief.[16]

In addition to strengthening the colony's military position, Shirley worked toward a solution of the financial crisis. He was always willing to meet with the bank directors, who were liquidating their organizations. Counseling peace and cooperation, he let it be known that he favored a return to office of the land bank supporters and that he would support Judge Auchmuty as a special agent for the colony in London.[17] His promises reduced tension and facilitated the directors' work; nevertheless, he adhered strictly to the law, though he regretted the conditions under which they labored. Parliament had anticipated interference from the local authorities by prohibiting all enabling legislation and by leaving the enforcement of its instructions to the courts. It had closed the banks, imposed personal liability upon the shareholders for all outstanding shares of the banks, and threatened any person who should fail to submit with triple penalties. As Shirley advised the directors, Parliament had left him only the legal responsibility of a prosecutor.[18]

In his conversations with the land bank directors, who had more difficult problems than the administrators of the other bank, Shirley discovered that only a few notes were issued, and that probably less than £47,000 of them were outstanding. Their redemption would have been easy if the notes could have been purchased at market value, but speculators were now demanding face value, or an approximate increase of one-fourth in price.[19] Although Shirley respected the rights of the speculators, he wanted justice done to the shareholders. The bank was legal before it was suppressed, and had been organized in good faith by its sponsors.

16. *Ibid.*, 141, 151-52; Mass. Archives, CVIII, 210, 215, 219-20, 222.

17. Thomas Hutchinson, *The History of the Colony and Province of Massachusetts-Bay*, ed. Lawrence Shaw Mayo (Cambridge, Mass., 1936), II, 305-8.

18. Davis, "The Currency and Provincial Politics," Col. Soc. Mass., *Publications*, 6 (1904), 168-70; Davis, "Provincial Banks: Land and Silver," *ibid.*, 3 (1900), 2-40. There are lists of shareholders in *ibid.*, 4 (1910), 169-200.

19. Davis, "Provincial Banks," *ibid.*, 3 (1800), 26-31; Andrew McFarland Davis, *Currency and Banking in the Province of the Massachusetts-Bay* (American Economic Association, *Publications*, 3rd Ser., vols. 1, 2 [1900-1901]), II, 130-67; Hutchinson, *History of Massachusetts-Bay*, II, 298-305.

The bank had been conceived as an institution that would render general public benefits to the colony. It was capitalized for £150,000, and any person could acquire up to four votes in its management by pledging from £75 to £2,000. Each subscriber would give the company mortgages on his land worth one and one-half the amount of the notes received and a personal bond for the same amount. Notes then would be printed and issued to the subscribers, repayable serially in notes or in acceptable commodities over twenty years. Since the bank would have colony-wide participation, it was expected that the notes would be accepted in trade and would circulate freely. Whenever there were sufficient profits, it was expected that these could be distributed or lent out to debtors on interest.

All shareholders suffered by the suppression of the banks because the notes were sold at market value, but some suffered even more by discounting notes in their haste to secure merchandise. They were anticipating a twenty-year period of repayment; the long term advantage in production from a new plow or an additional horse and cow would have offset the immediate loss. When Parliament outlawed the land bank, it upset these normal expectations. Many people were seriously in debt and obviously unprepared to repay the full value of their stock. But they were now obliged, under threat of triple penalties, not only to offer security for their stock, but to work for the liquidation of the banks—because they were personally liable for the entire debt until it was retired. Their attitude was the key to Shirley's administrative problems, and he decided to await the results of liquidation efforts by the directors of the bank. By persuasion and promises, he held off the legal actions of the speculators.

Through his good friend Judge Auchmuty, a prominent shareholder of the land bank, he was kept informed of its liquidation. In September, when the shareholders were invited to settle their accounts, there was some confusion, but those who hesitated were offered help in disposing of property or they were threatened with suits. By October almost

£30,000 of debt was cleared from the books. Confident of success, Shirley boasted to Newcastle that the "Malignant spirit . . . is now vanished."[20] Though his boast was not entirely valid, he was recording significant gains; popular feeling was not so bitter, and the legislature was again at work on colonial problems.[21]

III

To get public affairs on a firm footing, Shirley was engaged in many activities, divising plans for better defense and stricter enforcement of the trade and forest laws, and enlarging the support for his administration. Itemized as they are here, they appear to be easily separated as problems, but Shirley was attacking them simultaneously through corps of advisors and assistants. Basic to them all, however, were the financial problems of the government. He let it be known privately, soon after his accession to office, that he would consider a reform of the currency as the first order of business, and as a part of that reform he would grant a slight increase in the supply of paper money. This concession was a slight modification of Belcher's policy of resisting increases in the money supply. It was a minor violation of his Instructions and was against the expressed wishes of Newcastle and his London backers.[22] Writing to Charles Apthorp, Shirley asked him to explain the credit situation to the merchants and have Thomlinson obtain Newcastle's assent for an enlargement of the annual budget increase in the currency. "I have marked the clauses in the letter which I would desire to be pressed particularly upon his Grace."[23]

Shirley analyzed the currency problem as basically one of integrity. The legislature did not intend to redeem the yearly emissions of paper money and had allowed more paper money to be outstanding than was good for public credit. Since this

20. *Shirley Correspondence,* I, 79.
21. Shirley to Newcastle, Sept. 15, 1742, *Documentary History of the State of Maine: The Baxter Manuscripts,* 11, ed. James Phinney Baxter (Maine Historical Society, *Collections,* 2nd Ser., vols. 4-24 [Portland, 1889-1916]), 255-58. Hereafter cited as *Doc. Hist. of Maine.*
22. Shirley's Instructions arrived in Jan. 1742.
23. Shirley to Apthorp, Oct. 17, 1741, Shirley MSS.

paper was issued in anticipation of taxes, there was always a problem of balancing receipts and payments; and when the legislature deliberately permitted deficits to accumulate, it undermined confidence, inflated values, and drove the money from circulation. Shirley would do essentially what the bankers had been prohibited from doing; he would issue new money, guarantee its value, and put the legislature on record against unsecured paper emissions. He would momentarily please the inflationists by increasing the supply of new paper money, and then he would look out for the creditors by sponsoring policies that would provide safeguards for the value of the paper currency, that would tie debt contracts to sterling money, and that would slowly withdraw the unredeemed paper of past years.

The House of Representatives, however, drafted legislation that continued its past practice of unlimited inflation. It accepted Shirley's offer by increasing the supply of new currency to £36,000, but wrote few inflationary safeguards in the bill. Also the House deliberately violated an instruction from the Board of Trade that required legislative acts to be presented in a certain form, with a suspending clause for royal approval.[24] This dangerous legislation had to be rejected—even though a veto meant a delay in appropriations for salaries and other essential expenditures—because Shirley knew he could not justify it to his supporters in London. Still, he was obliged to explain the veto to the legislature in a manner that would not resurrect the bitterness of Belcher's administration. In consultation with Auchmuty and Willard, among others, the Governor examined the bill with unusual care. Whenever he objected to a provision, he cited statistical data and examples. He freely acknowledged that an adequate supply of money was essential; since the home government had not provided a hard currency and Massachusetts could not provide one for herself, a paper emission was the only solution. However, the colony had to guarantee the stability of the notes by putting a time limit on their circulation, voting taxes for their redemption, and accepting a definite schedule of retirement. Shirley desired,

24. *Shirley Correspondence*, I, 78.

above all, a law that would compel the repayment of private obligations in sterling equivalents. In brief, he wanted safeguards against inflation, and in return he would agree to a moderate expansion of the currency.

Shortly after his veto message Shirley recessed the legislature. He used the time before the next session to advise the home government concerning his problems—he had been doing this regularly since August—and to await the reaction of his London friends to the budget bill. The recess surprised the legislature and demonstrated to it his opposition to further currency inflation. The members tried to arrange a compromise with him. Eventually, negotiation centered upon two points: the Governor's insistence on inflationary controls and the legislature's objections to the suspending clause in money bills. Shirley finally agreed to an expansion of the currency if the legislature promised to incorporate certain minimum controls into its money bills. This understanding became the basis of a new writing of the budget legislation. The presentation of the revised bills in the House brought forth a fierce debate lasting for five weeks, but the delay gave Shirley time to await replies to his letters to England. Those replies (with his Instructions) arrived in January, granting him the authority to execute the terms of his compromise. Unfortunately, the legislature would not agree to the strong guarantees against inflation that he had recommended—particularly the formulation of sterling equivalents for all debts without regard to the value of paper money. In Shirley's opinion, however, the final bill represented the best bargain he could make, so he signed it.[25]

In describing these critical negotiations to the home goverment, Shirley did not minimize the weaknesses of paper money. But he was careful to point out that the final version of the bill contained some general guarantees against inflation: "By securing all private creditors from being hurt by any future depreciating of those bills, . . . [I have put] it out of the assembly's power to postpone . . . drawing them in beyond their

25. *Ibid.*, 80; *Mass. House Journals*, XIX, 105-11, 119, 140, 147.

limited periods of payment, which . . . seem to be the most effectual provision for securing the public faith, and private justice, that a paper currency will admit."[26]

Despite his enthusiasm for what he had accomplished, Shirley was not entirely satisfied that paper money could be properly regulated. He believed Parliament should create a provincial currency, using a system of token coins that could not be melted down without great expense. The use of paper money could then be prohibited.[27]

Though Shirley had made only a modest beginning in solving the currency problem in Massachusetts, he maintained his gains; later budget measures carried the minimal guarantees against inflation which he had won. He was unsuccessful, in spite of a persistent campaign, to tie debtor's contracts to British sterling and thus eliminate one incentive for depreciating the paper currency. He was able, however, to withdraw quantities of depreciated paper money still outstanding from the Belcher administration, reducing by December 1743 the total emission by nearly one hundred fifty thousand pounds. He also secured provision for an automatic tax levy to redeem the expiring notes if the legislature failed to act.[28] He was unable to limit the circulation of Rhode Island and Connecticut currencies, though he sponsored a conference with those colonies and denounced their paper money policies in his letters to the home government. But the foundations for a better currency were laid in Massachusetts, and Shirley had probably done all that he could within the limits of his governmental power.[29]

His merchant backers in London were enthusiastic over these initial legislative victories. Yeamans, Coswell, Lane, Hooper, Townshend, Burrell, Kilby, Sedgwick, Thomlinson, and Apthorp attended a tavern party and drank in honor of the Governor.[30] They met frequently, often with Thomlinson

26. *Shirley Correspondence*, I, 83.
27. Shirley to Board of Trade, Mar. 19, 1743, Bancroft coll., N. Y. Hist. Soc.
28. Shirley to Wentworth, Sept. 24, 1744, Mass. Misc., Lib. Cong.
29. Shirley to Board of Trade, June 20, 1744, Bancroft coll.
30. Shirley to Apthorp, Oct. 17, 1741, Shirley to Thomlinson, Mar. 13, 1742, Shirley MSS.

in the chair, to read the Governor's speeches and answer his requests for advice.

IV

With the budget legislation signed into law, Shirley raised the question of his salary; he wanted an annual payment of £1,000 sterling for the tenure of his office. This was the old and delicate issue that had driven Francis Burnett to despair and contributed to the political chaos of Belcher's governorship. Shirley's predecessors, however, were bound by instructions from the Board of Trade, long since modified, which had forced them to refuse salary until it was made a permanent grant for the tenure of their service. At the most Shirley was expected to raise the issue of a permanent grant and then accept an annual appropriation that would approximate the £1,000 sterling. Since Belcher had received far less, it appears that Shirley in contending for the larger sum also wanted to make a point of the insufficiency of the governor's salary.[31]

He was not willing, nevertheless, to give up the major issue of a permanent grant without testing the temper of the legislature; fresh from victories in the contest over the budget, he was ready to call the legislators' bluff. Knowing that they were in no position to begin a serious dispute when nearly half of them were facing bankruptcy and imprisonment for debt because of their participation in the land bank, he thought they could be pushed a little without risking a serious break. If he were forced to compromise, a retreat might gain supporters for his administration, and if he failed he would at least be praised by his backers for championing a good cause.

The battle began on January 21, 1742, when Secretary Willard read a message from Shirley to the House of Representatives:

I am commanded to acquaint you, that His Majesty expects . . . that you should . . . [settle] a fixed salary on One Thousand Pounds Sterling per annum, clear of all deductions, on me and my successors in the government. . . .
I need only observe to you . . . that the nature of the British constitution, which consists in a due balance of the three branches

31. *Shirley Correspondence*, I, 79-80, 87-88.

of the legislature, requires that such independency should be preserved in each of them. . . : that His Majesty is the head of the
legislature here, and the governor is but his officer; and that the
wisdom of the parliament has now made it an established custom to
grant the civil list to the King for life.
I must freely own, that I think [my salary is] . . . much below the
dignity of the station of His Majesty's governor of this province,
as it is below the assurances of that support which former assemblies
have given His Majesty . . . and I am assured it but little exceeds,
the ordinary expenses of some merchant families in this town, who
cannot be taxed with bad economy.[32]

Shirley's message obviously represented the imperial view
of relations between mother country and colonies. Like other
colonial governments, the Massachusetts legislature employed
its discretionary power to appropriate the governor's salary
as a means of controlling him and making him responsible to
itself rather than to imperial authority. The grant of a permanent, fixed salary would have eliminated this check and
rendered the governor responsible solely to his British superiors. The colonists would then have had to look to London
for satisfactory control of their executive; distance, unfamiliari-
ty with American customs, and patronage politics would have
stood between the colonists and any effective management of
their own affairs. Shirley, of course, did not see the problem
in this light; he merely saw a strong British executive as an
effective means of exercising imperial control and keeping the
colonies in a proper state of dependency. In his view, Britain
had an excellent constitution, a good king, benevolent laws,
and the dependence of the colonists on Britain preserved their
liberties.

The representatives, showing no inclination to engage in
battle, referred his message to a committee for study during
their winter recess. At their spring session, with the members
well aware of his position, Shirley again presented his arguments for a permanent salary. Finally, Speaker of the House
Roland Cotton delivered the following message to Shirley:

We humbly apprehend to settle a salary on His Majesty's governor
here, would greatly tend to lessen the just weight of the other

32. *Mass. House Journals,* XIX, 185-88.

two branches of the government . . . especially since the governor
has so great authority over, and check upon them;—the Council
depending on him for their very being, and both houses depending
on him for every law and act of government; since not one penny
can be raised, not disposed of when raised . . . without his consent;
—since he can call them together, and keep them so at pleasure,
or adjourn, prorogue, or dissolve them at his will, and can act in
very many other instances in a sovereign manner.[33]

Clinging to what he conceived to be the true interests of
the empire, Shirley marshaled an impressive array of arguments in reply. Yet he soon discovered that he was not argu-
ing a case in a court room, where a decision is rendered on
soundness of argument or rules of law. His words were getting little public response. The lawmakers seemed absorbed
in considering the other legislation that he had proposed in the
fall and winter. They voted funds for their new program of
defense, and Shirley may have found comfort in this, for
Belcher had never been able to initiate this vital program.
Hale, Choate, and Watts, men of influence in the House and
former land bankers, guided favorable bills through the committees and seemed friendlier to the Governor as the session
came to a close. But his salary demands were still hanging fire
at adjournment in April.

During the six-week period between legislatures, Shirley
welcomed his wife home; Frances arrived in mid-May on the
warship *Dover*. Although she must have been delighted to
see her family again—her first grandchild had been born in her
absence—she was ever the woman of public affairs and had
brought her husband detailed information on London politics.
After reporting on the activities of the new Whig government,
in which their friends Pelham, Newcastle, and Wilmington
were leaders, she assumed her role as the Governor's wife for
the first time. Dinners and receptions soon brought Boston's
social aristocracy to Province House.

These were also weeks for political discussion and bargaining. In May a new Council would be chosen by the House of
Representatives, and Shirley wanted to be represented on it.

33. *Ibid.*, 230-32.

He succeeded in getting Samuel Waldo, Samuel Watts, William Dudley, and George Leonard chosen as members. But many of Belcher's cronies and relatives were re-elected, such men as the former governor's brother-in-law Anthony Stoddard and nephew William Foye. The election of James Allen was even more serious, for that tireless troublemaker and critic was now in a position to disrupt the business of the Council. Shirley undoubtedly hoped to replace Stoddard, Allen, and Foye with men like the youngster Benjamin Lynde and Isaac Little.[34] In the House he had better luck—most of the land bank supporters were returned.

The election seems to indicate that Shirley obtained majority support in the House in getting his particular nominees on the Council, but that he did not have strength enough to block the candidacies of people he did not like. The return of Hale and Choate to House leadership shows that their policy of cooperating with him was popular with the majority of the members. And the restoration to Council membership of many councilors purged by the House in 1741 indicates that bitterness toward them had been lessening.

After the elections of officers were held in the House and Council, and Shirley had given his assent to the elections, he joined the legislature to hear the annual election sermon preached this year by the popular Nathaniel Appleton of Cambridge. They heard a familiar message: the "great blessing of good rulers depends upon God's giving his judgments and righteousness to them." After enlarging upon his thesis, Appleton spoke directly to Shirley, praising him for his "acquaintance with human laws, . . . his equanimity and modera-

34. *Ibid.*, XX, 3-4, 6-7. The full 1742-43 Council of 28 men consisted of the following:

William Dudley	Joseph Wilder	Nathaniel Hubbard
John Osborn	Daniel Russell	Shubal Gorham
Ebenezer Burrill	Samuel Danforth	George Leonard
Ezekiel Lewis	John Read	William Pepperrell
Francis Foxcroft	William Foye	Jeremiah Moulton
John Jeffries	John Greenleaf	John Hill
Josiah Willard	Samuel Waldo	James Allen
Jacob Wendell	Samuel Watts	Joseph Dwight
Anthony Stoddard	John Cushing	John Quincy
Thomas Berry		

tion of temper, . . . his wisdom, prudence, and steadiness of conduct."[35]

Four days later, in the closing remarks of his first address to the newly elected General Court, Shirley referred to Appleton's sermon, calling on the legislature to promote piety and frugality by enacting the necessary laws. Whether the invocation of the clergy had any appreciable effect may be doubted, but when the houses settled down to business, the members offered to compromise the salary issue. They found, to their surprise, that Shirley was ready to receive their terms.[36] A salary of £1,300 of the new currency was approved, a substantial increase over Belcher's last salary and an amount approximately equal to the £1,000 sterling that the home government considered adequate for the governor's position. But the legislature did not make the permanent grant for which Shirley had been agitating.[37] It is not certain why Shirley chose to settle without further debate. It would seem that he was satisfied to have Waldo and some former land bank people on the Council and was now interested in appropriating funds for colony defense; he would then have contracts for supplies at his disposal.

Perhaps of more importance in his decision was the peaceful solution of another problem. The legislature wanted Shirley to prosecute the land bank people who refused to settle their debts with the bank's liquidation committee. Under the Parliamentary edict, Shirley could not allow the committee to institute such suits. The House, attempting to circumvent the Parliamentary law, proceeded to claim the right to appoint the attorney general, its object being to replace the present holder of the office, John Overing, with someone who would undertake prosecutions in behalf of the liquidation committee. Shirley vigorously protested this encroachment on what had already been the governor's privilege; loss of the patronage would weaken his powers of appointment and reduce his con-

35. Nathaniel Appleton, *A Sermon Preached before his Excellency William Shirley* (Boston, 1742), 41, 53.

36. *Mass. House Journals,* XX, 8-10.

37. *Shirley Correspondence,* I, 87-89.

trol of law enforcement.[38]   But when the legislature persisted, a defensive maneuver seemed the best tactic to Shirley; he ordered Overing to institute proceedings against certain delinquent shareholders.   He then wrote the Board of Trade that the permission he gave Overing would make the act of Parliament enforceable.

Shirley said nothing more to the legislature about a permanent salary during his tenure as governor.   He described the nature of the controversy in a letter to the Board of Trade, concluding with the significant remark that the establishment of a permanent salary could never be secured by a direct effort.   It could only occur "at some unexpected juncture when their settled affection for a governor may give the representatives courage to venture upon a short settlement at first, out of a personal regard to him, which might easily perhaps be followed with a settlement of it during his administration, from which precedent it might be difficult for the province to recede upon the appointment of a new governor."[39]   Shirley was undoubtedly thinking of the future and of his own role in the politics of the governorship—however, his projection turned out to be overly optimistic, even for a governor of his abilities.

V

Throughout Shirley's maneuverings to end the monetary crisis in Massachusetts, he was unfailingly supported by his London backers.[40]   Their loyalty, in turn, won him the admiration of many Boston legislators.   Such powerful representatives as Robert Hale of Beverly and John Choate of Ipswich began to sponsor his proposals in the House.   Samuel Waldo and Paul Dudley worked behind the scenes, and Robert Auchmuty openly backed the administration's policies.   This assistance eased the burdens of office, but also compelled him to carry out

38. *Mass. House Journals*, XX, 34, 229.
39. *Shirley Correspondence*, I, 89-92; Board of Trade to Shirley, Aug. 18, 1742, C. O. 5/918, 76-79: "We must commend you . . . for your strict adherence to your Instructions, and can only hope the General Court will at their next sessions come to better temper."
40. Shirley to Apthorp, Oct. 17, 1741, Shirley MSS.

certain policies and make certain appointments.[41] None of his supporters imposed greater obligations upon him than Waldo, who wanted the forest laws enforced, and no crown directives required more tact and skill in their enforcement.

41. Shirley to Thomlinson, Feb. 27 and May 5, 1742, *ibid.;* Belcher to Waldron, Apr. 3, 1742, N. H. Misc., III, Lib. Cong. Belcher admitted that William Pepperrell had joined Shirley's administration.

IV

Smugglers, Politicians, and Clergymen

THE EVENTS OF Shirley's first year in office constitute, with the exception of a short period in 1748 and 1749, the most critical part of his career. He was closely tested and closely observed by his political colleagues. On the one hand, his few friends enthusiastically welcomed the change of administrations for the patronage it would release to them and eagerly pressed for a division of the spoils. They appreciated his connections with Newcastle and worked to strengthen them. On the other hand, his associates in government reluctantly accepted his leadership because they had no other choice. But they, drawn into the work of liquidating the banks and undoing the damage of the 1741 crisis, discovered a basis of understanding with him. Shirley, too, realized that he had a sounder and wider basis for ruling the colony than he had started with, when his party was composed almost entirely of the malcontents of the Belcher administration. He was now confronted with the problem of harmonizing the aspirations of his supporters with those of his newly acquired followers. He could easily fall, as Belcher had done, into the hands of the smugglers, or come under the influence of other American interests that would shatter the political foundations of his administration. There was equal danger that his older friends might press him to fulfill political promises that would alienate these governmental people.

Even before the May elections of 1742 were held Waldo and Wentworth, who were concerned with the interests of the naval contractors, had raised the issue of law enforcement against the timber smugglers. Shirley unsuccessfully tried to postpone this business until the salary controversy was settled with the legislature, but pressed by Waldo and Wentworth he reluctantly extended protection to the legal timber-gatherers.[1] Then, in the fall of 1742, when a bloody riot broke out in the timber area, he was forced to support them openly. He immediately issued a proclamation backing up Wentworth's activities and pledging his assistance: "I have endeavored to remove the obstacles in the way of the contractor's agents for hauling the trees they have cut for His Majesty's service by my proclamation; and shall be glad to take any other steps to make it more effectual."[2] He then advised Wentworth to secure proper affidavits and be certain that the authorities kept their timber cutting within the law.

To further the acting surveyor's work, Shirley sent Bollan into the timber region to speak with people. Wherever he went, the Advocate General left a profound impression. "He informs me," the Governor reported to Wentworth, "that your antagonists, the proprietors of the townships, had last fall voted Colonel [William] Pepperrell (who is king of that country) one of their propriety and made him a grant of a share in it for the sake of engaging him in that dispute; and he had been imprudent enough to talk big upon this affair and tell the people what money and interest he has at home to defend them. But he and the whole partnership have grown very sick since Mr. Bollan's discourse with them, and I believe they will be much more so before I have done with them."[3]

Despite these assurances of cooperation, Shirley knew that little could be effected without the cooperation of the legislature and courts. He turned first to the House of Representatives, but received no promise of help. He was then forced to exercise his power of judicial appointment, control over the court sessions, and influence with the Council to give the naval

1. Shirley to Admiralty, Feb. 1, 1742, Admiralty Records, I, 3817, 205-6.
2. Shirley to Wentworth, Jan. 7, 1743, Belknap Papers, Lib. Cong.
3. Shirley to Wentworth, Apr. 6, 1743, *ibid.*

contractors a better chance to win their cases.[4] Progress was slow, but Shirley assured Thomlinson in 1743 that "I shall make [the timber smugglers] . . . sick of their suits at the Superior Court, . . . and you may depend upon everything in my power for that purpose."[5] In the succeeding weeks, the Governor kept his word, frequently going into court himself to aid Bollan and securing postponements of hearings until Waldo had witnesses ready for their court appearances.[6] Shirley also served the contractors by counseling Wentworth, who, besides being lazy and unimaginative, had to cope with the Belcher faction in his conduct of the New Hampshire governorship.[7] Shirley consulted with Wentworth's private secretary, Theodore Atkinson, who was constantly making trips to Boston, and entertained the Governor and his lady when they were in town on business.[8]

Forest law enforcement did not become a legislative issue until 1743, when Shirley, in a strong speech that included recommendations for colonial defense, raised the matter of lawlessness in the forest areas: "[I have received complaints from the] Surveyor-General . . . that the workmen employed by the undertakers for furnishing the royal navy with masts, yards and bowsprits here, have been greatly obstructed in that service by the unreasonable opposition of some people, and harassed with vexatious suits upon groundless pretences, [and] I must recommend it to you to pass some act for the protection of such workmen from the beforementioned injuries."[9]

The representatives received the speech in good spirits, and Robert Hale, who had helped Shirley repeatedly in the House, volunteered to head an investigating committee. Hale was a relative of the Gilmans and friend of the Pepperrells, all of whom were connected with the timber interests; he conducted immediate hearings on the timber laws and drafted a bill.

4. Shirley to Thomlinson, Jan. 26, 1743, Shirley MSS; Richard Waldron, Jr., to Richard Waldron, June 20, 1743, Mass. Papers, N.Y. Pub. Lib.
5. Shirley to Thomlinson, May 1, 1743, Shirley MSS.
6. Shirley to Thomlinson, Mar. 21, 1743, ibid.
7. Shirley to Wentworth, Sept. 25, 1744, Belknap Papers, Lib. Cong.; Waldron to Belcher, June 25, 1743, Waldron-Belcher Papers, Mass. Hist. Soc.
8. Shirley to Wentworth, Aug. 22, 1744, Belknap Papers, Lib. Cong.
9. Mass. House Journals, XX, 290.

It provided for a general clarification of the various British laws dealing with the forests of Maine and Massachusetts "so that it not only takes in all White Pine Trees, which have grown up to such diameter since the date of the Charter, . . . but perpetuates the preservation by extending it to all such trees, as shall be suffered to stand 'till they arrive to those dimensions."[10]   There were also provisions requiring licenses for cutting trees and imposing penalties of triple fines for "vexatious" lawsuits.

Times had changed.   No opposition to the bill was recorded, for attached now to Waldo's forest interests was the major opponent of the remedial legislation, William Pepperrell. An old friend of former Governor Belcher, an influential member of the Council, and a merchant of wealth and influence in Maine, he had changed sides politically when he gave his daughter in marriage to Nathaniel Sparhawk, Waldo's stepbrother, and agreed as part of the contract to share his Boston mercantile business with the firm of Sparhawk and Colman. Waldo, in turn, gave Sparhawk and Colman some of his naval contracting work with the British navy.   Their disagreements over timber suspended, Waldo and Pepperrell also reached agreements on military defense policies of the administration. Both had lands vulnerable to Indian raids, and their friends on the frontiers (many of whom were timber cutters) were threatened by the French in Canada.[11]   Both looked to the administration for help, and this unity of political and economic interests brought the leaders into cooperation.   The bill was passed on to Shirley for his approval.   Pepperrell's change of heart was evident of June 29, 1744, when he praised the Governor as the "father of this country" and Waldo for his "hearty regard" for Maine.[12]

Considering the difficulty of enforcing the forest laws, Shirley would have been exceedingly bold to have predicted the happy outcome of his attempt.   As it was, he was able to

10. Shirley to Admiralty, Nov. 14, 1743, Admiralty Records, I, 3817, 319-24.
11. Gulston to Waldo, July 13, 1742, Mass. Archives, LIII, 135; *Mass. House Journals*, XX, 291-92, 314, 316.
12. Pepperrell to Waldo, June 29, 1744, Waldo Papers, Mass. Hist. Soc.

satisfy Governor Wentworth (who had also taken on Dunbar's work as surveyor-general of the King's woods), Waldo, and their English friends, and he won the support of William Pepperrell.

I

Shirley was not so fortunate in his enforcement of the trade laws. He was committed by his own policies to a vigorous search for smuggled goods, and his new advocate general was a dedicated foe of smuggling. The bell on the Court House rang repeatedly as cargoes were seized. Excitement ran high, and the crowds of intent spectators followed the court procedure. The loss of ship after ship brought a demand in Boston and London for a relaxation of the enforcement. Bollan's answer was to have some of the seized cloth made into a suit and to wear it about Boston as a reminder to the smugglers that he was in hot pursuit.[13]

Since much of the illicit trade was with enemy Spain, no one could openly defend it, but there were ways in which the smuggling merchants could strike back and reduce the efficiency of the Admiralty officials. The opposition's favorite device, a threat to procure the dismissal of officials, was well-known to Shirley. When in 1743 a Rhode Islander tried to undermine the position of one officer, Charles Paxton, the Governor informed the Admiralty: "[I think Mr. Paxton] has executed his post . . . with diligence, fidelity, and good conduct, and particularly distinguished himself in it within the colony of Rhode Island (where there was ever a turbulent opposition . . .) in one instant with no small hazard of his life."[14] Before Paxton was eventually rescued, other enemies tried to remove Shirley's son from office.

This harassment was annoying to Shirley and dangerous to his interests. He was trying to serve the Admiralty and, indirectly, to show his loyalty to Newcastle. In desperation, he informed the Admiralty that "until all breaches of the acts . . . are made triable in the courts of vice admiralty, . . . illicit trade

13. Admiralty Court Records, Mass., V, June 16, 1744, and May 20, 1746, Lib. Cong.; Corbett to Shirley, June 9, 1744, Admiralty Records, II, 1054, 238.
14. Shirley to Admiralty, Nov. 14, 1743, ibid., I, 3817, 323.

... will be carried on ... and perhaps grow."[15]   Even when the law was clear, he complained, rum-runners were hard to catch and even harder to keep in jail.   When he imprisoned seven or eight witnesses for refusing to testify, a local judge released them on the pretense that to hold them in city jail was illegal.   Shirley re-arrested them under another warrant and housed them in the county jail.   But he could not prevent a wealthy Boston merchant from showering them with luxuries; nor could he stop their lawyers from securing a writ of habeas corpus that gave the witnesses immunity from further arrest.[16]

No general enforcement of the law was possible under these circumstances, and Shirley informed the home government of his predicament.   Since Judge Auchmuty was then in London as special colonial agent, Shirley asked him to take these problems directly to the Admiralty.[17]   Auchmuty's twenty-five years of service as judge and advocate general gave unusual authority to his opinions, and Shirley hoped that the Judge's remarks in addition to his own and Bollan's, would persuade the Board. Agreeing to perform the service, Auchmuty presented his opinions to the Board in writing.   The strongest part of his long discourse was his description of perjured custom declarations.   The solemnity of the oath, he affirmed, was violated in countless ways.   Ship masters sent their subordinates to enter false declarations.   Frequently the oath was tendered in a noisy coffee house and administered in a digested form, and the examination of ship papers was so hastily made that the oath had become an administrative formality.[18]

The Board was impressed, but it did nothing to help Shirley enforce the law; he did not win the commendation of Newcastle and the London merchants, who were, in fact, most alarmed by colonial opposition to the seizures and advised him to be more lenient on certain offenses.   Some merchants, apparently, thought of proposing that he be asked to resign.   In

15. Shirley to Board of Trade, Feb. 26, 1743, Boston Pub. Lib.
16. Shirley to Admiralty, Oct. 3, 1743, Admiralty Records, I, 3817, 281-88.
17. Shirley to Admiralty, Oct. 1, 1743, *ibid.*, 269-86; Shirley to Pelham, May 1, 1744, Huntington Lib. MSS, 9699.
18. Auchmuty to Admiralty, Nov. 23, 1743, *Historical Manuscripts in the Public Library of the City of Boston* (Boston, 1900-1904), No. 1, 1-16.

Boston, the feeling of local merchants was intensified in 1743, when Shirley replaced Andrew Belcher with Samuel Auchmuty as register of the admiralty court. He took this action primarily to favor the son of a friend, but he also wanted to assure himself control over the enforcement of the trade laws. The appointment raised a storm of protest, and forty-three merchants, led by Jacob Wendell, Thomas Hutchinson, and John Erving, Sr., old associates of Jonathan Belcher, presented Shirley with a petition.[19] Their number and the fact that many were supporters of his legislation in the General Court made Shirley reconsider this action. He restored young Belcher to the registery and petitioned the Admiralty to withdraw the appointment of Auchmuty.[20]

Opposition to Shirley's trade law enforcement also broke out in the legislature, when it was learned that Francis Wilks would be retiring from his post as Massachusetts agent in England. Old and in ill health, Wilks had long been a Belcher supporter and had remained loyal to the former governor. His powers as agent, however, had been reduced during the controversies over the banks; special agents had been sent to England to handle this matter. Christopher Kilby, one of them, had joined Shirley's forces against Belcher and now was putting himself forward as Wilks's successor. Kilby was not acceptable to Shirley's opponents, who wanted to assure themselves, through an agent of their choosing, of an official means of expressing their dislike of the Governor's trade policies.

A clique of Belcher's friends, led by Thomas Hutchinson, secretly threw their weight behind the English merchant Eliakim Palmer, nominated him before Shirley realized what was happening, and pushed for a confirmatory vote of the Council. The speed of their action revealed the importance of the issue. Shirley blocked the appointment in Council and then, by enlisting members of the "Land Bank as well as the

19. Shirley to Admiralty, May 5, 1743, Admiralty Records, I, 3817, 263-65. The merchant's petition carried the date of Apr. 30, 1743.

20. Shirley to Admiralty, Oct. 19, 1742, ibid., 247-49; Commissioners to Penrice, July 13, 1743, ibid., II, 1054, 138.

opposite party to break Palmer's interest," won enough votes in both houses to elect the popular Kilby.[21]

But the merchants were not ready to accept defeat. There was pending in London a disputed boundary issue with Rhode Island. Someone familiar with the problem was necessary, and Shirley looked upon Judge Auchmuty as a suitable agent. Auchmuty was a firm friend of the administration, deserved some reward for his loyalty, and wanted a chance to visit London. But he was as unacceptable to Hutchinson and the merchants as Kilby, and Hutchinson moved quickly again to nominate Palmer, using the powerful connections of James Allen in an attempt to overwhelm the Governor's supporters. Allen's Boston friends were not able to muster the votes, however, for Shirley with the assistance of Hale and Choate employed the strength of the land bankers and was again successful against Hutchinson.[22]

Though Shirley had the legislature on his side, these elections were a mixed blessing. Kilby's appointment had especially complex ramifications. A former Boston merchant, Kilby undoubtedly owed his victory in part to the powerful support of his friend Thomas Hancock. (Kilby's daughter was Hancock's ward and the men were also in close correspondence on business matters.) But Hancock was as bitter as his fellow merchants over the enforcement of the trade laws and was still refusing his full support to the Shirley administration until he could be compensated for his trade losses. His support of Kilby, however, had the immediate effect of separating him from the merchant group fighting the Governor's trade policies. As Kilby established himself as a merchant in the capital, he became a junior partner of Sedgwick, Barnard, and Kilby, which he hoped to make a supplier of war materials to the New England governments. Kilby wanted to tie Hancock's firm with these merchants, so they, with the Governor's cooperation, would furnish Massachusetts her military supplies. In short, Kilby would use the position of Massachusetts agent

21. Shirley to Thomlinson, Feb. 27, 1742, Shirley MSS.
22. Shirley to Thomlinson, Feb. 27 and Aug. 27, 1742, and Shirley to Yeamans, May 5, 1742, ibid.

to increase the business of his London firm, and Hancock, in exchange for loyalty to the Shirley administration, would become its Boston representative.[23]

Kilby's growing position in trade and politics disturbed Shirley's other London friends. Thomlinson, their spokesman on many occasions, warned the Governor that Kilby was taking unfair advantage of the agency and was exercising influence through Waldo. Wanting some of the trade that was flowing into Kilby's hands, they protested these encroachments and questioned the basis of Shirley's hostility to Eliakim Palmer;[24] before Shirley could conciliate Thomlinson, he received another protest from his London friends. This time they did not like Auchmuty's presence in London. The Judge was remembered as one of the land bankers and as an advocate of strict trade law enforcement. Everywhere he went he was quizzed about Massachusetts politics, and when his son replaced the younger Belcher in the registery, the merchants interpreted the appointment as dangerous to the stability of the Shirley administration. In several sharply written letters Yeamans and Thomlinson told the Governor that the Judge's agency in London was harming the administration and that harsh enforcement of the trade laws was hurting business. Surprised by the vigor of the attack, Shirley withdrew his strong support of Auchmuty and assured the London merchants that their interests came first.[25]

Stung by opposition at home and abroad, Shirley thought of resigning the governorship and went so far as to consult his London allies about future patronage. If he had his choice of position, he would prefer an English judgeship—though he admitted to Thomlinson that he would have to refresh his knowledge of the law. In reply, Thomlinson merely advised him to prosecute fewer smugglers. Shirley did not respond. The number of prosecutions continued large in 1743; however

23. Shirley did not permit Hancock and Kilby to have the full defense business of Massachusetts; he forced them to share it with Charles Apthorp and John Thomlinson.
24. Shirley to Thomlinson, Jan. 24, Sept. 20, and Oct. 3, 1743, Shirley MSS.
25. Shirley to Thomlinson, May 2 and 17, 1743, ibid.

advice from Newcastle may have brought a shift of policy, for in later years prosecutions declined.[26]   In spite of the vocal opposition to trade law enforcement, Shirley could count on solid support for his administration.   Besides his friends Waldo and Apthorp, Pepperrell remained friendly; the land bankers gave him continuous support; and Hancock, putting aside old bitterness, spoke for the Governor.   In England, Shirley enjoyed consistent backing of his policies, except that the merchants disapproved his appointments;[27] there was no opposition faction, and even when Hutchinson and his associates raised their protest, there was no one commissioned in London to put the petition before the ministry.

Shirley persisted in his enforcement of the trade laws far longer than he should have.   For one who was as politically astute as he the continuation of unnecessarily hostile policies seems out of character; it is well, however, to emphasize that catching smugglers was lucrative business for the Governor and his admiralty associates.   One-third of the profits from all seizures went to him, and in 1744 his salary was doubled by his share of the booty.[28]   Undoubtedly the profits had a large influence upon him, for he could not have forgotten the pinched years of his youth.   He was also reluctant to give up the prosecutions out of consideration for Bollan's interests.[29]   The Advocate General was a close friend and a valued member of his staff.   Their relationship was deepened when, in September 1743, at a solemn church service conducted by Roger Price of King's Chapel, William Bollan wed Frances Shirley, the eldest daughter of the Shirleys.   The young couple rented a large house not far from the Governor's mansion.[30]

26. Bollan to Board of Trade, Feb. 28, 1743, *Historical Manuscripts in the Boston Public Library*, No. 1, 7; Freiberg, "William Bollan," *More Books*, 23 (1948), 90-100.
27. Bourryan to Hancock, June 9, 1743, Hancock Papers; III, Admiralty Court Records, Mass., V, 1744-1745, Lib. Cong.
28. *Ibid.*, V, 1744.
29. Freiberg, "William Bollan," *More Books*, 23 (1948), 140; Shirley to Admiralty, Feb. 1, 1742, Admiralty Records, I, 3817, 205-6.
30. Boston Record Commissioners, *Report . . . Marriages from 1700 to 1751* (Boston, 1898), 275; *The Boston Weekly News-Letter*, Sept. 15, 1743.

II

As a colonial governor Shirley was expected to be all things to all men, and like his other supporters, Shirley's friends in the Anglican Church had great expectations of his help. The Reverend Mr. Price of King's Chapel, commissary of the church in New England, was elated by his appointment, predicting "great advantages" in having an Anglican governor.[31] Church officials in England reflected Price's enthusiasm by enrolling Shirley as a member, patron, and lay missionary in the Society for the Propagation of the Gospel (S. P. G.), bundling off to him collections of sermons, pamphlets, and prayer books, which they hoped he would distribute in the colony. They designated him an advisor of the Anglican clergy in New England and put matters of church discipline and relations with the legislature in his hands. Accepting these responsibilities, the Governor helped to secure passage of a law which allowed taxes for religious purposes collected from members of the Church of England to be turned over to the minister of the church usually attended by the taxpayer. This was a significant achievement; it went a long way toward bringing religious peace during Shirley's administration.[32]

Though a firm Anglican, Shirley was no zealot and refused to use his office to promote the missionary activity of the Church; when books and pamphlets arrived from the S.P.G., he gave them to the Harvard College Library. A vigorous pro-Anglican policy, in any case, would have brought new religious friction, for the colonists were stirred by the Great Awakening. But Shirley's denominational ties were apparent in his regular attendance at the services of King's Chapel and his willingness to free the Church of England from discriminatory legislation.

Much to Price's irritation Shirley enjoyed supervising Church affairs in Boston; he recommended appointments of local clergy and occasionally offered advice on religious policy.

31. Price to S.P.G., Aug. 19, 1741, Manuscripts of the Society for the Propagation of the Gospel, London, B Ser., IX, 1741-1743, No. 1.
32. S.P.G. to Shirley, Oct. 25, 1742, *ibid.*, X, 1741-1743, No. 186; Shirley to S.P.G., July 8, 1743, *ibid.*, XIII, 1743-1746, 134-36.

He rarely agreed with Price as to what was best for the Church. When Trinity Church had a vacancy in the pulpit, Shirley backed the vestry and congregation over Price's opposition in the selection of William Hooper. When this energetic, eloquent orator of a Presbyterian church in Boston indicated a willingness to exchange pulpits, Shirley was delighted. He went over Price's head to urge his ordination, listing Hooper's good qualities: "agreeable [in] conversation, . . . a prompt elocution, a winning address, and good sense and learning in the pulpit."[33] Hooper was soon confirmed as Trinity's minister.

Observing the habits of Congregationalist ministers, the Governor wondered why the Anglican clergymen did not bestir themselves during the week and offer lectures. He cited for the S. P. G. the opinion of a member of the Council, who told him that the week-night lectures of the Congregational ministers were responsible for the strength of that church in Boston.[34]

Shirley was also concerned about Anglican education in Boston. He was careful to see that his three sons were well prepared in their religion, taking pains to instruct them and say his prayers with them. He even composed a morning prayer that was one of the prized possessions of his family:

Almighty and infinitely good and gracious God who has restored me to a new day and thereby given me another opportunity of approaching the throne of thy mercy . . . O Lord, I beseech thee, strengthen my faith, enliven my hope and increase my charity, that my soul may advance from one degree of virtue to another, from perfection to perfection in the course of this mortal life. . . . Bless the whole family to which I belong, let thy Holy Angels guide them in the ways of thy commandments, and in what ever they do, give each of us grace to do our duty in our several stations toward each other.[35]

33. Henry Wilder Foote, *Annals of King's Chapel: From the Puritan Age to the Present Day* (Boston, 1882-1940), I, 534; Mary Plummer Salsman and Walter H. Stowe, "The Reverend Roger Price (1696-1762) Commissary to New England (1730-1748)," *Historical Magazine of the Protestant Church*, 14 (1945), 220-22.

34. Shirley to S.P.G., Dec. 1, 1746, Perry, *Papers of Mass. Church*, 403-4.

35. Dated 1745, James G. King coll., New York City.

He advised the S. P. G. to establish a grammar school, with a curriculum strongly classical and free from the "Antiquated Jargon of the Schoolmen and Calvinistical Tenets." Undoubtedly, he was observing the progress of his son Thomas, then in the Boston Latin School, and was concerned by the fact that Thomas had been given less "taste of Classical Learning" than he had gained in his own education. From the objectives of his plan, Shirley seems to have desired greater emphasis on the writings of the church fathers, the great Roman and Greek philosophers, and a substantial treatment of the Reformation, together with the standard languages, disputation, logic, and mathematics—a considerable change in the work load of the average Latin School. The school which Shirley advocated was established, and a schoolmaster named Stephen Roe was placed in charge, but the merits of Shirley's ideas on education were not now to be tested, for Roe soon proved unfit for the responsibilities. His past life involved "debauching a young girl" and marrying "an actress of low morals." Both Shirley and Price, in rare agreement, had Roe replaced.[36]

When Price resigned his King's Chapel post in 1746, Shirley exerted influence upon the vestry through his son-in-law Eliakim Hutchinson to find a different type of minister. Several vestrymen made a very careful survey of candidates, undoubtedly conferring with Shirley during the negotiation, and the eventual selection of Henry Caner of Fairfield, Connecticut, was most agreeable to the Governor. An American convert, a competent scholar, and a good preacher, Caner brought distinction to the pulpit of King's Chapel.[37]

III

These were years of the Great Awakening, when towns and hamlets of the colony witnessed intense religious revivals.[38]

36. Shirley to S.P.G., July 8, 1743, S.P.G. MSS, London, B Ser., XIII, 1743-1746, 134-36.
37. Shirley to S.P.G., June 6, 1747, *ibid.*, XV, 16-19.
38. Leonard W. Labaree, "George Whitefield comes to Middletown," *William and Mary Quarterly*, 3d Ser., 7 (1950), 588-91; Charles Chauncy, *Seasonable Thoughts on the State of Religion* (Boston, 1743); Joseph Haroutunian, *Piety Versus Moralism* (New York, 1932), xi-xxv, 15-21, 97-

The ground had been well prepared for the first coming of the revivalist preacher George Whitefield. The stories of his conversions in the Carolinas, New Jersey, and Connecticut had instructed the masses as to what was expected of a converted Christian. Then, too, New England had her own Jonathan Edwards, whose revivals at Northampton had aroused uncommon interest.[39] Whitefield, on his first visit to New England in the fall of 1740, came and went in less than five weeks, but his ten days in Boston and four days in Northampton were dramatic beyond expectation. "Great multitudes attended at every place"; sermons at Old South Church, in the Boston Common, in the meeting houses, and on the streets were heard by thousands. The vivid language of his sermons took his listeners to the pits of hell, lifted them to the heights of heaven, struck their souls with "arrows" of accusation, and compelled them to repent. Whitefield undoubtedly knew his stage, for his graceful presence, mellow voice, and vivid descriptions imparted a message of salvation that had a hypnotic effect on his audiences.[40]

After Whitefield left Massachusetts, the local ministers Thomas Prince and Benjamin Colman, at first, then the itinerant revivalists James Davenport and Gilbert Tennent lent their voices to the "battle against Satan." They were even more blunt in their predictions of doom than Whitefield. Davenport climaxed one of his sermons, "You poor unconverted Creatures, in the Seats, in the Pews, in the Galleries, I wonder you don't drop into Hell."[41] The congregations reacted violently; night prayer sessions followed the sermons, public testimonies revealed the sinner, and the saved Christian emotionalized his religious experience. "Some were present with the Lamb and saw Him write their names in the Book of Life, and could describe the Book, Character, Hand and Pen."

101; Edwin Scott Gaustad, *The Great Awakening in New England* (New York, 1957), 42-60.
    39. Ola Elizabeth Winslow, *Jonathan Edwards* (New York, 1940), chap. IX; and *Meetinghouse Hill* (New York, 1952), chap. XIII; William Warren Sweet, *The Story of Religion in America* (New York, 1939), chap. IX.
    40. Cutler to Bishop of London, Jan. 14, 1742, Perry, *Papers of Mass. Church*, 350-52; *The Boston Weekly Post-Boy*, Apr. 5, 1742.
    41. Chauncy, *Seasonable Thoughts*, 98.

Some "have seen the very Blood of Christ dropping on them, and His Wounds in His side; some have seen a great light shining in the chamber."[42] These excesses disturbed many people who had at first welcomed Whitefield's preaching. Charles Chauncy, minister of the First Church of Boston, became a leader of the reaction, with a powerful attack on the New Lights, in a volume entitled *Seasonable Thoughts on the State of Religion* (1743). He denounced the itinerant preachers as "Busie-Bodies," poked sarcastic jabs at the "terrible Tempest and Thunder," and ridiculed their revelations.[43]

These criticisms apparently had Shirley's full sympathy; he contributed his support as one of the sponsors of Chauncy's book. As a devoted Anglican, he was distressed by the excesses of revivalism, but like many of the Congregational clergy, he held his opinion and awaited the eventual reaction. Similarly, he recommended to Price that their church publicize the doctrinal soundness of Anglicanism. He supported the mission churches in Scituate, Salem, Hopkinson, and Marchfield, and sponsored a move to rebuild an enlarged King's Chapel, giving an initial contribution of £250.[44]

Shirley's discretion in handling religious matters was rewarded by the praise of such diverse people as Secretary Willard and acting vice-admiralty judge George Cradock. Willard, a revivalist, was at the Governor's side during these years and was not offended by Shirley's opinions. In a letter to Dr. Benjamin Avery of December 31, 1743, he wrote: "I am not apprehensive that he [the Governor] will ever use his power to oppress us. . . . There [never was] a greater harmony and agreement between the several parts of the legislature than since the beginning of his administration, nor have any of our governors had more of the affection of the people than he."[45] Judge Cradock, a strong churchman of King's Chapel,

42. Report to Price, Oct. 15, 1741, Fulham Palace MSS, Mass., Box 1, fol. 162.
43. Chauncy, *Seasonable Thoughts*, 242-43, 256-57, 271-74.
44. Foote, *Annals*, II, chap. XIV; King's Chapel Vestry to Bishop of London, Oct. 25, 1749, Fulham Palace MSS, Mass., Box 1, fol. 85; MacSparran to S.P.G., June 14, 1748, S.P.G. MSS, London, B Ser., XVI, No. 16 and Jan. 3, 1750, XVII, No. 87.
45. Willard to Avery, Dec. 31, 1743, Foote, *Annals*, II, 130.

told the Bishop of London that the colony was blessed with "a true son of the church . . . who by his steady principles, exemplary life of affable temper has gained him the universal esteem of the whole province, even the most rigid separatist."[46] It should be added that, in 1745, out of regard for the Governor, such prominent Congregationalists as Thomas Hancock and Andrew Oliver helped contribute new bells for the Anglican Christ Church of Boston.

As the war against Spain became more serious in 1744-45, Shirley shared the deep feelings of New Englanders that the war had religious significance. The defenseless frontiers seemed a threat to Massachusetts's way of life; war with France would undoubtedly subject the colony to invasion. Thomas Prince, one of the revivalists, turned his energies to an explanation of the international situation. He found the French base of Louisbourg on Cape Breton Island to be the "Dunkirk of North-America, and in some respects of greater importance."[47] The danger of that fortress, he believed, had cast a shadow across Protestant America for twenty years and, in each passing year, the menace grew darker. By the time Prince published his essay, Shirley was himself aware of the danger to Massachusetts and was laying down a policy of defense.

46. Cradock to Bishop of London, Oct. 8, 1743, Fulham Palace MSS, Mass., Box 2, fol. 179.

47. Thomas Prince, *Extraordinary Events the Doings of God, and Marvellous in Pious Eyes* (Boston, 1745), 18-19.

V

Louisbourg

W HILE SHIRLEY was consolidating his power during these difficult years, he was fortunate in having the benefits arising from increased defense expenditures to offer his followers. Recruiting fees, provision contracts, and visits from naval vessels brought supplies of sterling money into the colony, giving the economy a generally prosperous appearance. Better times had the effect of reducing political tensions and the moderation of the Shirley regime caused many people to contrast it favorably with the bitterness of Belcher's. But thoughts of war remained far from the minds of most citizens; they were primarily concerned about the religious revival, inflationary controls, and the prosecution of smugglers. Some ministers and a few frontiersmen worried about defense and the spread of popery from Canada. Although petitions from such fretful people were sympathetically received, the legislature was not impressed with the need for spending more than a minimum for defense.

To Shirley the defenses of Massachusetts were a constant source of worry. The Spanish war could easily spread into a general European war, and if France entered the conflict as an ally of Spain, Massachusetts would be faced with enemy territory along hundreds of miles of its frontier.[1] In order to spur defense preparations, Shirley invited legislative committees to go with him to Castle William, located in Boston harbor, where they could hear Spencer Phips, the Castle commander, explain the deficiencies of harbor defense. The fortress's only substantial fire power, Phips said, consisted of several guns

1. *Shirley Correspondence*, I, 76; Shirley to House, Oct. 13, 1741, Mass. Archives, CVIII, 220.

regularly used for official salutes. Its faulty stone walls were neither thick nor high enough; the roofs of its inadequate barracks were leaking; and most serious of all, its garrison was untrained and poorly paid.[2]

When the House of Representatives heard the report on Castle William, members raised questions about the fortifications at Marblehead, Gloucester, Plymouth, Martha's Vineyard, Salem, and Falmouth. No detailed information was available, but the committee on defense admitted that the colony was unprepared to withstand enemy attack. At Shirley's suggestion, the legislature authorized a fact-finding tour of the defense areas of Massachusetts and Maine. Selecting Samuel Waldo, William Pepperrell, John Choate, and John Osborn as leaders, the General Court instructed a delegation of twenty-five legislators to aid the Governor in meeting with the Indians and examining seaboard defenses.

Before the legislature adjourned in the spring of 1742, Shirley agreed that if immediate funds were voted to improve fortifications, he would petition the home government for the necessary cannon. His promise and the help of Choate and Hale brought enough money to begin construction work on Castle William and eight other forts. Opposition from economy-minded members delayed a more intensive consideration of defense requirements until September, when a report on defense was to be placed before the legislature.[3]

During the early summer the Governor prepared for his journey to Maine; in August he embarked with the legislative delegation. Arriving at Fort Georges on the St. Georges River, he was saluted by the cannon of the half-finished fortress, and several hundred Indians rowed out to his ship. He went ashore for a conference, and for three days he and the legislators listened to complaints from settlers and Indians against each other. One Samuel Green, for example, declared

2. *Mass. House Journals*, XIX, 65, 191, 197, 208, 240-44; House to Shirley, Aug. 18, 1741, Mass. Archives, CVIII, 210.

3. *Mass. House Journals*, XIX, 242-44; Message, Dec. 4, 1741, Mass. Archives, 242. The House committee which supervised these repairs on Castle William consisted of the following men: Timothy Prout, Edward Bromfield, and Samuel Watts.

"that he saw at the wigwam three skins of the mares and two heads."[4] Indian after Indian told his story of being cheated in trade, of wormy corn at the public storehouses, of abuse of his women and children. Shirley consoled the participants by offering promises and presents. On the day of his departure, he noticed British flags flying from many wigwams.[5]

At Richmond, on the Kennebec River, he heard the details of the fort's reconstruction from John Storer and the workmen. Carefully inspecting the plans, he left orders to hasten the job, ignoring the complaints of some legislators who grumbled about the expense of providing elaborate quarters for the garrison. From Benjamin Larrabee, commander of Fort George at Brunswick, he listened again to tales of neglect: "The fort itself wants but little repairs, only shutters to the gun ports and a small matter done to the lodgings to make them tight and comfortable. But we have 4 carriage guns and 4 swivels and the carriages of them—all are partly rotten and out of repair; . . . in case of a sudden rupture [with France, we] would . . . want . . . soldiers. My number of soldiers allowed this fort is but six." From Commander Arthur Savage of Fort Frederick at Pemaquid came another pitiful account: "I . . . must . . . observe . . . the impossibility of my being able to subsist upon the poor wages the government is pleased to allow me at present, and your Excellency must be sensible there can be but little perquisites, where there is but six men, and [I] do assure your Excellency I do spend more in a year than I can possibly get in a just manner."[6]

Many of these settlers were friends of Samuel Waldo and looked to him to present their case to the Governor and emphasize their reliance upon the forts of their area for defense against sudden Indian attack. The Penobscots, Pigwackets, Norridgewocks, St. Francis, St. Johns, and Cape Sables were

4. *The Boston Weekly News-Letter*, Aug. 19, and Sept. 9, 1742; Shirley to Newcastle, Aug. 30, 1742, *Doc. Hist. of Maine*, XI, 251-53; Proceedings of Meeting, Aug. 6, 1742, *ibid.*, XXIII, 284.
5. *Ibid.*, XI, 252-53 and XXIII, 285-86, 298-99; *Shirley Correspondence*, II, 375; Roland Oliver MacFarlane, "The Massachusetts Bay Truck-Houses in Diplomacy with the Indians," *New England Quarterly*, 11 (1938), 48-65.
6. *Doc. Hist. of Maine*, XI, 224-25, 231.

not large tribes, but if they fell under the influence of France they could easily destroy the prospering farms of Maine and the timber trade. For some years Massachusetts had been trying to win Indian friendship through the regulation of trade between the natives and the merchants. By hiring public factors to sell merchandise at reasonable prices, the colony had sought to deal fairly and realistically with the Indians. But finding good traders was most difficult, and trade abuses were always present.

On his return to Boston, Shirley recommended to the General Court increased appropriations for the forts and a better selection of Indian traders and truckmasters. He counted heavily on the support of those legislators who accompanied him on the junket. He was not disappointed. In addition, both Waldo and Pepperrell were delighted with the Governor's policies and rallied their followers in the legislature. Within a week the legislature had approved £700 for work at Saco, St. Georges, and Pemaquid, and additional funds for Castle William. Later, some new truckmasters were chosen, presumably in response to the Governor's request for better men. Shirley, in summarizing the new legislation for Newcastle, told him that the people of Maine had been in danger of being abandoned, but the colony had now granted them "equal protection with its other inhabitants."[7]

Though pleased with the spirit of the legislature, the Governor knew that he still must prod the lawmakers to appoint chaplains, hire better truckmasters, build additional vessels for the navy, and provide annual grants for soldier pay. His messages to the lawmakers, often no longer than a hundred words, served as reminders of their joint responsibility to king and people. He was fortunate in having the warm support of Choate and Hale. Their help smoothed Shirley's relations with the legislature and placed more friends on the Council. In 1743 Benjamin Lynde, Jr., Isaac Little, Ezekiel Cheever, and John Chandler replaced John Read, Anthony Stoddard, John Quincy, and James Allen. In 1744 Eliakim Hutchinson, William Browne (who often served as Shirley's private secretary),

7. *Ibid.*, XI, 252; *Mass. House Journals*, XX, 68-70, 77, 79.

Daniel Russell, and James Bowdoin, Sr., were elected. To show his gratitude for these favors, the Governor redistributed colonial patronage on a grand scale in the summer of 1744.[8]

I

Defense activities raised a political tide in Shirley's favor. Speculators, contractors, and merchants prospered, and their profits attached them to the new administration. The new defense policy won the support of many of Belcher's allies; their defection was undoubtedly encouraged by Belcher's departure from the colony in 1744. So valuable, however, had friendship with the Governor become that Thomas Hancock, a long-time critic of Shirley now drawn into profitable contracting, outdid himself in soliciting the Governor's favor.[9] Gone were his hesitations about Shirley's trade policies; with Charles Apthorp and Jacob Wendell, he sang the Governor's praise. Lesser men, in turn, looked to the contractors; a chain of favors spread war business to a large number of people.

Shirley's preoccupation with defense was especially popular with Waldo, who had extensive business interests in Maine. In some of Waldo's enterprises the Governor was a minor partner, although there is no evidence that his concern for colonial defense was strongly motivated by these interests.[10] Waldo's relations with the Governor gave him unusual opportunities to reward his friends. The growing fear of war with France brought solicitations for better defense, and Waldo, known to be close to the Governor, was besieged with petitions for governmental patronage: "I thank the Lord who hath put a gentleman in the chair of government to whom you have a ready access, with whom you have a good understanding, and whose impartial administration gives us great consolation in this day of trouble."[11]

8. *The Boston Weekly News-Letter*, Mar. 8 and Aug. 30, 1744; Prout to Pepperrell, Mar. 10, 1746, Belknap MSS, 1745-1776, 46, Mass. Hist. Soc.
9. W. T. Baxter, *The House of Hancock*, 95-100; Bourryan to Hancock, June 9, 1743, Hancock Papers, III; Business agreement among Williams, Stoddard, and Wendell, June 17, 1743, Williams Papers, Berkshire Athenaeum.
10. Indenture between Shirley and Waldo, July 3, 1738, Knox MSS.
11. Clenachan to Waldo, May 23, 1744, Waldo Papers.

Shirley, nevertheless, was careful that no one usurp his own position as chief dispenser of patronage. Always aware himself of political advantage, he used his closer relations with Pepperrell to enlarge his connections with the conservative elements in Boston—with Benjamin Colman in particular. The ancient pastor of the Brattle Street Church was pleased with Shirley's overtures: "His Excellency seems to venerate me for my age, and does me the justice to number me among his friends."[12] Shirley had become better entrenched in office each year; almost all the local officeholders now owed their appointments to his favor, and in England, his chief benefactors, the Duke of Newcastle and Henry Pelham, were more firmly established in office, though Lord Wilmington had recently died.[13]

Shirley's English friends, like himself, owed their rise to the Spanish war. Almost five years old, the war thus far was more important for its stimulation of business than its military exploits, but there was a new and serious development in 1744. This was noted in Newcastle's dispatches to the American governors, when he warned them that the conflict was spreading to Europe and that hostilities with France would bring conflict to North America. Shirley took measures to meet the imminent crisis. He ordered the colonels of the militia to ready their forces for war and urged Wentworth to strengthen Fort Dummer, a key post on the upper Connecticut River: "I am in pain for the danger, I apprehend it to be in, from the French Fort at Crown Point. Be pleased to let me know whether you can take it into your protection or not."[14]

II

The attack was sudden and brutal. The French assaulted Canso, a rocky isle almost hidden by clouds of fog off Nova

12. Colman to Belcher, Aug. 22, 1743, Mass. Hist. Soc., *Collections*, 2nd Ser., 2 (1814), 187.
13. *The Boston Weekly News-Letter*, Mar. 8 and Aug. 30, 1744; Livingston to Wendell, Sept. 4, 1744, Livingston Papers, 7118, Museum of the City of New York; Richard Waldron, Jr. to Richard Waldron, Sr., June 20, 1743, Mass. Papers, N. Y. Pub. Lib. The Waldrons were noting the very close relations now between Waldo and Pepperrell.
14. Shirley to Wentworth, June 18, 1744, Essex Institute, Salem, Mass.

Scotia's northern shores. Taken by surprise, the garrison capitulated; the loss of men and materiel was a severe blow to the defenses of Nova Scotia. The French moved down the peninsula toward the tiny capital of Annapolis Royal, held by Paul Mascarene and an undermanned garrison. Mascarene notified Shirley that unless help arrived swiftly from New England, he would be compelled to fight to the death.[15]

In the fall of Annapolis Royal, Shirley perceived irreparable damage to Massachusetts's commerce: the fishing banks would be lost, the northern trade imperiled, and the frontiers of Maine violated. To meet the emergency, he dispatched seventy militiamen northward on the armed snow *Prince of Orange*. Meanwhile the French had reached Annapolis Royal.[16] The fort was peppered with gun shot, its outer buildings burned, and many of the defenders killed or wounded. Just when surrender seemed inevitable, the garrison saw, through the smoke of the burning town, the white sails of the Massachusetts relief party. The reinforcements turned the battle, and Mascarene wrote Shirley: "I can hardly find expressions to thank you. . . . We every day drink your Excellency's health."[17]

During the remaining weeks of summer Shirley sent more men and provisions to Annapolis Royal in anticipation of a new assault. When it came in late September, the garrison had the advantage of greater manpower and stronger defenses. Water-filled ditches and the earth-supported walls of the fort held off the besiegers. When the battle became too fierce and the season too short, the French commander withdrew his men to winter quarters.[18] Shirley considered this successful resistance most fortunate, but he was aware that the crisis had not terminated. Although he had sent Mascarene a total of 180 men from Massachusetts, the reinforcements were not enough if the French population of Nova Scotia would rebel and join the French forces. The fall of Nova Scotia would

15. Mascarene's Letter Book, July 4, 1744, Add. MSS, 19071; Shirley to Board of Trade, June 16, 1744, Bancroft coll.
16. Mascarene to Shirley, July 28, 1744, Letter Book, Add. MSS, 10971; Shirley to Thomlinson, Aug. 12, 1744, Shirley MSS.
17. Mascarene to Shirley, July 7, 1744, Bancroft coll.
18. Shirley to Board of Trade, July 25, Aug. 10, and Oct. 4, 1744, *ibid.*

leave the New England colonies unprotected from raids originating at the great fortress of Louisbourg on Cape Breton Island.[19] The Governor was especially disturbed by the terms under which he had been obliged to raise the relief party. Its service was limited to three months and the expenditures of the expedition were restricted to approximately two thousand pounds. Shirley warned the home government that the General Court would do little more to relieve Annapolis Royal, where Mascarene was already enfeebled by lack of resources. Mascarene had provisioned the relief party by drawing unauthorized bills upon the British Treasury and had pledged his property as security to merchants; nonpayment of the bills could tie up his estate and bankrupt him. Some of the bills were honored at Boston only with a personal guarantee of payment by Shirley himself. Shirley's friends had advised him to avoid financial responsibility, but he realized that all of Nova Scotia would be lost unless someone was willing to hazard funds. With help from Apthorp and Hancock, his military contractors, he secured food and clothing and hastened a request for money and reinforcements to Henry Pelham: "I forthwith gave orders to a merchant here, agent vitualler for His Majesty's ships, to supply me with . . . provisions, . . . clothing for 172 men, and shall hire a vessel."[20]

Shirley counted on his good relations with Newcastle and Pelham, whom as reasonable men, he expected to recognize the peril to trade of a French attack on Nova Scotia, approve the expenditures, and order additional preparations. Until he knew their decision, he did what he could to improve the Massachusetts defenses. Although he could not send more men northward, he secured an extension of enlistment for the Massachusetts garrison. This action indicated a different spirit in the legislature; however, its members were less concerned with the remote menace of the French in Nova Scotia than with strengthening the colony's immediate defense lines. De-

19. Shirley to Pelham, Nov. 15, 1744, Huntington Lib. MSS, 9700.
20. *Ibid.;* Shirley to Admiralty, Dec. 7, 1744, Admiralty Records, I, 3817, 399-400.

fense committees conferred with Shirley, and the legislature
voted funds for three new forts in the western part of the
colony—Shirley, Pelham, and Massachusetts. Money for Fort
Dummer in western New Hampshire would be supplied until
that colony assumed the responsibility. Shirley also proposed
a second line of defense along the Connecticut River and secured authorization to build fifteen blockhouses. To supervise these military preparations, he appointed John Stoddard,
one of the most influential men of the west.[21]

Increased funds for coastal defense enabled him to strength-
en Castle William, erect a new breastwork on Governor's Island, and make soundings of Boston harbor preparatory to the
sinking of ships on the sandbars in the event of an enemy attack. He won larger garrisons for the Maine forts, a declara-
tion of war on the Cape Sable and St. Johns Indians (who
were apparently cooperating with the French), and money to
reward scalping parties. The keel was laid for an additional
warship, the frigate *Massachusetts*, which was finally commissioned in January 1745 under the command of Edward
Tyng. Its 400 tons and 20 guns doubled the fire power of the
fleet, which hitherto consisted only of the *Prince of Orange*
and several armed fishing vessels.[22]

The cooperation of New Hampshire was essential in these
plans. Shirley still conferred regularly with the Governor's
secretary on policy matters and maintained a correspondence
with Wentworth himself. Now he was careful to keep Wentworth informed of his progress. In one letter of October 1744,
his subtle humor broke into an otherwise serious discussion:
"I wish you a good deliverance of Whitefield [the religious
enthusiast], and a safe arrival of the gun powder."[23]

III

Late in 1744 an exchange of prisoners with the French
repatriated a number of British seamen and Massachusetts

21. *Shirley Correspondence*, I, 138-41; Shirley to Board of Trade, Oct. 4
and 16, 1744, Bancroft coll.; Wheelwright to Williams, Oct. 18, 1744, Williams
Papers.
22. Waldo Lincoln, "The Provincial Snow, Prince of Orange," Amer. Antiq.
Soc., *Proceedings*, New Ser., 14 (1900-1901), 251-305.
23. Shirley to Wentworth, Oct. 14, 1744, Belknap Papers, Lib. Cong.

soldiers who had been imprisoned at Fort Louisbourg and had secretly observed the town and fortress. The information was primarily from three men—John Bradstreet, William Vaughan, and Joshua Loring—who told him that the fortress lacked sufficient fire power, and that the garrison was discontented and would be unable to withstand a sustained assault. The Governor questioned his informants closely. If their information was correct, there was much to recommend a British attack on Louisbourg before the French reinforced the garrison in the spring.[24]

The capture of Louisbourg was obviously the best way of saving Nova Scotia and preserving the New England fisheries; but the expedition was not to be undertaken lightly. The French had spent twenty-five years and millions of livres building and defending the fortress. Although Shirley's ultimate decision to make the attempt was heavily influenced by the reports of the British prisoners, other factors probably contributed. He was being warmly praised for his efforts in Nova Scotia, and as the home government accepted responsibility for supporting the Nova Scotia garrison, his merchant friends were benefitting from contracts.[25] In Massachusetts a popular demand for an attack on Louisbourg had been fostered by the stories of the returned prisoners, and many people pressed Shirley for a decision. Some offered to enlist men; others were willing to petition the General Court for an expedition; and still others were content to proclaim that an attack on Louisbourg was a golden opportunity to strike a blow at popery.[26]

While calculating the personal and political risks of an attack, the Governor gathered data on the fortress and weighed

24. *Shirley Correspondence*, I, 145-48; Shirley to Pelham, Nov. 15, 1744, Huntington Lib. MSS, 9700; Usher Parsons, *The Life of Sir William Pepperrell* (Boston, 1856), 48-53; Gerald S. Graham, *Empire of the North Atlantic: The Maritime Struggle for North America* (Toronto, 1950), 120; Vaughan to Shirley, Jan. 14, 1745, C. O. 5/753; Shirley to Greene, Jan. 29, 1745, Rhode Island Archives, Providence, Letters II, 89; George Arthur Woods, *William Shirley* (New York, 1920), 250-56; Shirley to Warren, Jan. 29, 1745, Admiralty Records, I, 3817, 407-13.

25. Kilby to Newcastle, Oct. 8, 1744, C. O. 5/309-19.

26. Shirley to Warren, Jan. 29, 1745, Admiralty Records, I, 3817, 407-13.

the practicability of mounting an expedition from Boston. Finally, on January 9, 1745, in a secret session of the General Court, he unfolded his plan: "I have good reason to think that if two thousand men were landed upon the island [of Cape Breton] . . . such a number of men would . . . be masters of the field at all events, and not only possess themselves of their two most important batteries with ease, break upon their out settlements, destroy their cable and magazines, ruin their fishery works, and lay the town in ruins, but might make themselves masters of the town and harbor."[27]

The legislators responded sharply to the scheme, branding it foolish and impractical. Thomas Hutchinson said that the strategy for battle was "like selling the skin of a bear before catching him," and his opposition led others to demand detailed information about Louisbourg's defenses and the availability of a naval convoy from the British fleet. When the lengthy sessions ended and the vote was taken, the legislature rejected the proposal by a small margin—primarily because the colony was without professional soldiers, ample cannon, and financial resources. Shirley and Vaughan continued to agitate for the expedition.[28] Vaughan circulated petitions among fishermen, merchants, and traders, asking their aid in putting pressure on the General Court. Shirley promised to seek British repayment for the costs of the expedition, get a convoy from the British Admiralty, and give commissions and contracts to local men.[29] While continuing secret negotiations with his followers, Shirley laid before Newcastle the precarious condition of the northern defenses and outlined the steps he had taken to protect the area. Possession of Louisbourg, he stressed, permitted the French to interrupt "the coasting trade and navigation of the northern colonies as far as Pennsylvania, but especially of . . . the New England fishery, which . . . has been half ruined . . . in time of peace, [and] will be now in danger of being quite destroyed and lost to the enemy." He also asserted that control of Canada would give Britain a

27. *Mass. House Journals*, XXI, viii; Prout to Pepperrell, July 3, 1745, Belknap Papers, 61B, 135, Mass. Hist. Soc.
28. Vaughan to Waldron, Jan. ——, 1745, Photostat coll., Mass. Hist. Soc.
29. Shirley to Waldo, Feb. 5, 1745, C. O. 5/753.

monopoly of the fur trade and possession of a vast country whose climate and resources would guarantee the development of prosperous colonies: "If the value of a territory to the mother country may be computed by the increase of her natural wealth and power, which it occasions, [then the possession of French America] may be reckoned a more valuable territory to Great Britain than what any kingdom or state in Europe has."[30]

Two weeks after his initial proposal to the legislature, Shirley delivered another message to both houses, he emphasized that colonial troops could hold Louisbourg until they were reinforced by British land and sea forces. He promised to seek aid from the home government, and in addition to formal assistance he believed their venture "might probably" be supported by British naval units on duty in American waters.[31]

The Governor's new speech was studied by a committee of the two houses chaired by William Pepperrell, and a bill that embodied Shirley's recommendations was drafted. After two days of debate, the bill won approval by good margins. Shirley was given authority to raise 3,000 volunteers, 1,000 more than he had originally requested, and to purchase the necessary supplies. He was further instructed to solicit cooperation from neighboring colonies as far south as Pennsylvania. Within an hour of this vote, Shirley had dictated letters to the governors of these colonies inviting them to join the enterprise; and he had arranged for Captain Joshua Loring to take a report of the legislative action to the British ministry. He then dispatched instructions to the militia colonels and selectmen of the outlying towns to raise the required number of men. A committee of the General Court, acting in an executive capacity, took measures to insure secrecy, procure supplies of food, place an embargo on shipping, and establish facilities in the Boston area for housing and feeding recruits.[32]

30. *Shirley Correspondence*, I, 162-63.
31. *Ibid.*, 168.
32. Shirley to Wentworth, Feb. 9, 25, and 26, Mar. 2 and 6, 1745, Belknap Papers, Lib. Cong.; Shirley to Thomas, Feb. 4, 1745, Dreer coll., Pennsylvania Historical Society; Shirley to Board of Trade, Feb. 5, 1745, Mass. Archives, LXIV, 261.

Making military decisions was entirely new to Shirley, and
he sought the advice of Waldo, Wendell, and his sons-in-law
Bollan and Hutchinson. He would not accept personal leadership of the expedition because the administration of the government of Massachusetts was too important to be left to
subordinates; in any case, he supposed that military command
was no business for a lawyer. Who should be the commander-
in-chief? Shirley may have considered Waldo, but new honors
for him would increase jealousy and particularly offend William Pepperrell, Waldo's competitor for the timber of Maine.
On the whole, Pepperrell seemed a safer choice politically,
and Shirley offered him the post. Pepperrell was at first reluctant to assume responsibility for such an important enterprise, but he favored the expedition, and when Jacob Wendell
urged him to accept, he obliged the Governor. The appointment of Pepperrell paid enormous political dividends to Shirley, closing the political ranks which had been broken since the
banking crisis of 1741. Shirley then appointed as brigadier
generals Waldo and Joseph Dwight (an influential landholder
and military man of western Massachusetts); Hale, Choate,
and Shuball Gorham were among those named colonels.[33]

Honors aside, the colonelcies were enviable posts, for deductions were allowed colonels in the purchase of clothes and
handling of soldier pay, in addition to the privileges of selling
certain luxuries to enlisted men and of taking spoils from
enemy territory. Shirley frankly told Dr. Hale that he had
been commissioned as colonel to help him meet his financial
obligations.[34] And despite Shirley's need for haste, he was very
much the politician in making arrangements for commissions
and contracts. He commissioned Waldo's son a commissary,
Pepperrell's son-in-law a contractor, and Auchmuty's son a
lieutenant. Members of his family, like Eliakim Hutchinson

33. Mass. Hist. Soc., *Collections*, 1st Ser., 1 (1792), 5-11; *Pepperrell
Papers, ibid.*, 6th Ser., 10 (1899), 99-114, hereafter cited as *Pepperrell Papers;*
Shirley to Warren, Jan. 29, 1745, Admiralty Records, I, 3817, 407-13; Shirley
to Newcastle, Feb. 1, 1745, Parkman Trans., XXXVIII, 28-35, Mass. Hist.
Soc.; J. S. McLennan, *Louisbourg from its Foundation to its Fall* (London,
1918), 360.

34. Shirley to Hale, June 23, 1745, Gilman MSS, Mass. Hist. Soc.

and William Bollan, were charged with recruiting and provisioning. He was equally ready to refuse favors to those who had not fully supported his administration.

During the weeks of mobilization, the need for funds was especially urgent, and the emission of paper currency seemed to be the only solution. Shirley secured several tax levies that provided for the immediate issuance of £50,000 paper currency and its redemption in the tax years 1747 and 1748. He jeopardized his record as a sound money advocate, but he expected Britain to subsidize the campaign costs before the paper money depreciated. In any case, he decided that the expedition was worth the risk. He revealed his attitude when Wentworth asked him for recommendations on a New Hampshire bill supporting the expedition but not providing for repayment of the paper money. Shirley was uncertain. Admittedly, the expedition was all important, "but I might veto the bill; [however] I must leave you to better judgment than my own to advise you."[35]

While preparations were getting underway, Shirley notified the home government of his actions and sent a letter to Commodore Peter Warren, the commander of naval operations in American waters, asking for a naval escort. He did not inquire whether Warren had authority to support the expedition, merely assuming that the ministry's plans to protect Nova Scotia would include an attack on the source of the trouble, the fortress at Louisbourg. He believed that if Warren would release naval ships in North American waters, these vessels, together with those commissioned by the colonies, would give ample protection to the British expedition.[36]

The letter was written on January 29, when Warren was cruising in the West Indies. As he waited for an answer, Shirley appreciated more fully the dangers of conducting the expedition in hostile waters and the absolute necessity of a strong naval support. He arranged to outfit additional vessels, but these were hardly a substitute for warships. Meanwhile,

35. Shirley to Wentworth, Feb. 9, 1745, Belknap Papers, Lib. Cong.; Wentworth to Newcastle, C. O. 5/10, 229-36.
36. Shirley to Warren, Jan. 29, 1745, Admiralty Records, I, 3817, 405-13.

he attended to a plethora of administrative details that demanded his attention: writing scores of letters, signing commissions and proclamations, setting policy, clearing information, and working with hundreds of people.[37]

In February he welcomed 200 men from New Hampshire and promised to pay for any additional recruits; he reminded Wentworth that "the essential thing is the number of the men."[38] There were many discouragements, not the least of which was the procrastination of the colonies to the south. Only Connecticut was making any effort to supply recruits. Nevertheless, Shirley worked steadily and without loss of enthusiasm. Apthorp, Osborn, Hancock, Sparhawk, and Shirley's sons and sons-in-law were contracting for the supplies. Reports of progress were rushed to Wentworth, who was a little confused by the pressure of the mobilization, and to Pepperrell, who was recruiting in Maine. "I write in a great hurry," Shirley began one letter to his commanding general, "and have only at present to assure you that no attention and vigilance of mine shall be wanting and that I think the affair has a very good aspect."[39]

With so much activity everywhere, complications were inevitable. Reports of smallpox, which were later proved false, appalled the expedition's leaders, for the spread of that dread disease would have ended their plans. Tempers exploded as men worked at cross purposes in their jobs. Sometimes duplicate commissions were issued, and contractors found themselves bargaining for the same supplies. Seamen were often scarce, and impressment was necessary to complete the crews; riots occurred when indignant townspeople protested seizures to town meetings.[40] Shirley hoped the Council would avoid

37. Shirley to Newcastle, Feb. 1, 1745, Parkman Trans., XXXVIII, 2; Shirley to Admiralty, Mar. 27, 1745, Admiralty Records, I, 3817, 435-45; Shirley to Greene, Jan. 29, 1745, R. I. Archives, Letters II, 89.
38. *Shirley Correspondence*, I, 187.
39. Shirley to Pepperrell, Feb. 14, 1745, Pepperrell MSS, 61A, 142, Mass. Hist. Soc.; Byron Fairchild, *Messrs. William Pepperrell: Merchants at Piscataqua* (Ithaca, 1954), 173-77. Mr. Fairchild placed at my disposal his very large film collection of Pepperrell MSS.
40. *The Boston Weekly News-Letter*, Feb. 21, 1745; Graves to Shirley, Jan. 21, 1745, Mass. Archives, LXIV, 269; Waldo to Pepperrell, Feb. 19, 1745, Belknap Papers, 61A, 146, Mass. Hist. Soc.

making impressment a political issue: "I suppose there will be
no hesitation at the Council Board in passing a warrant for
impressing twenty men or thereabouts for Captain Durell. It
is impossible to avoid it. The request is modest; he has four
mast ships depending upon him, and he personally deserves all
favors from us."[41]

In this critical period the Shirleys were deeply grieved by
a death in their family. For several days in early February
their daughter, Frances Bollan, suffered a protracted child-
birth and after giving birth to a daughter, she died. Her
prolonged agony and the funeral ceremonies at King's Chapel
depressed Shirley and his wife, but did not interrupt work in
the mounting preparation for war.[42]

As the days of February passed, Shirley manned three
twenty-gun ships, two sixteen-gun snows, and a brigantine,
and sent them into northern waters to pick up intelligence
reports of Louisbourg. When their reports proved favorable,
he readied a snow and several smaller vessels waiting at Boston
to act as convoy for the fleet of transports and supply ships
that would take the troops to Louisbourg. In reviewing these
preparations for the Admiralty, he was satisfied that the work
of mobilization was progressing well, but without the necessary help he expected from British naval commander Warren
and the home government. When Shirley eventually received
word from Warren in late March, he was very disappointed.
Warren refused to allow any of his vessels to be used, asserting
that he had no authority to engage in an expedition. He would
do no more than send two warships into the coastal waters of
New York and New England to relieve those colonial vessels
drawn into the Louisbourg campaign. Shirley pleaded with
Warren, but he dared not delay the expedition.[43] Forced to
depend upon the navy he had assembled, he hoped the element

41. Feb. 5, 1745, Mass. Archives, LXIV, 261.
42. Shirley to Pepperrell, Feb. 17, 1745, Belknap Papers, 61A, 142, Mass.
Hist. Soc.
43. Shirley to Admiralty, Mar. 27 and Apr. 4, 1745, Admiralty Records, I,
3817, 435-45, 457-59; Osborn to Pepperrell, Feb. 18, 1745, Belknap Papers,
61A, 145, Mass. Hist. Soc.; Shirley to Wentworth, Mar. 26, 1745, C. O. 5/10,
229-36.

of surprise would make up for its weakness. He allowed for possible defeat and had planned a pattern of retreat, but like those around him, he was satisfied with the preparations and willing to take the gamble.[44]

Weighing anchor at Boston on March 28, 1745, a bitterly cold day, the little fleet moved away in a heavy fog. As it disappeared, the shadows of Louisbourg extended to Boston. Shirley, now having time to reflect on the consequences of what he had done, admitted later to Pelham that the expedition was constantly "upon my mind . . . You would easily conceive, Sir, that . . . [my] duty might make a deep impression upon firmer constitutions than mine."[45] Defeat was a grim consideration. From Shirley's standpoint, however, the political stakes were high—business flourished, contracts and offices multiplied, and the heady scent of glory was in the air.

IV

Within a week of the fleet's departure, Shirley received a remarkable letter from Warren. The Commodore had received new orders which gave him authority to harass the enemy, and he interpreted them as empowering him to aid the expedition. He would cooperate fully, with ships, supplies, and leadership. Unfortunately, Warren's earlier orders had been issued before word of the Louisbourg expedition reached London. Shirley's communications had impressed Newcastle with the peril to Annapolis Royal, and the ministry had ordered Warren to reduce the French in Nova Scotia, calling upon the governors for any necessary aid. Warren, of course, was to exercise high command of an attack which now had to be adapted to the expedition against Louisbourg.

Shirley was greatly encouraged; British assistance seemed to guarantee victory if Warren and Pepperrell did not contest

44. *Shirley Correspondence*, I, 198-99.
45. Shirley to Pelham, July 27, 1745, Huntington Lib. MSS, 9706; Joseph P. Edwards, "Louisbourg: An Historical Sketch," *Nova Scotia Historical Society, Collections* (Halifax, 1879-1938), IX, 137-96. It is interesting that Auchmuty had urged an attack on Louisbourg as early as Apr. 1744, and that Kilby had written a long letter to Newcastle in October on the value of the Nova Scotian fisheries.

the position of commander. Shirley wrote Pepperrell of the news, warning him that to make an issue of authority "might prove fatal to His Majesty's service in the expedition."[46] All members of the expedition were obliged to serve under Warren's command, and, as Shirley explained to Pepperrell, "this is not a preference given to . . . [Warren] by me, but [I am] only acting in obedience to His Majesty's orders."[47]

Settlement of command problems awaited Warren's arrival, but in the meantime there were immediate difficulties in maintaining communications with Pepperrell. The Governor was never certain of the expedition's progress and the safe arrival of supplies. Frequent letters from Pepperrell complained of shortages, and Shirley, often bewildered by the delay, tried to reassure him: "This is the sixth sloop's load of provisions . . . sent to Canso since the news of your arrival. . . . I spoke to the committee [of war] for more shells a month ago, who twenty times assured me . . . 100 more [were] . . . made. But at last it turned out that . . . [the armorer] received no orders concerning them. . . . I will call upon the committee every day for an account of their proceedings."[48]

To avoid shortages of this kind, the Governor tried to anticipate the needs of the expedition—not an easy task when there were no data on the number of combatants, the condition of the provisions on arrival, and the rate of consumption. "Since my last letter," he wrote Pepperrell on April 26, "I have apprised the Committee of War that they must compute the number of men in the army and on board the fleet at 4400 at least. . . . [I] have obtained from the Assembly . . . a vote impowering the Committee to purchase and send you provisions for one month more over and above the four months. . . . I have put 50 more barrels of powder for you on board Captain Gayton, who is equipped and full manned after

46. Shirley to Pepperrell, Apr. 10, and Pepperrell to Shirley, Apr. 28, 1745, Mass. Hist. Soc., *Collections*, 1st Ser., 1 (1792), 14-16, 22-25; Shirley's Journal of the Siege of Louisbourg, 1745, Huntington Lib., MSS. 899.
47. Shirley to Pepperrell, Apr. 22, 1745, Pepperrell MSS, 71A, 57; Shirley to Warren, Apr. 16, 1745, Admiralty Records, I, 3817, 467-70.
48. Shirley to Pepperrell, Apr. 8, 1745, Belknap Papers, 61B, 20, Mass. Hist. Soc.; Shirley to Newcastle, Apr. 18, 1745, Parkman Trans., XXXVIII, 54.

infinite trouble in getting it done, and will, I hope, sail by Sunday morning."[49]

Provision ships continued to be sent, but there were many supply problems at Boston. British warships regularly entered port for repairs, men, and provisions. The arrival of the *Princess Mary* and the *Hector* in early May brought, in addition to the usual problems of supply, the return from England of Shirley's messenger, Captain Loring, who had dispatches from the Admiralty and reinforcements for the expedition. This news Shirley rushed to Warren and Pepperrell. Loring, he wrote, "stayed but twelve hours in London, before he was ordered to go on board the *Princess Mary*. The Duke of Newcastle being out of town, his secretary, Mr. Stone, instantly laid my letters before his Majesty, who upon reading them, was pleased to express his approbation of the expedition, and referred the letters to the Lords of Admiralty, whereupon a Board was called at eleven o'clock at night. I understand their lordships received the scheme with great pleasure, and ordered away those two ships upon the spot, and would scarce give Loring leave to sleep."[50]

The news of these reinforcements reached Louisbourg in June. By this time Warren had arrived safely. His fleet was blockading the harbor and assisting Pepperrell's men to storm the land defenses. The commanders had divided their responsibilities, tactfully avoiding questions of rank and authority until Louisbourg fell, and Warren had been sufficiently aware of American sensibilities to reassure Shirley that "I have the success of this expedition so much at heart that nothing shall break the harmony that now subsists between me, the general, and troops."[51]

With everything going well at Louisbourg, there was time for the routine duties of the governorship. May was the month of elections to the legislature, and Waldo and Eliakim Hutchin-

49. *Shirley Correspondence*, I, 210-11; Shirley to Pepperrell, Apr. 23, 1745, Belknap Papers, 61B, 21, Mass. Hist. Soc.; Shirley to Admiralty, May 12, 1745, Admiralty Records, I, 3817, 485-93.

50. *Shirley Correspondence*, I, 214-15.

51. Warren to Shirley, May 12, 1745, Admiralty Records, I, 3817, 499-502; Shirley to Admiralty, May 12, 1745, *ibid.*, 487-93.

son, as well as Pepperrell and Wendell, were returned to the
Council. The election sermon for the year was preached by
Ebenezer Gay, pastor of the Congregational Church in Hing-
ham. Its serious tone reflected the anxiety of Boston awaiting
news of the expedition. The next day Shirley opened the
legislature with an optimistic address that contrasted with the
gloom of Gay's sermon: "We have reason to hope, that if we
are not wanting to ourselves at this important crisis, the . . .
expedition may . . . answer all our labor and expense in the
prosecution. . . . How different will the scene be, if instead
of losing Annapolis Royal, His Majesty should gain Cape
Breton [Louisbourg] by this expedition? How invaluable in
its effects to the province in particular, as well as to His
Majesty's other neighboring colonies, would be the acquisition
of that island and its dependencies?"[52]

A miscellany of bills was presented to further the expedition
and strengthen local fortifications. Castle William needed
money for garrison pay; Fort Dummer was about to be abandoned unless Massachusetts again provided funds; blockhouses
and forts on the Connecticut River and in Maine required repairs and ammunition. Funds for these necessities were easily
voted, but Shirley encountered opposition when his salary was
budgeted and appropriations for Louisbourg were approved.
Some members still branded the expedition as a "Wild goose
chase."[53]

Amidst these problems of political management, Shirley
continued to be harassed by troublesome difficulties of military
recruitment and logistics. When British captains wanted men
to fill their crews, he secured the replacements by impressment.
Often the draftees had to be escorted by a small army of
constables, and these episodes created a reservoir of bitterness
against naval recruiting. He also had to answer all requests from Louisbourg. To Pepperrell on June 22, he

52. Ebenezer Gay, A Sermon Preached Before . . . William Shirley . . .
May 29, 1745 (Boston, 1745), 21; Mass. House Journals, XXII, 8-9; Shirley
to Newcastle, June 2 and 17, 1745, Parkman Trans., XXXVIII, 88, 90; Waldron
to son, June 21, 1745, Louisbourg Papers, 19, Clements Lib.
53. Prout to Pepperrell, July 3, 1745; Belknap Papers, 61B, 135, Mass.
Hist. Soc.

pledged 1,000 more men, 400 to be sent immediately, and promised that extensive quantities of powder, shot, and shells would be shipped the next day. To Hale on June 23, he promised more medicine and a surgeon. To Governor Gideon Wanton of Rhode Island on June 24 he reported an acute shortage of powder and asked the Governor "to lay an embargo upon all the powder now lying in your stores."[54]

V

Less than forty-eight hours after writing this letter, Shirley heard that Louisbourg had capitulated on June 17. The news touched off a frantic celebration in Boston. Crowds gathered outside the picket fence of Province House and shouted for Shirley. Cannon at Castle William, Governor's Island, and the city's breastwork pounded out messages of victory. Fireworks and bonfires expressed the joy of the colony. It was said that one could see the gladdened hearts of the people from their faces—which may also have been illuminated by the emptying of many punch bowls in honor of the occasion.[55]

The capture of Louisbourg was acclaimed in other colonies. Cadwallader Colden of New York thought that "Governor Shirley and the people whom he governs have remarkably distinguished themselves and have very deservedly obtained the applause of the world." Another New Yorker told Jacob Wendell that "I wish we had a Shirley to govern us."[56] From Boston Benjamin Colman wrote his kinsman William Pepperrell: "You will ever stand next to our excellent Governor Shirley in their hearts and in the history of New England. . . . Never was a man . . . [as] universally loved as his Excellency."[57] Not all

54. *Pepperrell Papers,* 288; Hale to House of Representatives, June 8, 1745, Osborn to Pepperrell, June 23, 1745, 61B, 104, 61, 125, Belknap Papers, Mass. Hist. Soc.; Shirley to Hale, June 23, 1745, N.H. Misc. Corres., Lib. Cong.; *Shirley Correspondence,* I, 231; Shirley to Wanton, June 6 and July 3, 1745, R. I. Archives, Letters, II, 116, 135.

55. *The American Magazine,* Dec. 1745; *The Boston Weekly Post-Boy,* July 8, 1745.

56. Colden to Collinson, June 20, 1745, *The Letters and Papers of Cadwallader Colden* (N. Y. Hist. Soc., *Collections,* vols. 50-56, 67-68 [New York, 1918-1937]), III, 120. Hereafter cited as *Colden Papers.* Richard to Wendell, June 19, 1746, N.Y. Hist. Soc.

57. *Pepperrell Papers,* 352-53.

Bostonians were as enthusiastic as Colman about the victory.
One called it a wild goose chase that was only justified because
"we got the goose," and he cynically noted that "we were told
in a . . . sermon . . . that there is such a strange work of God
in it that it will convince all but Atheists that the whole of the
work was from His immediate hand."[58] Nevertheless, the
victory enormously enhanced Shirley's prestige.

Indeed, it gave him confidence to speak out on British
imperial policy and reawakened his ambitions of knighthood
and preferment. He lost no time describing the magnitude of
the victory to Pelham, Newcastle, the Board of Trade, and the
London merchants. Generous as was his praise of Pepperrell,
Warren, and the colonels, his gratitude to the volunteers was
boundless. For 3,600 raw militiamen to have reduced "the
French King's strongest" fortress, captured 2,000 troops, and
lost only 100 men seemed to him a deed which deserved
universal admiration. Their victory, he believed, should mark
the start of a campaign that would eventually drive the French
"off this continent." He stoutly advocated the retention of
Cape Breton Island and strongly emphasized its value; it was
worth the cost of maintaining a strong garrison.[59]

While he drew spacious plans for expansion into Canada,
Shirley took up matters of patronage with Henry Pelham.
He wanted a British regiment, more favors for the family, and
a baronetcy. "It is a dignity not unknown to my family, and
which has not been many years extinct in it."[60] He complained
that his service in behalf of the empire was not adequately
compensated by the emoluments of his office; the hard work
and tensions of the governorship had not only "sensibly de-
cayed my health," but had not substantially increased his income, which was "very little more than what has sufficed to

58. Prout to Pepperrell, July 3, 1745, Belknap Papers, 61B, 135, Mass.
Hist. Soc. A letter to the *Boston Evening-Post*, July 14, 1745, called the victory
"scarce to be paralelled in history."
59. *Shirley Correspondence*, I, 239-46.
60. Shirley to Pelham, July 27, 1745, Huntington Lib. MSS, 9706; Shirley
to Pelham, Sept. 27, 1745, *ibid.*, 9707. Shirley's great grandfather was a
baronet, and the last Shirley to hold the title was Sir Richard who died in
1705. His granddaughter married William Shirley's son Thomas in 1768.

support the ordinary expenses of my family with a decency suitable to my station."[61]

Considerations of empire and patronage did not distract Shirley from safeguarding Louisbourg. The task of holding the fortress until a British garrison took it over was as vital as the conquest. The great stone ramparts had to be rebuilt and a garrison assigned to guard them through the winter. In undertaking these measures, contracts were handled by Apthorp, Hancock, Sparhawk, and Kilby, who took their profits—and sometimes enormous ones—as they helped Warren and Pepperrell reconstruct the fortress before the winter ice closed the area.[62]

But the excitement of fighting an enemy no longer served to unify the men and keep them working; there was only homesickness and the realities of hard labor. Issues of authority and discipline divided the British and American officers; camp rumors magnified differences among the foot soldiers. Discontent was not confined to the troops. Pepperrell, a wealthy merchant who had few characteristics of the professional soldier, questioned the need of rigid discipline. All Warren did, he complained, was "to find fault," because "the soldiers did not march as handsome as old regular troops, their toes were not turned enough out, etc. I thought we encamped as regular as the hills and valleys would admit of."[63]

As misunderstandings among the officers became known, colonials spread rumors of a British plot to deprive them of Louisbourg. It was an American victory, they insisted, and not even the "High-Admiral of England" was going to steal the honor from them. Little by little the happiness of victory turned to gall, and people from all parts of Massachusetts called upon Shirley to talk with Warren and describe the importance of the victory to the home government. He assured them that he would visit Louisbourg; but he had a difficult task before him, trying to protect the American interest in the

61. Shirley to Pelham, July 27, 1745, *ibid.*, 9706.
62. Kilby to Pepperrell, Nov. 6, 1745, Pepperrell MSS, 355; Baxter, *The House of Hancock*, 95-107.
63. *Pepperrell Papers*, 330.

face of the hostility of a British commodore.[64] Charles Chauncy put the problem very well to Pepperrell: "I believe the Governor will come down with a firm resolution to do all honor to you and the New England troops. I doubt not his being well received by you; though if he should exert himself in giving you the full power and glory that belong to you, I do not know how the commodore would look upon him."[65]

Shirley's impending visit to Louisbourg aroused much speculation. He would not leave Boston until the General Court provided additional funds for defenses in Maine and western Massachusetts, where Indians were imperiling settlements, and until plans were completed to send an agent to London, where petitions would be presented for a subsidy to cover the recent military expenditures. Shirley wanted William Bollan to undertake this mission and, perhaps, look after patronage matters at the same time.[66] Bollan was quickly commissioned and, with the other legislative problems out of the way, the Governor sailed in early August, accompanied by his lady and a shipload of officers' wives.

64. Shirley to Pepperrell, July 29, 1745, *ibid.*, 338-42; Payne to Hale, Aug. 6, 1745, N.H. Misc. Corres., 1745-1787, Peter Force Trans., Mass. Hist. Soc.

65. Chauncy to Pepperrell, July 27, 1745, Mass. Hist. Soc., *Collections*, 1st Ser., 1 (1792), 51; Allen to Pepperrell, July 9, 1745, Belknap Papers, 61B, 141, Mass. Hist. Soc.

66. Bollan left Boston in the fall of 1745, accompanied by Shirley's son William. Freiberg, "William Bollan," *More Books*, 23 (1948), 90-100; Shirley to Bedford, Oct. 31, 1745, Admiralty Records, I, 3817; Hodshon to Wendell, Nov. 14, 1745, Wendell Papers, Mass. Hist. Soc.

VI

The Canadian Expeditions

The HARD WORK and monotony of garrison duty were forgotten as the Louisbourg soldiers prepared a royal welcome for Shirley. When they saw the sails of the *Hector* in the evening sky of August 16, they shouted their welcome from the fortress walls and gave him an impressive cannon salute. Early the next morning, the Governor, his wife, their daughter Judith, Mrs. Warren, and the wives of the Louisbourg officers came ashore, with "a great deal of drumming, trumpeting, and other instruments of music" filling the air.[1]

Shirley took his place in the public ritual, but his visit was more than ceremonial. With tact and understanding, he investigated disciplinary matters and ascertained the degree of preparation for the winter. He discovered that death was taking a frightening toll of the men. Wind, dampness, salt pork, and dry peas were as hard on health as they were on military discipline. The Governor insisted on cooperation, and the prestige of his position soon restored harmony among the officers and men.[2]

As the weeks passed, the garrison worked to rebuild the fortress before winter set in. Roofs were repaired, and a hospital, barracks, officers' quarters, and mess hall were constructed.[3] Preparations were taken for the health of the troops; latrines were built and trash receptacles provided—the

1. Louis Effingham de Forrest, ed., *Louisbourg Journals 1745* (New York, 1932), 37, 103; McLennan, *Louisbourg From its Foundation to its Fall*, 169; Parson, *Sir William Pepperrell*, 116-19.
2. Warren to Corbett, Oct. 3, 1745, Admiralty Records, 480, I, 9-21; Shirley to Wentworth, Sept. 2, 1745, Belknap Papers, Lib. Cong.
3. Shirley to Pepperrell, Oct. 26 and 29, 1745, Pepperrell MSS, 71A, 216, 217.

men were so unaccustomed to camp life that it was difficult to enforce the regulations. The wives of the officers organized entertainments and provided dancing and music for the troops. The Governor presented barrels of rum to the men as a token of his esteem, but did not neglect to have a meetinghouse erected where chaplains preached Sunday sermons and held week-night lectures.[4]

In September, Shirley received the first dispatches from London in reply to his announcement of the Louisbourg victory. The Governor was congratulated for his devoted service to the crown, and the expedition was generously praised. All this was to be expected; then he read the news that Warren and Pepperrell were to be honored for their courage in leading the expedition. Both were to be knighted, and Warren given an admiral's flag and the governorship of Nova Scotia. Pepperrell and Shirley were jointly promised colonelcies of new American regiments whenever these were commissioned.

Although Shirley knew the vagaries of imperial favor, he was deeply hurt by this action. He wrote Pelham that the ministry's decision was unfair, for the expedition was "wholly formed, set on foot, and carried into execution, in New England by myself." Warren was acting under orders and had sacrificed the expedition at one time in order to seize a French prize. Pepperrell was but the personal representative of the Governor. This treatment by the King, Shirley complained, "gives me no small concern and makes me less able to bear the loss of my health."[5]

The reluctance to reward Shirley was due in part to the political implications of the Louisbourg victory. In England popular reaction was explosive: Louisbourg "became the darling object of the whole nation [and] . . . ten times more so than ever Gibraltar was."[6] Pamphleteers pronounced it the greatest of conquests, and the First Lord of the Admiralty vowed that he would hang the man who dared surrender

4. Shirley to Pepperrell, Nov. 6, 7, and 22, 1745, *ibid.*, 223, 233; Shirley to Warren, Dec. 14, 1745, Warren MSS, Clements Lib.
5. Shirley to Pelham, Sept. 27, 1745, Huntington Lib. MSS, 9707.
6. Richard Lodge, ed., *The Private Correspondence of Chesterfield and Newcastle, 1744-1746* (London, 1930), 75.

Louisbourg.[7] He personally pronounced the victory the deed of Admiral Warren and his captains. Pelham was distressed by the popular outburst. Tired of war and its disasters, he had urged peace with France only to see the possibility of peace diminished by the victory's effect on politics. His brother, the Duke of Newcastle, confronted with grave military losses on the continent, a rebellion in Scotland, and hostility from King and Parliament, considered Louisbourg as one more episode likely to split his party. The Pelhams were then looking about for additional support to reinforce their coalition, which was not easily sustained when military events continued unfavorable and the erratic behavior of men like William Pitt kept the House of Commons on edge. Seeking alliances, they were content to let Shirley be deprived of major credit for the Louisbourg victory in favor of the protégés of other factions. Finally, in February 1746, the ministry resigned, and the Pelhams formed a new coalition.[8]

Even before the crisis was resolved, Newcastle secured the regimental commissions for Shirley and Pepperrell, and instructed them to go ahead immediately with recruiting the necessary men. The new appointment did not satisfy Shirley, but a colonelcy had financial advantages worth more than a thousand pounds, patronage opportunities, and all the implications of prestige that arose from a new royal favor. He tentatively set aside captaincies for his sons John (Jack) and Thomas —the latter was a boy of sixteen years—and a lieutenancy for James Auchmuty, the younger son of his good friend. Still, he could not forget that the Pelhams had not rewarded him as generously as Pepperrell and Warren.

Until their return from Louisbourg in November, the Shirleys lived luxuriously in the quarters of the late French commandant. Whenever it was possible, the Governor invited Pepperrell and Warren to exchange ideas on the war; at other times, often with Waldo, Hale, and Choate present, their discussions ranged from regimental business to patronage matters.

7. Arthur H. Buffinton, "The Canadian Expedition of 1746: Its Relation to British Politics," *The American Historical Review*, 45 (1939-40), 563.
8. John B. Owen, *The Rise of the Pelhams* (London, 1957), 279-97.

Waldo was seeking commissions, war prizes, and additional profits. Hale hoped to restore his finances from the disasters of the land bank crisis—in spite of the advice from one of his correspondents that there was a lighter side to life at Louisbourg: "a bowl of punch, a pipe, and a pack of cards . . . and whatever else you desire (I forgot to mention a pretty French mademoiselle)."[9]

Apparently the Governor and Pepperrell agreed that their best patronage, the London agencies of the regiments, should go to Bollan and Kilby, with shares given to Sparhawk, Eliakim Hutchinson, and such people as Apthorp, Hancock, Benjamin Colman, and Wendell.[10] There were other agreements. Pepperrell's friends Jeremiah Moulton and Simon Frost were to be appointed, respectively, justice of probate and justice of the peace for York County.[11] Dr. Hale was to be named sheriff of Essex County; Paul Dudley, chief justice of the superior court.[12] And Waldo, always ready for his share of the spoils, secured a captain's commission for his son, Samuel Jr., who was then in charge of supply for their regiment.[13] Through his stepbrother Sparhawk, he arranged for the sale of French war loot in Boston. There were also some intangible gains in cementing friendships. Mrs. Shirley and Pepperrell exchanged recipes, and she promised to send him a goose and turkey pie and some minced meat for Christmas. After her departure, she sent him several letters from Boston relating messages from the Governor and the social news.[14]

During the intervals between politics and patronage, Shirley was captivated by the spacious pattern of conquest opening before him. The reduction of Canada, he assured Newcastle, "seems to be the most effectual means of securing . . . not only Nova Scotia, and this acquisition [of Louisbourg], but the whole northern continent as far back as the French settle-

9. Payne to Hale, Apr. 24, 1745, Gilman coll., Mass. Hist. Soc.
10. Sparhawk to Pepperrell, Dec. 16, 1745, and Feb. 5, 1746, Pepperrell MSS, II, 5, 93.
11. Kilby to Pepperrell, Nov. 6, 1745, ibid., 355.
12. The Boston Weekly News-Letter, Jan. 30, 1746.
13. Sparhawk to Pepperrell, Apr. 29, 1745, Pepperrell MSS, 108C.
14. Frances Shirley to Pepperrell, Jan. 8, 1746, Belknap Papers, 61C, 30, Mass. Hist. Soc.

ments on the . . . Mississippi, which are about 2000 miles distant."[15]   He suggested sending British and colonial armies from Louisbourg up the St. Lawrence River into Quebec, not to stop until French power was swept from North America. His ideas had changed since January 1745, when he justified the siege of Louisbourg primarily as a means of saving the fishing banks and Nova Scotia.   He now visualized the conquest of all Canada.   He conceived of a North American empire reaching to the Mississippi, based upon shipping, fishing, fur trading, and commerce.   If the empire were developed along these lines, he prophesied that Britain could use the expanded power of America to offset the power of her rivals in Europe. Warren apparently agreed with him and offered to recommend that the ministry undertake a campaign against Canada in 1746.   They sent their proposal to London and awaited the reaction.

I

Sailing from Louisbourg, Shirley's ship entered the choppy waters of Boston Harbor after a rough passage of four days. For the first time during the voyage, the Governor and his family came on deck, where toasts were drunk to George II and the men of Louisbourg.   As they passed Castle William, Frances Shirley laughed at the little cannon "popping" their barrels out of the battery walls to fire the royal salute.[16]   Shirley's arrival was signaled by the church bells of Boston and fires on the distant hills.   A launch brought news of a large reception for the Governor, and Shirley agreed to delay his disembarkation until the next morning, when he could walk up King Street in military procession.   One of Belcher's friends observed that no "governor [had] received . . . more joy and

15. *Shirley Correspondence,* I, 284; Warren to Corbett, Oct. 3, 1745, Admiralty Records, I, 480, 14.   Warren recommended that Louisbourg be made a free port.

16. Frances Shirley to Pepperrell, Jan. 8 and 17, 1746, Belknap Papers, 1745-1746, 30, 49, Mass. Hist. Soc.   There are only a few letters in existence which show Frances' vitality and sparkle; in the Jan. 8th letter she writes thus of women and women correspondents: "I think I have heard you say that the first things that girls should learn should be to write and cast accounts that latter may still be your opinion, but I fear you'll give up the first when you find what troublesome correspondents women are by me."

fervent affection by any people" than Shirley had during that morning's festivities.[17]

With the ceremonies of his arrival concluded, the Governor devoted his time to the accumulated business of four months' absence. In addition to matters of budget and local defense, he had to make a large number of civilian appointments. There were also the problems of supplying Louisbourg, recruiting men for his regiment, and laying plans for the projected campaign of 1746. An enormous logistical problem caused by rivalry among the contractors, distance, and bad weather had to be overcome. As always, the difficulties of supply were closely involved with political considerations. Among his first visitors was Pepperrell's son-in-law Nathaniel Sparhawk, who reported on the provisioning of Louisbourg and requested more favors for the firm of Sparhawk and Colman. Shirley had already agreed with Pepperrell to help him, providing the additional contracting did not violate agreements with Apthorp and Hancock.[18]

The Governor was willing to favor the youth, not only to bind his friendship with Pepperrell, but to win the esteem of Pepperrell's sister and brother-in-law Mary and Benjamin Colman. After fifty years of godly service, the old minister was an influential citizen of Boston, and his erudition and urbanity made him a delightful acquaintance. The Colmans often had the Shirleys as visitors in their home and remembered them in family prayers.[19] Friendship for the Colmans had much influence upon Shirley's attitude toward Sparhawk, but the young man had other valuable family alliances. His partner Benjamin Colman was the minister's favorite nephew and his stepbrother Samuel Waldo the Governor's firmest supporter. Waldo himself was hoping to strengthen these family alliances by wedding his son to Pepperrell's daughter.

Sparhawk was well aware of his family connections and was determined to exploit their ties with Shirley. Not in a position to bargain with Shirley himself, he questioned his father-in-law

17. Colman to Pepperrell, Dec. 12, 1745, Belknap Papers, 61C, 16, *ibid.*
18. Sparhawk to Pepperrell, Dec. 16, 1745, Pepperrell MSS, II, 5.
19. Sparhawk to Pepperrell, Feb. 5, 1746, *ibid.*, II, 93.

closely. Had the Pepperrells done Shirley any favors for which rewards had not been collected? If William Bollan were to be chosen Pepperrell's regimental agent in London, what patronage might be exacted from the Governor in exchange?[20]

Distracted though he might be by considerations of patronage, Shirley nevertheless had to meet the responsibilities of his office. He pressed Sparhawk to explain the deficiencies in the supply system, and he described what remedial measures had been taken. Sparhawk was lectured—as were Apthorp, Hancock, and the committees of the legislature—on the serious disaster that would ensue if the garrisoned men were forced to subsist during the remaining months of winter on a diet of salt food. Without some relief Shirley insisted that the troops would be wiped out, and the popular reaction to the tragedy would threaten plans for the conquest of Canada. The contractors replied that the stormy December weather was keeping vessels in port, and some captains, frightened by the prospects of mid-winter voyages, were refusing to risk their ships.

Despite his best efforts, Shirley succeeded in dispatching only a few ships to Louisbourg. He was exasperated to realize that he could do nothing else to supply the garrison. The weather would not break until March,[21] and by that time hundreds of soldiers would be dead, and the rest, sick and mutinous, would be demanding release. For the moment, he could only try to enlist men for the American regiments to relieve the garrisoned militia in early March. Even here he encountered difficulties. He and Pepperrell had planned to offer company commissions (still worth much in prestige and money) to American youths as rewards for recruiting their neighbors and friends; but he now learned that the clients of English aristocrats had won the patronage. The news of their appointments

20. *Pepperrell Papers*, 406, 433; Sparhawk to Pepperrell, Jan. 13, 1746, Belknap Papers, 61C, 31, Mass. Hist. Soc.

21. Shirley unified the supply in Mar., taking it out of the hands of John Osborn and the legislative committee and putting it directly in those of Sparhawk, Apthorp, and Hancock. Apthorp, in a letter to Pepperrell of Apr. 16, 1746 (Pepperrell MSS, II, 139), recognizes this closer relation to the Pepperrells and promises to favor William Tyler, another of the General's kinsmen, in the business arrangements. "[I] shall continue to let Mr. Tyler with a kinsman of mine supply everything they can in the brazury and ship chandlers business."

hampered recruiting.[22] Shirley objected to Pelham, and while he awaited a reply, a major, two captains, and several other officers appointed in England were lost at sea on the voyage to America. Shirley immediately suggested American replacements for the drowned officers.[23]

It was well that his request was granted, for he had already promised his sons and several other young men commissions if they succeeded in locating volunteers. There was some competition with Pepperrell's agents, but he pressed his officers hard during the early months of 1746, and by using his governmental influence he filled nearly half his regiment by April. A sufficient number of recruits was available when the first ships left for Louisbourg to relieve those veterans who wanted to return home. Many of the returning men were critical of the contractors and business interests responsible for provisioning Louisbourg. They had many stories to tell; the cold months of winter's isolation had killed nearly one out of three New England soldiers, approximately nine hundred men.

Public resentment was further aggravated when the British fleet returned to Massachusetts waters, bringing the sick soldiers home and using press gangs to round up crews to sail the ships back to England. Apparently the shortage of sailors was caused in part by local seamen who helped discontented navy personnel to jump ship. Eliakim Hutchinson, Shirley's agent in procuring seamen, tried unsuccessfully to find men without causing a disturbance; however, his own interest in the contracts for supplying Louisbourg was too well known for him to be regarded as an impartial official. When press gangs began rounding up likely victims, anger was directed against him as much as it was against the impressment. Members of the legislature from the seaport towns reacted with hostility; and Hutchinson was first censured, then removed from the Council in the 1747 election. Shirley was unable to help him in the election, but he resisted pressure to remove him from

22. Chauncy to Pepperrell, Jan. 18, 1746, Belknap Papers, 1745-1776, 33, Mass. Hist. Soc.: "Tis a most scandalous contempt of our brave officers that they should not be thought worthy, after they have behaved so well."

23. Shirley to Pelham, Jan. 20 and Feb. 20, 1746, Huntington Lib. MSS, 9701, 9703.

appointive offices he held in the court system and in the army.[24]

II

Facing public indignation about his provisioning of the Louisbourg garrison, Shirley was relieved to receive the campaign plans for 1746 from London. Though they arrived late, he was delighted by their majestic promise—a great fleet, seasoned regular troops, and a large war chest. By contrast with the resources available for the Louisbourg expedition, these were tremendous.[25] The object of the campaign was Quebec, which would be attacked by a joint land and sea expedition under Sir John St. Clair and Sir Charles Warren. Another expedition, commanded by Governor William Gooch of Virginia, was to proceed first against Crown Point, the fortified French post on Lake Champlain, and then march on to Quebec.

The plans for attacking Canada pleased Shirley, but he was disappointed that no New Englander was given a position of authority in the expeditions. Lack of appreciation of New England's part in the Louisbourg conquest was partly responsible for this slight of American leaders. The British navy had taken credit for the victory in its traditional rivalry with the army, and the London newspapers followed its lead by making Warren the hero of the expedition. But Shirley was also advised that the ministry was divided on the importance of the American war. Both Pelhams had hardly thought of North America as a war zone before the capture of Louisbourg and then had opposed anything that would distract attention from the war in Europe.[26] Like many of their associates, they did not see any military value in taking Canadian territory when the war in Europe was often more than they could handle. They favored a policy of coexistence in colonial areas, and in fact they wanted to drop even the Caribbean operations

24. Shipton, "Eliakim Hutchinson," *Sibley's Harvard Graduates*, VIII, 726-29; *Mass. Acts and Resolves*, XIII, 720-21.

25. Shirley to Newcastle, May 31, 1746, Parkman Trans., XXXVIII, 212.

26. Richard Pares, "American Versus Continental Warfare," *The English Historical Review*, 51 (1936), 429-65.

in order to concentrate forces in Europe. The 1746 Canadian campaign, it appears, was sanctioned less as a military operation and more as a way to win friends for the ministry. The Pelhams needed the Bedford interest, and the Duke himself was an enthusiast for a Canadian war. In exchange for his help, the Pelhams agreed to his plans for a campaign, but Bedford, fearing the rise of colonial military power, wanted the campaign directed by Britons. The Pelhams accepted this further condition in bargaining for his political help.[27]

Shirley's interests and those of his patrons were no longer identical, a fact which accounts, perhaps, for the limited patronage he was given in the new campaign. Nevertheless, he could not allow it to dampen his spirit toward the Canadian conquest. He formed plans on a large scale. "It is my opinion," he wrote Governor Greene of Rhode Island, "that a body of 6000 men, at least, should enter enemy country by the way of Albany; and that the colonies ought to raise 10,000 among themselves in order to proceed in the proposed plan."[28]

Few, even of Shirley's associates, shared such visions of conquest, and although leaders of the Massachusetts legislature were ready in theory to support the mobilization proposed by the crown, a growing number resisted new taxes. Finance was a stumbling block. Some legislators proposed a lottery as a money-raising device, though it was hardly enough to provide the vast funds necessary. Some merchants were willing to accept military notes in anticipation of payment in sterling, but again, such notes were no substitute for taxes. Refusing to tax war profits, the House of Representatives risked inflation by issuing more paper money, expecting it to be redeemed by the British government. Shirley, in putting military needs first, felt that he had no alternative but to accept the new paper issue, though a few of his followers were worried about the mounting inflation.

Enlistment of men also proved supremely difficult. The growing apathy, together with the fear of garrison duty and a

27. Richard Lodge, *Studies in Eighteenth-Century Diplomacy, 1740-1748* (London, 1930), 170, 239-40.
28. Shirley to Greene, May 29, 1746, R. I. Archives, Letters, III, 19.

late campaign, soured colonists against military service and forced Shirley to draft men from the frontier garrisons. The militia colonels who were expected to find men for the resulting vacancies flooded Shirley's office with protests that frontier defenses were being critically weakened.[29] However, by using these desperate methods Shirley was assured of a fast mobilization in Massachusetts. Neighboring colonies had equally difficult problems raising men, but Connecticut voted 600 men, increased later by another 400; New York provided 1,600; New Jersey, 500; and New Hampshire, Rhode Island, and Pennsylvania supplied lesser numbers.[30]

While the men were assembling, Warren took up quarters in Boston, where he could confer with Shirley. Their plans were complicated by a lack of information from London about the date of St. Clair's arrival and the supplies he would require. Yet there was a need for preliminary preparations. The task of provisioning a large army required more supervision than Warren was physically capable of. Disabled by running sores on his legs, he walked lamely from place to place during his rounds of chores. Shirley, feeling the intensity of the work, complained of nervous pains in his shoulders, but attended to the endless details of preparing a military operation; he sent recruits to Louisbourg, shipped provisions to Mascarene's men at Annapolis Royal, and dispatched powder, equipment, and garrison pay to John Stoddard, whose western forts were constantly being annoyed by French attacks.

As the summer months slipped by, and the transports from England did not appear, Shirley surmised that the rebellion in Scotland had drawn "off the thoughts of the ministry from everything else." He realized with despair that the delay had necessitated abandonment of the expedition. It meant, too, that the fate of the colonial auxiliaries had to be decided. Since there was no adequate fleet or army for an amphibious attack on Quebec, perhaps the Americans should be employed against

29. Shirley to Stoddard, June 18 and Aug. 2, 1746, Shirley MSS.
30. Townshend to Admiralty, Sept. 1746, Admiralty Records, I, 480, II, 169. Victor Hugo Paltsits, "A Scheme for the Conquest of Canada in 1746," Amer. Antiq. Soc., *Proceedings*, New Ser., 17 (1905-6), 69-92.

Crown Point. When Shirley put the question to Warren, the Admiral agreed that a decision was necessary, and suggested that the neighboring governors be consulted. Plans for assailing Crown Point were complicated, however, by the refusal of Governor Gooch to serve as commander of the expedition. Shirley made Waldo the new leader and appointed as the major generals Joseph Dwight and Theodore Atkinson.[31]

The project was not completed when news was received of French troop movements on the Bay of Fundy. Shirley pressed the General Court for permission to dispatch to Nova Scotia half of the Massachusetts contingent for Crown Point, although he carefully assured the legislature that "I have not altered my sentiments concerning . . . Crown Point." With the help of Wendell and Hale the required permission was won; however, Shirley was firmly reminded that the men were not to do garrison duty.[32]

Nova Scotia was not the only trouble spot. The inaction of the summer had bred discontent in garrison and camp. Men were deserting from the army, and some merchants, short of hands for their fishing and lumber vessels, were enticing sailors from warships anchored in the ports. Constables had trouble arresting deserters as the local population flaunted the law by attacking their subordinates.[33] In western Massachusetts Indians ravaged the countryside and terrorized the frontiersmen. Fort Massachusetts was burned in August after its thirty defenders were taken prisoners. The single casualty was an English settler; a French soldier and his Indian allies cut up and roasted the body—an incident that symbolized to inhabitants the promiscuous cruelty of Indian warfare.[34]

Before a relief party could set out for Fort Massachusetts, Boston was thrown into panic by frightened sailors who claimed

31. Shirley to Newcastle, Aug. 15, 22, and Sept. 19, 1746, Parkman Trans., XXXIX, 7, 14, 30. Warren and Shirley to Waldo, Oct. 20, 1746, Knox Papers, L, 71.

32. *Shirley Correspondence*, I, 346-50.

33. Townshend to Shirley, Aug. 17, 1746, Admiralty Records, I, 480, II, 195-96; Shirley to Townshend, Sept. 12, 1746, *ibid.*, 245-49.

34. *The Boston Evening-Post*, Sept. 1, 1746; John Norton, *Narrative of the Capture and Burning of Fort Massachusetts*, ed. Samuel G. Drake (Albany, 1870), 9-51.

to have seen a French fleet sailing towards the colony's coast. Colonists armed themselves and rushed toward the capital. Soon the town was filled with thousands of men, helping the merchants clear the docks of merchandise and take small vessels up the Charles River to safety. At Providence House, Shirley conferred with Colonel Dwight on city defense and prepared for the safety of the government in case of an invasion.[35] Yet he was not completely convinced that this information from the sailors was reliable. It seemed ridiculous for the enemy to attack in the south when the north was vulnerable and had a French population ready to rise. Shirley gambled that he was right, hurried more soldiers to Nova Scotia, and urged Wentworth to do the same. He was vindicated when the reported French fleet, which had in fact been sailing off Massachusetts, passed northward and entered the Bay of Fundy.

Without knowledge of the fleet's whereabouts, Shirley was nevertheless careful to supply Mascarene at Annapolis Royal as best he could. But it was the weather, a long-time foe of Massachusetts, which effected a temporary rescue. While seas off Massachusetts remained smooth, September gales in the north brought heavy seas; storms in the exposed harbors off Annapolis Royal ripped the enemy fleet and drove it into northern bays. Fishermen, seeing the warships, took flight for Boston. Their reports intensified preparations and kept Boston an armed camp.

Disaster soon struck. Some of Shirley's dispatches to Nova Scotia fell into enemy hands. Their references to British naval movements frightened the French commander into weighing anchor and sailing into open water. Before departing, however, he put ashore strong reinforcements for the local French army. News of this landing reached Mascarene, who was determined to prevent the consolidation of the enemy armies, but he made the error of ordering his men out of the fixed defenses of Annapolis Royal. When the French and English met in open country, the British forces were nearly annihilated.[36]

35. Shirley to Stoddard, Oct. 7, 1746, Shirley MSS; Shirley and Warren to Townshend, Oct. 5, 1746, Admiralty Records, I, 480, II, 350.
36. Shirley to Newcastle, Feb. 27, 1747, Parkman Trans., XXXIX, 98.

The defeat especially distressed Shirley, because he was convinced that Mascarene's army was a victim of ministerial indecision, and his opinion was doubly confirmed when, after a summer of waiting, he learned that the army destined for America had been deployed in Europe. To Shirley it seemed a poor excuse for abandoning the campaign. If there was to be another one—and he insisted that there should be—he wanted better support from home. He and Warren planned a campaign for 1747 that included an expedition against Crown Point and an amphibious assault upon Quebec. Warren was assigned the task of taking these recommendations to London and also of aiding Bollan to secure reimbursement for the military expenditures of the past campaigns. Warren's distinguished service during the Louisbourg expedition, they agreed, would be an invaluable asset in the negotiations, and a reimbursement of expenses was essential if the home government expected Massachusetts to contribute to a campaign in 1747.[37]

Throughout the winter of 1746-47, Shirley pressed for better northern defenses. His anxiety for Nova Scotia, he admitted to Newcastle, was ever upon his mind: "I am afraid your Grace will think, from my incessant representations of the state of Nova Scotia, that I imagine that province should be the sole object of your attention." His letters show that he wanted a reconsideration of British policy in that region: plans for defense and settlement, with provisions for Protestant colonists and ministers, civil government, Indian trading houses, and forts.[38] When Warren gave up the governorship of Nova Scotia in 1746 in order to devote full attention to leading the Canadian campaign, Shirley applied for the position, as well as the command of the principal regiment in the area. He received a promise from Newcastle that he would be given

37. Warren and Shirley to Newcastle, Oct. 12, 1746, C. O. 5/901, 51. The 1747 plan was indeed impressive, especially in the light of the preparations of 1759 when Canada was finally conquered. Twelve ships of the line and auxiliaries were to attack Quebec and six of the line and auxiliaries were to guard Louisbourg and blockade the St. Lawrence Gulf. Eight thousand regulars and about three times that number of colonials were to provide the manpower of the armies.

38. Shirley to Newcastle, Oct. 31, Nov. 1, 1746, and Feb. 27, Apr. 29, 1747, Parkman Trans., XXXIX, 75, 77, 98, 126.

priority in the naming of a successor to the colonelcy of Phillips's regiment when there was a vacancy, but nothing was said about the governorship. Undeterred, Shirley again put his name forward on the resignations of Warren's successors, Charles Knowles and Edward Cornwallis. He believed that unity of Massachusetts and Nova Scotia under the same governor would contribute greatly to military effectiveness, for it would put Nova Scotia under the control of an official who was concerned about its safety and able to rally Americans in its cause. Union of the colonies would also assure control of military contracts to New Englanders.

III

The abandonment of the 1746 campaign only increased Shirley's desire for an attack on Canada. He favored an assault on Crown Point as soon as possible, believing the fort to be a threat equal to what Louisbourg had been. He was ready to support an attack in December; but Waldo, Stoddard, Dwight, and Wendell counseled delay, and the leaders of Rhode Island, New Hampshire, and Connecticut did not share his sense of urgency. While they wanted to remove French forces from British territory, Crown Point was a long way off, and the cost of taking men over ice and snow might be too high. Their reaction compelled Shirley to alter his calculations, for he did not feel that Massachusetts could make the sacrifice alone.[39] Under the circumstances, there was little that could be done until the arrival of the 1747 campaign plans. During this delay of four months, he spent his time reinforcing Nova Scotia and rebuilding Fort Massachusetts; he also provided Forts Pelham, Shirley, and Dummer with more men and instructed Stoddard to establish better relations with the local Indians. In April and May he had large supplies of Indian presents sent to Albany for distribution among the Iroquois, who were growing weary of the procastination of the colonies in carrying war into Canada.[40]

39. Shirley to Board of Trade, Jan. 10, 1747, Admiralty Records, I, 3818, 149-51; Shirley to Wentworth, Feb. 8 and 9, 1747, Belknap Papers, Lib. Cong.; Shirley to Pelham, Mar. 25, 1747, Huntington Lib. MSS, 9711.
40. Shirley to Wentworth, May 18, 1747, Belknap Papers, Lib. Cong.

A French attack on Saratoga in late spring precipitated a crisis in Shirley's plans, for the Iroquois demanded British protection. Would the northern colonies continue to await the ministry's plans, already months late, or would they open their own campaign? Shirley called a special session of the Massachusetts legislature for August 12 and suggested that the other governors do likewise.[41] On that hot morning he spoke long and forcefully to the members of the General Court. The ravages of the enemy, he said, compelled the colonies to aid the Iroquois before "the spreading power of the French" destroyed ties of friendship, ruined settlements, and deprived the colonies of their western heritage. "Nothing is wanting but a union of councils in the several governments. . . . The only difficulty that can arise will be to state the just quota to be furnished by each of them for such an expedition, and agree upon a general plan of operations."[42] His call for men and money was heard patiently, but without enthusiasm. On returning to their chamber the representatives appointed a committee to consider the message, and the next day held debate on the committee's report. A joint committee of both houses was then selected to study the Governor's recommendations.

Before any vote was taken, Shirley received unsettling news: Newcastle had called off the 1747 campaign. His letter announced the withdrawal of all support from the projected expeditions and the disbandment of the expeditionary army. Shirley and Charles Knowles, military governor of Louisbourg, were put in charge of the demobilization.[43] This order did not put an end to projects for attacking the French. New crises would arise in 1748 and new plans would be formulated. However, the colonies were henceforth on their own resources, and they would not again support another expedition like the force sent against Louisbourg.[44] Shirley yearned to fall upon Canada, but he had to admit there was no enthusiasm for an

41. *Shirley Correspondence*, I, 392.
42. *Mass. House Journals*, XXIV, 103.
43. *Shirley Correspondence*, I, 386-89.
44. Shirley to Clinton, Feb. 1, 1748, Parkman Trans. XXXIX, 188.

expedition; indeed there was pressure in Massachusetts to reduce garrisons and cut taxes.[45]

One cannot easily separate the imperialist from the politician in Shirley. Undoubtedly he saw war as a golden opportunity for expansion, and he dreamed of spreading New England across Canada. At the same time, as governor of Massachusetts he was associated with land speculators, contractors, merchants, and military officers. War had increased his political capital; the discontinuance of war threatened to reduce it. Superficially, he had motive to avoid peace. Demobilization brought problems of shrinking patronage and the political controversy engendered by hard times, deflation, and taxes. Within Shirley's circle of friends and supporters, some who had become rich from war contracts became disaffected when their opportunities faded. Christopher Kilby, who had formed a company with Barnard of London and gained wealth from profitable contracts lapsed into sullen ill-humor when Shirley could not give him any more.[46] Even Waldo and Hancock were pressing the Governor for more profits. Shirley found himself with greedy supporters whom he could no longer favor and whose friendship he could easily lose.[47] Was his party about to split apart?

IV

The governorship wore heavily upon Shirley's health. In the absence of Jack, who had always assisted him with the details of administration, Shirley relied more and more on his secretaries, Eliakim Hutchinson and Josiah Willard. But he

45. Shirley to Clinton, Mar. 22, 1748, E. B. O'Callaghan and Berthold Fernolds, eds., *Documents Relative to the Colonial History of the State of New York* (Albany, 1856-87), 421.

46. Baxter, *The House of Hancock*, 103-5.

47. The greed of Shirley's friends was well pointed up by Kilby, who told an associate, Thomas Hancock, "I am sure the colonies will be greatly benefitted in the first instance by the expense of so vast a sum of sterling money amongst them. This I have constantly had my eye upon and have never suffered it to slip out of my thoughts." But Kilby was not alone, as is indicated in a letter of Zachary Bourryan to Hancock: "I . . . thank you for the share you have got me of Mr. Apthorp's business and hope he will have no cause to repent of his new correspondent." Kilby to Hancock, Aug. 25, 1746, fol. 1, 48-50, Boston Pub. Lib.; Bourryan to Hancock, Jan. 31, 1746, Hancock Papers, VII.

had not been able to delegate much of the burden of supervising the recent mobilization. Though he loved writing, his twelve-to-fifteen page dispatches to his superiors, his instructions to subordinates, and his advisory letters to his fellow governors must have exceeded his inclinations. Often conferring with Willard at sunrise and finishing his correspondence at midnight, he had found himself pressed for time and would turn to Willard for help in drafting a letter of proclamation. Sometimes he also made work for himself; when a draft letter was sent him by the Secretary, he would take the trouble to edit it, scratching lines and rearranging words. Since the Governor was exceedingly cautious, ever watchful, of the impression he created, few letters passed through his hands without some editing. Over the years, moreover, he favored certain expressions and took an unnecessary amount of time in making unessential changes. Though he complained increasingly of fatigue, rheumatism, and "loss of exercise," at fifty-three he had remarkable energy. He had gained considerable weight, his face was fuller, and his tall frame looked more bulky.[48]

Now that the tension of imminent war had relaxed—for better or worse—Shirley seemed about to settle down to a more comfortable middle age. Three daughters were still living at home, but Shirley's sons were widely scattered. Jack was temporarily garrisoned at Louisbourg as a captain in his father's regiment; William and his brother-in-law William Bollan were in London. Young Shirley was in England ostensibly representing his father in ministerial affairs but hoping to purchase a commission in a British regiment. Tom Shirley, then nineteen, was captain in a British regiment in Europe.

From his own war profits (and they were considerable), Shirley had bought thirty-seven acres in suburban Roxbury, isolated by hills and farms from the city and port of Boston. He and his wife hoped to build a two-story house of brick and wood. For a family of their social position, the plans were

48. Shirley to Pelham, July 27 and Sept. 27, 1745, Huntington Lib. MSS, 9706 and 9707; Shirley to Willard, Jan. 5, 1747, Mass. Archives, LIII, 207. There are many examples of Shirley's editing in Mass. Archives, LVIII and LXIX.

modest; the house was to be severe in its architectural lines, crackerbox in appearance, with similar entrances at the front and back.[49] Their neighbors, the Auchmutys, the Dudleys, the Hallowells, and the Thomas Hutchinsons, had much finer homes,[50] but the Shirley's land gave a finer view of the distant harbor.

Before the house was completed, the Shirley family experienced an unexpected tragedy. After a lifetime of devotion and service to her husband, Frances fell ill during mid-August and died on the evening of the thirty-first, just a few months short of her fifty-first birthday. She was buried in a crypt beneath King's Chapel, near the resting place of her daughter. Shirley did not express his emotions easily, and grief made his words seem stiff when he wrote Governor and Mrs. Wentworth: "I have lost a very dear companion, and most valuable friend, and I think I may say as great a treasure of good qualities and happiness as a woman can bring to her husband."[51]

49. W. W. Cordingley, "Shirley Place, Roxbury, Massachusetts, and its Builder, Governor William Shirley," *Old-Time New England* (*Bulletin* of the Society for the Preservation of New England Antiquities), 12 (1921), No. 2, 51-63. There are excellent diagrams of the floor space and several prints of the house.

50. Francis S. Drake, "Roxbury in the Provincial Period," *The Memorial History of Boston* (Boston, 1880-1881), II, 342-45.

51. Shirley to Wentworth, Sept. 13, 1746, Belknap Papers, Lib. Cong.; *The Boston Weekly News-Letter*, Sept. 4, 1746.

VII

New Alliances

AFTER HIS WIFE's death the Governor engaged a widowed relative from London to be his housekeeper and relied upon his daughters to act as hostesses. The country home that he and Frances had planned was furnished in 1747; the grounds were landscaped with hedges and shrubs, arranged in geometric patterns like those of his English estate in Sussex. These personal matters interrupted the duties of a busy official life only momentarily, for he had to face the rising opposition to his administration. Many events helped bring on the discontent, but none was more important than the cessation of British military operations. The years of free spending, easy credit, and easy discharge of perennial debts to British merchants were ending, and in their wake were the hard realities of deflation, accumulating debts, and heavy taxes.

For the previous six years Shirley had depended upon a coalition of business and agricultural interests to support his governmental program. The coalition had never been tested under peacetime conditions; it was held together largely by contracts and commissions growing out of wars in the Caribbean and North America. He had initially brought the land bankers into his administration by promising help in a financial crisis; he later indulged their desire for cheap money by the inflationary spending of the military campaigns. He had labored less successfully for merchantile creditors, but they were more satisfied with the prosperity of the war than he might have expected. His expansionist policies broadened the popular base of his support by multiplying patronage opportunities and gratifying sentiments of religion and patriotism; Louisbourg became a symbol of colonial courage and ingenuity. His personal adroitness as a compromiser went far to cement political alliances. He had to moderate the force of his prosecutions of smugglers; he had to accept the followers of former Governor Belcher into his government; and he had to secure the cooperation of the Congregationalists. The give and take of his policies benefited almost the whole colony, but they had special significance for a group of men headed by Apthorp, Waldo, and Hancock. They and their friends—Pepperrell, Kilby, Sparhawk, Wendell, and Stoddard—shared especially heavily in the spoils, though the patronage of office reached into the community and gave the administration substantial popular roots. The spread of patronage on a geographical basis was most beneficial. Waldo and Pepperrell represented Maine, with its timber, fishing, and land speculation; Choate and Hale, coastal Massachusetts outside of Boston, with its desire for soft money and increased trade; Hancock, Apthorp, and Wendell, the city of Boston, with its commercial interests and governmental patronage; and Wendell, Stoddard, and Dwight, the colony's west, with its Indian trade, defense needs, and land speculation.

The least happy were a core of merchants who had Thomas Hutchinson and James Allen as their spokesmen. But although Hutchinson objected to the inflation that Shirley tolerated, his relations with the Governor had warmed considerably since 1741, especially when Shirley's friends accepted him as speaker of the House of Representatives in 1746. Most of Hutchinson's friends supported the Governor's war policies; even his brother-in-law, Andrew Oliver, was a backer of the administration. Hutchinson did not like the Governor's supporters and probably hated Waldo, but he let himself be drawn into measures favored by the Governor. Less can be said of Allen, who was never consistent in his political support. At one time he was the best friend of former Governor Belcher; at another, his bitterest enemy. Allen's politics were obviously motivated by personal considerations; a denial of patronage may have engendered his hostility toward Shirley. Whatever the reason, his opposition was bitter and determined.

Allen had now allied himself with the discontented, who apparently wanted cheap money and a continuation of the war, but without casualties and without heavy taxes. Newcastle's letter, however, had put an end to British finance of colonial war, making the colonists face up to taxes for defense and a correction of the money system. When Shirley took steps to have the colony represented at a military conference in September 1747, the legislators reluctantly accepted his proposal to send delegates, then refused to receive the report. Finally they refused Shirley's request to continue maintaining garrisons at certain western forts. The Governor accused them of "being cold and indifferent," but his words had little effect, for without crown support, they were spending their own funds and were therefore infinitely careful.[1]

Nor was the Governor more successful in raising the question of currency reform. During the war funds had been procured by successive issues of paper bills until over a million pounds was put into circulation. The money was depreciating. Deeply concerned over the situation, Shirley urged Bollan in London to get reimbursement of the colony's war expenditures; the sterling could then be used to redeem the paper money. However, Shirley was dependent upon the Pelhams for securing repayment from Parliament, and they had neglected to act. In fact, Bollan was finding extreme difficulty in presenting the colony's case, for there was a lack of appreciation of its part in the expedition.[2] Further, no cost estimate of the Louisbourg expedition was prepared for some time, and the accounting of actual military expenditures for it and the 1746 and 1747 campaigns had not yet begun. Bollan was also plagued by a disagreement among the London merchants on the use the colony should make of its reimbursement; most wanted to require Massachusetts to use it as the basis for conversion to a hard money system.

The currency problem was the single most important issue

1. Messages to General Court, Oct. 28, 1747, Mass. Archives, CVIII, 246.
2. Bollan to Willard, Nov. 15, 1746, and Feb. 29, 1747, Mass. Archives, XX, 367-68, 411-13; Bollan to Oliver, Apr. 18, 1763, Dana Papers, Mass. Hist. Soc.; *Journal of the Commissioners for Trade and Plantations from . . . 1741-2 to . . . 1749* (London, 1931), 227-36.

facing Massachusetts. Shirley was not ready to lead a reform movement—nor had he decided upon an appropriate solution. But he and his associates had done much to explain the general purposes of the Louisbourg campaign to the British public. Shirley had published *A Letter to the Duke of Newcastle with A Journal of the Siege of Louisbourg;* Pepperrell and Bollan had also put their ideas into print; and Kilby flooded the home offices with memoranda and letters.[3] No complete reimbursement, however, was possible until Commodore Knowles, the military governor of Louisbourg, and Shirley set the rules for auditing expenditures. They finally conferred in October 1747 and quickly devised instructions for auditing and preparing the accounts that would satisfy the British Treasury. They required accurate militia rolls, receipts for disbursed funds and used provisions, and a return of the military equipment, especially the muskets, ammunition, and cannon. Responsibility for these audits was placed upon the governor of each colony. When completed, the accounts were to be submitted to Shirley and Knowles for final audit.[4]

Funds for these military expenditures were to be provided by the colonial legislatures or, if compensation was received, by drafts on the British Treasury. When the accounts were closed, the records would be reviewed by the local governor, who in the meantime had been collecting receipts for all other charges—rental of ships, recruiting services, and special provisioning. For those in charge, like Waldo and Dwight in Massachusetts, there were opportunities to change sterling into local currency, because some money had to be raised by drafts on London. The possession of these drafts was particularly

3. William Shirley, *A Letter to the Duke of Newcastle with a Journal of the Siege of Louisbourg, and other operations of the forces during the Expedition against the French Settlements of Cape Breton* (London, 1746); William Pepperrell, *An Accurate Journal and Account of the Proceedings during the Expedition against the French Settlements on Cape Breton, to the Surrender of Louisbourg* . . . (Oxford, 1746); William Bollan, *The Importance and Advantages of Cape Breton Truly Stated and Impartially Considered* (London, 1746); Bollan to Willard, Apr. 23, 1752, Mass. Hist. Soc., *Collections*, 1st Ser., 1 (1792), 53-54.

4. Newcastle to Shirley, May 30, 1747, C. O. 5/45, 247-57; Shirley to Pelham, Sept. 13 and Dec. 10, 1748, Treasury I, 330, 54, 65, P.R.O.; Shirley to Wentworth, Nov. 24, 1747, Belknap Papers, Lib. Cong.

valuable, since the reduction of military purchasing had glutted the provision market and put a premium on sterling for the satisfaction of British trade deficits. To show his regard for the Massachusetts agents, Shirley waived the usual requirements of a bond and allowed them to handle the funds in settling the accounts.[5]

I

Shortly after the audit got underway, Commodore Knowles received sailing orders for Jamaica. Because his ships were battered and his provisions low, he asked the Governor for help. At Shirley's order, the fleet was readied for departure, and by the evening of November 16 only one task remained: to find men to replace the numerous British crewmen who had died or deserted. Before dawn on the crisp morning of the seventeenth, press gangs boarded vessels in the harbor and swept down upon laborers on the docks. Men were dragged into launches and carried to the anchored warships. By daylight rumors of the impressment had covered Boston's water front, and a crowd gathered. Stung by the memory of former impressments, the crowd's temper became dangerous. At length, a mob of several hundred people, said to have been mostly sailors, Negroes, and laborers, surged through the streets looking for British seamen and British property. The sheriff was severely wounded and his deputies beaten. The town militia took cover.

About ten o'clock Shirley heard the noise of the mob of sailors and workingmen pursuing some British officers, who fled to Province House for safety. Giving the officers sanctuary, he learned that others of their group had already been captured by the mob. Before he could hear more, the mob had surrounded the house, and men were pounding at the front door. He "immediately went out to them and demanded the cause of the tumult, to which one of them, armed with a cutlass, answered me in an insolent manner [that] it was caused by my unjustifiable . . . warrant [of impressment]."

5. Shirley to Waldo, Oct. 28, 1747, Knox Papers, L, 86; Shirley to Wentworth, Oct. 10, 1747, Belknap Papers, Lib. Cong.

Shirley denied any knowledge of an impressment order for New England subjects of the crown. He said the order was directed against outsiders, but his "words were barely audible over the derisive shouts of the mob." An American sailor on the steps cursed, and when Shirley objected, the sailor became more belligerent. Eliakim Hutchinson knocked his hat off. This act of daring momentarily silenced the mob and gave Shirley an opportunity to speak. "I demanded of them where the [other] King's officers were that they had seized; and they, being shown to me, I went up to the lieutenant and bid him go into my house. And upon his telling me the mob would not suffer him, I took him from among them and, putting him before me, caused him to go in, as I did likewise . . . three [others] and followed them without exchanging more words with the mob."

Remaining on the porch, Eliakim and Thomas Hutchinson, with another gentleman or two, tried to reason with the mob, but when it pushed steadily forward, the speakers retreated. Inside the house the defenders held their muskets as they waited for the mob to force an entry. The front door was battered, stones were thrown on the windows, and a deputy sheriff, who had not got inside the house quickly enough, was beaten and "put in the public stocks." Despite its anger, the mob was not desperate enough to break the doors and, getting no satisfaction from Shirley, went off toward the water front.

Soon after the mob left, Shirley issued orders for the militia to assemble. The officers arrived, but no men turned out. In the afternoon Shirley ventured the short distance to the Court House, where the Council was holding its bi-weekly meeting, intending to ask for help and criticize the local militia for not aiding in the crisis. He found that the representatives had already taken steps to investigate the riot, and the councilors were on the point of similar action. He advised more direct measures, and the Council issued a proclamation to apprehend the ringleaders.

At this point in their deliberations the legislators heard the noise of the mob. A cacophony of shouts and splintering wood grew in intensity until advance elements of the mob were hammering on the council chamber door. Two of the councilors went to the balcony and attempted to appease the crowd in the street, which was loudly demanding the release of the impressed seamen. The councilors, failing to quiet the mob, urged Shirley, much against his will, to speak. His deep voice and commanding appearance did not calm the mob, but convinced its leaders, at least, that the Governor and Council could not do anything to help them.

Frustrated again in its attempt to get public backing for its protest, the mob then moved to a local dockyard "to burn a twenty gun ship now building there for His Majesty," but the way was diverted by "the sudden coming to shore of a barge" –a better object for its revenge. Someone cried that the barge should be burned in the Governor's yard; all shouted approval, and the mob charged toward Marlborough Street.

In the meantime, Shirley had returned to Province House under armed escort, accompanied by many councilors and representatives who feared further violence. The lawmakers had appropriated muskets from the Court House, and taken battle stations inside the Governor's house. The mob approached. Unimpressed by the sight of the legislators turned soldiers, the mob hooted and tried to force the gate leading to the yard. The noise of splintering wood was a signal for the defenders to aim their guns and prepare to fire, but General Pepperrell "instantly" shouted to the men. He saw boys on the fence and bystanders who would be killed. Motioning these people out of the way, he rejoined the lawmakers, who again took hold of their muskets. The delay had given the sailors time for a second thought about their foes' courage or desperation, and they retreated into the evening shadows. Sometime later, Shirley heard their voices coming from the direction of the Common and saw the night sky brighten with a huge bonfire—the sailors were burning the royal barge.[6]

Shirley thanked the members of the legislature for their assistance, but he feared for the safety of some British officers still in the hands of the mob. The complaisant attitude of the

6. *Shirley Correspondence*, I, 406-19; Shirley to Admiralty, Dec. 1, 1747, Admiralty Records, I, 3817, 209-21.

militia and citizenry had permitted mob rule, and there was little for him to do other than to show his disgust for the lawlessness. Accompanied by the few British officers he had rescued, he took a launch for Castle William, where he intended to await proper apologies from the townspeople "for insults to His Majesty George II."

Knowles was incensed over the imprisonment of his officers. Bringing his warships closer to the town, he was ready to shell the docks. Such desperate means of retaliation appalled Shirley, who believed that more violence was not the answer. Instead, he begged Knowles to take the first step toward conciliation by releasing the impressed men. When Knowles reluctantly obliged, Shirley commanded the mob leaders to free the British officers. By Friday, November 20, the townspeople had regained control of Boston, and the militia was patrolling the streets.

Shirley remained at the Castle, insisting upon an apology before he would re-enter Boston. "I shall be concerned at fixing a lasting brand upon the town for their failure . . . [to] exert themselves vigorously."[7] This ultimatum delivered to the already aroused selectmen by Secretary Willard brought into session a town meeting, in which suitable resolutions of regret were passed and a committee was appointed to present them to Shirley at the Castle. Shirley returned to the town Saturday afternoon, escorted up King Street to the Court House by a large assembly of the militia and applauded by a huge crowd of spectators who lined the narrow street. On Sunday morning, he signed a proclamation of the General Court ordering the rioters to surrender and submit themselves to the King's mercy. Although no one came forth, the townspeople offered apologies to Shirley and the navy, and the Governor was wise enough to accept these tokens of good will rather than insist on mass arrests.[8]

Hardly had Boston settled down when another calamity occurred. On the morning of December 9, some minutes after

7. *Shirley Correspondence*, I, 406-9.
8. Albert H. Hoyt, "Pepperrell Papers," *The New-England Historical and Genealogical Register*, 28 (1874), 451-66.

six o'clock, the city was awakened by the fire bells. The noise brought Shirley into the street, and he saw the Court House aflame. It was impossible to come close to the burning building; the heat was so intense that snow on the roofs of nearby buildings melted, and water poured down on the icy streets. Although the firemen were able to save some furnishings and records on the first floor, many papers were destroyed, and treasures of wine, whisky, and brandy in the cellar were lost.[9] While the ashes of the building were still smoking, a disaster council of seven men was formed to save the official records from the weather and find a temporary meeting place. The Boston selectmen offered Faneuil Hall, and those quarters were hastily prepared for a meeting of the General Court on the tenth. On that evening the weather turned bitter cold. Snow and wind blew in from the Atlantic and huge drifts paralyzed business in the town. Overheated and improperly ventilated stoves started several small fires; one blaze nearly took the lives of several sailors whose ship was tied to the Long Wharf for safety. Troubled by these "Frowns of divine Providence," the representatives begged Shirley to declare a "Day of Humiliation and Prayer." In granting their petition, he set January 28, 1748, as the day and promised to join them in prayer.[10]

The Court House fire complicated the clerical work involved in the demobilization of the army. Partial destruction of the financial records multiplied accounting difficulties, and the remaining papers had to be inaccessibly stored in various warehouses. Shirley gave Waldo and Dwight possession of the papers, and they attempted to procure copies of the missing documents either from the colonists concerned or from the British government; but it took months to put the records into usable condition. In the meantime there was considerable chaos. When Wentworth asked Shirley for vouchers for the

9. *The Boston Weekly News-Letter,* Dec. 10, 1747; *Mass. House Journals,* XXIV, 230-31.
10. *The Boston Weekly News-Letter,* Dec. 31, 1747; *Mass. House Journals,* XXIV, 235.

New Hampshire regiment, he had to apologize, "I can't readily find them."[11]

These problems were contributing annoyances to a political situation that was exacerbated by hostility over monetary affairs. The issues of inflation, salaries, and defense appropriations were being debated in the legislature, but no solution seemed forthcoming.[12] In fact, criticism of the administration was the only issue which unified the members. Some legislators blamed the administration for depressed conditions that were unsettling trade, while others accused it of supporting Knowles and impressment.[13] In answer to this last group, Shirley released to the newspapers his correspondence with Josiah Willard which seemed to infer that during the riot some local citizens had taken pleasure in the embarrassment of the administration. This accusation was shocking to the selectmen, who called a special meeting of the town and again presented an official apology to the Governor. After some private discussions, the Governor and selectmen agreed upon an exchange of messages; the Governor's dignity was vindicated.[14]

But an exchange of messages could not settle the basic economic problems facing the colony. The opponents of the administration were not silenced. For months a public debate on impressment and Knowles's behavior took place in the columns of Boston's newspapers. An anti-administration paper, The Independent Advertiser, did not hesitate to attack Shirley's war policies, deprecating the value of Louisbourg and enlarging upon the dangers of inflation. Joining in these assaults was Dr. William Douglass, a hard-chinned Scot whose barbed criticisms in the newspapers were well known to Bostonians. Douglass accused Knowles of stupidity and once described him as a "monster of wickedness." Though Shirley apparently did not dare to have Douglass arrested, Knowles was convinced—

11. Shirley to Wentworth, Jan. 15, 1748, Belknap Papers, Lib. Cong.
12. Shirley to West, May 10, 1749, Treasury I, 335, 110; Mass. House Journals, XXIV, 202-3; The Boston Evening-Post, Dec. 14, 1747.
13. Mass. House Journals, XXIV, 252, 256; The Independent Advertiser (Boston), Feb. 8, 1748.
14. The Boston Weekly News-Letter, Dec. 17 and 31, 1747; The Boston Evening-Post, Dec. 14 and 21, 1747, and Jan. 4, 1748.

in spite of a cautious warning from the Governor—that a libel action was justifiable. Accordingly, Knowles put Apthorp and Hancock in charge of a suit that was litigated for several years and brought a weak apology from Douglass, but not a cessation of his newspaper attacks on the administration.[15]

At first, Shirley tried to ignore the invective and derision of *The Independent Advertiser*, but its continued abuse forced him to consult the Council. Finally, it seemed clear to all his friends that the legislature must censure the newspaper, and the Council sent a committee of such respected men as John Osborn, Samuel Welles, Benjamin Lynde, and Andrew Oliver to solicit approval of the House of Representatives. So decisively was the proposal rejected by the representatives that Shirley never dared present another similar bill.[16] He turned, instead, to Bollan and Kilby, to urge an intensified campaign for an immediate repayment of the military expenditures, without waiting to present the full accounts that he was preparing with the help of Waldo and Dwight.[17]

II

Although Shirley's working majority of merchant, land speculator, and inflationist had been temporarily disrupted, party ranks closed to back an expedition to Crown Point in 1748. Indian relations in New York had deteriorated as a result of French encroachments, and the capture of Crown Point seemed the only way to secure the defense of western Massachusetts and upper New York.[18] With Newcastle's approval, Shirley worked to mount an attack, and won from the House of Representatives a pledge of full cooperation if neigh-

15. John Noble, "Notes on the Libel Suit of Knowles v. Douglass in the Superior Court of Judicature," Col. Soc. Mass., *Publications*, 3 (1900), 213-36; *The Independent Advertiser* (Boston), July 11 and 25, 1748; William Douglass, *A Discourse Concerning the Currencies of the British Plantations in America, &c.*, ed. Charles J. Bullock, Amer. Econ. Assn., *Economic Studies*, II, no. 5 (New York, 1897), 266-89; Suffolk Superior Court Records, 6550, doc. 22, 25, 28, Suffolk County Court House.

16. *Mass. House Journals*, XXIV, 252, 256.

17. Bollan to Willard, Nov. 15, 1746, Feb. 29, June 9, 1747, Apr. 2, 1748, Mass. Archives, XX, 367-68, 411-13, 392, 221-22.

18. *Mass. House Journals*, XXIV, 331-32; *Shirley Correspondence*, I, 425-28.

boring colonies would send assurances of help and if an inter-colonial conference would set quotas of men for each partici-pating colony.[19] It was clear that the colonial legislatures could not count upon a British subsidy to repay the costs of the expedition.

Financing a new expedition while Massachusetts was still burdened with the debt of the recent campaigns was a per-plexing matter. Ten emissions of paper money since 1744 had flooded the colony, and another emission would accelerate currency depreciation. The guarantees of tax levies to main-tain the value of these paper issues now reached to the tax year of 1760, which was too distant to assure public confidence. Only Thomas Hutchinson, then speaker of the House, was bold enough to suggest a way out of the chaos, but his measure would depend upon using the subsidy that Britain was expected to give the colony for establishing a hard currency.[20] Shirley may have sympathized with Hutchinson's attack on inflation, but he was faced with a frontier crisis that took preference in his mind over anything else.

His sense of urgency, however, was not shared by his fellow governors. His correspondence with them was pro-tracted and proved to be disappointing, though a conference was eventually planned for the summer at Albany. Jacob Wendell, who favored an expedition, was repeatedly warned by friends in New York that Governor George Clinton was not ready or able to back an assault upon Crown Point. Philip Livingston wrote Wendell, "You have quite different manage-ment in . . . [Massachusetts]. You have men of Public Spirit . . . [who] can do everything easy."[21] Undoubtedly Wendell passed his private information on to Shirley, and the Governor made allowances for Clinton's weakness.[22]

Shirley's negotiations with other colonial governors were not very encouraging, whether over matters of defense and

19. Shirley to Wanton, Feb. 29, 1748, R. I. Archives, Letters, III, 66.
20. Hutchinson's memorial to Governor, Council, and House, Feb. 3, 1748, Mass. Archives, CII, 366-69.
21. Livingston to Wendell, June ——, 1747, Livingston Papers, 47, 100, 173, Museum of the City of New York.
22. Livingston to Wendell, Jan. 17 and Feb. 13, 1747, ibid., 47, 173, 81, 85.

Indian relations, or over the demobilization of the army assembled for the abortive Canadian invasion of 1747. He frequently inquired of other governors about the progress of the demobilization under his and Knowles's instructions and urged the correspondent to hasten the accounting: "I am uneasy least I should be blamed for delay in the execution of those orders."[23] He found the governors increasingly hostile to the demobilization plans; some were setting higher rates for the soldier pay than were permitted; others were corresponding directly with the home authorities. In fact, he was discovering that the governors and their assemblies gave little weight to his opinions. Whenever difficulties arose, they passed the responsibility to him, then frequently appealed his decisions to the British Treasury and secretary of state. Rhode Island and Connecticut challenged his right to make decisions, and when their accounts were put in final form, they dispatched them directly home, leaving only copies for his personal examination. Both colonies granted greater pay and more allowances for provisions to the soldiers and more funds for incidental charges to the offices than Shirley had permitted in Massachusetts. He observed in disgust that "the more the King grants, the more the people in this part of the world seem to crave." But after reviewing his problems with the secretary of state, the Duke of Bedford, he requested authority to extend to Massachusetts those benefits taken in Rhode Island and Connecticut.[24]

The weakness of Shirley's position was readily apparent to Waldo, who decided to force his hand in Massachusetts, as the governors were doing elsewhere. Waldo demanded the full perquisites of a regimental officer. Besides taking deductions from the soldiers for such services as providing clothing, arms, and medical care, he was pocketing the pay of deceased soldiers and selling the returned muskets. When Shirley insisted upon seeing the records, Waldo refused to discuss the

23. Shirley to Wentworth, Aug. 24, 1748, Belknap Papers, Lib. Cong.
24. Shirley to Clinton, Apr. 19, 1748, Bedford to Shirley, May 10, 1748, Clinton Papers, Clements Lib.; Shirley to Pelham, Jan. 25, 1749, Treasury I, 333, fol. 93; Shirley to Bedford, Oct. 24, 1748, O'Callaghan, ed., *N. Y. Col. Docs.*, VI, 457-58.

matter, asserting that he was directly responsible to the British Treasury.[25]

Shirley hoped to avoid a break with Waldo. The contractor had been a firm supporter through seven years of the governorship, a person of wealth and connections in Massachusetts, the leader of his political faction. Waldo's friends and relatives— Kilby, Pepperrell, Sparhawk, and Wentworth—had materially assisted Shirley's rise to power. Could he count upon their loyalty if he and Waldo parted company? Shirley decided not to take the risk. Despite the unreasonableness of Waldo's requests, he would back them in an application to the British Treasury, insisting only that until the necessary amendment of the regulations was received, Waldo would abide by the existing rules. Shirley tried unsuccessfully to reach Waldo with this message, then asked mutual friends to speak with him, and finally sent his own son with his plea: "I am sensible of your former attachment to me. And my attachment to your interest has ever been reciprocal. I have not only embraced but sought opportunities of serving you . . . and I should have been glad to have had it more in my power to have served you than it has been. The continuation of your friendship I should be glad of; but if it is . . . to be purchased . . . [by] exposing my fortune and interest, as you now insist . . . [this] I won't do to gain or keep the goodwill of any person whatever."[26]

These were strong words, but Shirley reduced the sting by sending Waldo £3,600 in paper currency to pay salaries of regimental officers and by applying for authority to grant him the perquisites he demanded. Waldo was not satisfied with these overtures and decided to put further pressure on the Governor. Several of Shirley's officers were taking up a subscription among officers who had served at Louisbourg in order to purchase a gift in Shirley's honor. The proposal seemed innocent enough; the money was to be used as a contribution to

25. Memorial to the Treasury, 1748, Treasury I, 340, fol. 23. See John A. Schutz, "British Marine Accounting and Auditor Edmund Herbert," *The Huntington Library Quarterly*, 20 (1957), 269-80. Shirley accepted personal financial responsibility for these disbursements of funds, and until the accounts were passed by the Treasury, he was liable for the funds.

26. Shirley to Waldo, July 7, 1748, Knox Papers, L, 93.

the King's Chapel building fund, of which Shirley was the leading patron and honorary chairman, and to buy a number of muskets to decorate his home. For most of the officers it was no doubt a voluntary offering, but inevitably there were some who felt that they were obliged to participate. Waldo seized upon their complaints to discredit the whole undertaking, asserting that contributions were being forced. The publicity, breaking at election time, compelled Shirley to ask the officers to abandon the project.[27]

III

While the May elections did not appreciably change the political composition of the House, nor affect the membership of the Council, there was a stiffening of opposition toward the administration. This is surprising, for in the preceding winter and spring Shirley had appointed more people to office than he had done during any comparable time in former years. Nevertheless, representatives from seaboard communities, led by Joseph Heath, James Allen, and John Tyng, attempted to cut his salary. Exchanges of messages with Shirley did not compromise the issue, and the June session closed without a decision.[28]

The session ended prematurely because Shirley agreed, apparently against his personal wishes, to join a legislative delegation to the defense conference at Albany. Although he had been promoting the meeting all winter and spring, he was now so involved with Waldo, the legislature, and the governors that he was reluctant to give time to it. Also, late reports from London indicated that hostilities were nearly ended in Europe; the only thing still remaining to terminate the war was the signing of the peace treaty. He may have realized, however, that the conference offered an opportunity to confer with Thomas Hutchinson, Andrew Oliver, and John Choate, the legislative delegates, and regroup his followers with their help.

27. Shirley to Pelham, Sept. 13, 1748, Treasury I, 330, fol. 54.
28. *Mass. House Journals*, XXV, 52-53, 57-58; Shirley to Bedford, July 2, 1748, C. O. 323/12, 15-20.

It may be significant that Peter Oliver, brother of Andrew, was honored with a judgeship in early May.[29]

Since the legislature delayed voting funds for the trip until the last minute, the delegates were not able to go part way by sea, but had to take a land route across the hills of Massachusetts and Connecticut and travel by barge up the Hudson River. When they arrived, Albany was crowded with thousands of Iroquois waiting for the proceedings to begin. For five days and nights, speeches were made, toasts drunk, and pipes smoked. Had not peace between France and Britain been expected, the conference would have been a great military success, for the Iroquois placed themselves definitely on the British side. As it was, the negotiations laid foundations of friendship and raised prospects of closer alliances in the future. Shirley described the success of the negotiations in a sweeping manner: "All was obtained from them that could be proposed. They promised either to drive the French, who privately reside among them, out of their country, or to deliver them up to Governor Clinton. They also promised to send no deputations to Canada, and that they would keep their warriors or fighting men in readiness, whenever Governor Clinton should call for them."[30]

The Crown Point expedition was, of course, abandoned. After the conference, Shirley joined Clinton in a leisurely journey down the Hudson River discussing the politics of their colonies. Shirley must have thought his own dispute with Waldo trifling as he listened to Clinton's story of the intrigue and almost unparalleled bitterness that existed in the New York government; the hatred of Clinton's former friends James and Oliver de Lancey; the aggression of an assembly that had taken to itself the management of finance. Such proceedings against a royal governor incensed Shirley. He sympathized with Clinton and offered his assistance.

29. *The Boston Weekly News-Letter*, May 19, 1748.
30. Shirley and Clinton to Board of Trade, Aug. 18, 1748, C. O. 5/407-18; *Mass. House Journals*, XXV, 54, 62, 64; Clinton to Johnson, July 5, 1748, James Sullivan and A. C. Flick, eds., *The Papers of Sir William Johnson* (Albany, 1921-51), I, 172-73, hereafter cited as *William Johnson Papers*; Clinton to Bedford, Aug. 15, 1748, O'Callaghan, ed., *N. Y. Col. Docs.*, VI, 428-32.

By the time they joined Mrs. Clinton in New York, the governors had decided upon a plan in which Cadwallader Colden, Clinton's advisor, had agreed to participate. Shirley was to be introduced to the leading politicians and familiarized with local issues and was then to send a fact-finding report to the home authorities. It is not clear why Shirley agreed to this plan. Perhaps he liked Clinton's family connections with the Earl of Lincoln or anticipated some reward for helping a fellow governor. He may simply have been flattered by the request for his advice. Clinton needed more power to change his Council and eliminate the de Lanceys from office, and he expected Shirley's report to attract the attention of the ministry to his many letters on these subjects. Whatever Shirley's reason for helping Clinton, he was saddled with the responsibility of mixing into politics where he had little accurate information and where he could receive few personal advantages. He took his notes and prepared to write the analysis.

On his return to Boston, Shirley reconsidered his promises —probably upon the advice of Jacob Wendell, who was well acquainted in New York—and decided to make his report directly to Clinton. In this way, he avoided ministerial criticism for leaving his government without permission and for performing a task unauthorized by the ministry. His report thus became an informal service to a fellow governor: it outlined the major causes of discontent, placed the major blame for governmental turmoil on the legislature, and suggested some commonplace methods for solving political problems.[31]   While Shirley did not entirely fulfill his promise, perhaps because Clinton was personally responsible in part for the divisions in New York politics, he was sorry for the Governor and tried whenever he could to counsel him. Many letters passed between them. Sometimes Shirley added incidental advice to a letter about accounting business or regimental recruiting; other times he included observations on governmental policy in letters introducing personal friends who were visiting New York. But whatever the occasion, he emphasized caution,

31. Colden to Shirley, Aug. 22, 1748, *Colden Papers,* IV, 73-74; Shirley to Pelham, Aug. 24, 1748, Huntington Lib. MSS, 9714.

understanding, and tactical maneuvering in handling the New York Assembly. One letter, especially, reveals Shirley's disposition to avoid controversy:

I perceive from the copies of the late messages of your assembly, [that the legislators] make a great point of your denying them access to you by any message they think proper to deliver to you, and depend much upon that as . . . justification . . . for not proceeding upon business, till they are redressed in that point. I won't take upon me to say, that you are not right in refusing to receive indecent messages from them. But I must acknowledge, it seems to me the only disputable matter between you and them: And I could wish things were not pushed to extremities on that account. . . . It seems to be a punctilio to deny the assembly's committees access to you, to deliver them. And since they so fondly lay hold of it to embroil the government, . . . I would recommend it to your consideration, whether taking away the pretense of putting everything to a stand in the government might not be advisable, and whether it might not be done with a good grace by suspending the point . . . till it shall be determined at home. At the same time I don't take upon me to say that the assembly is in the right, but it is certainly a tender point. And how far your Excellency's answer to the assembly upon it will hold in the case of his Majesty's governors, I am not clear.[32]

IV

When Shirley returned to Boston after his six-week absence in New York, he found that Waldo had become increasingly self-confident; apparently Kilby and other London merchants were helping him spread opposition to Shirley's administration. It was finally necessary to secure a court order to place Waldo's military accounts in the neutral possession of Thomas Hutchinson.[33] Though not the best solution for a difficult situation, it allowed Shirley to delay action until the ministry answered his queries.

Opposition was also multiplying in Connecticut and Rhode Island, where officials, taut with indignation, had discovered that they could not by-pass Shirley's scrutiny of their accounts.

32. Shirley to Clinton, Aug. 1, 1749, Clinton Papers.
33. Shirley to Waldo, Oct. 19, 1748, Suffolk Court Records, 65640, doc. 90; Waldo to Shirley, Feb. 21, 1749, *ibid.*, doc. 89.

Though they had sent the originals to London and only copies to him, he had examined the copies anyway, finding discrepancies in their statements. What was more, Secretary of State Bedford backed his decisions. The governors hoped to discredit him through Eliakim Palmer and Richard Partridge, agents of Connecticut and Rhode Island, respectively, who were peculiarly suited to perform the task. Both were merchants of London, with very good official and non-official connections. Both had been Shirley's enemies from Belcher's day, and Palmer boasted to Governor Jonathan Law of Connecticut that he would do everything in his power to blacken Shirley's name.[34]

Judging that the danger was acute, Shirley sent his son William to London with letters for Newcastle, Pelham, and Bedford; significantly, none was addressed to the London merchants, not even to such a good friend as John Thomlinson, who were the principal backers of the administration in 1741. This marks a sudden break with the merchants, and it probably indicates that Shirley was uncertain of their help in his disagreement with Waldo. In any case, he instructed William to secure secret permission for him to visit London; he could personally mend political fences. In the meantime, he prepared for that visit by completing the accounts. Although the strain of his argument with Waldo and the burden of legislative business had sapped his strength, he elicited the help of Eliakim Hutchinson and managed to finish them by working day and night. It required endless hours to arrange, adjust, copy, and explain hundreds of pages of computations; but he checked and rechecked until the accounts of nine colonies were completed. At the same time he decided that direct action was the best way to handle Waldo's opposition and instituted proceedings against him to force a return of the muskets and a disbursement of funds to soldiers, doctors, and merchants.[35]

34. Palmer to Law, July 23, 1748, Law Papers, Correspondence and Documents during Jonathan Law's Governorship of the Colony of Connecticut, 1741-1750, 3 vols. (Connecticut Historical Society, Collections, vols. 11, 13, 15 [Hartford, 1907-1914]), III, 257-59. Hereafter cited as Law Papers. Shirley to Pelham, Dec. 10, 1748, Treasury I, 330, fol. 65.

35. Mass. House Journals, XXVI, 81-82; Waldo to Shirley, Feb. 21, 1749, Suffolk Court Records, 65640, doc. 89.

Shirley's labor was continuously interrupted by the demands of politics. In the House, James Allen of Boston, who had joined forces with Waldo, was expelled, re-elected, and re-expelled for some audacious remarks on the Governor's policies.[36] Allen criticized Hutchinson's connection with impressment in 1746 and 1747 and accused the Governor of benefiting from the suffering of impressed Bostonians. Allen's bitter tongue and sharp tactics, though often a liability to him, attracted a large following in the town and made him a leader of the opposition to Shirley in the House.[37] Gathering around him, too, were representatives of the seacoast towns, where impressment had aroused citizens, also a number of veterans, some of them Waldo's friends from Maine.

Allen's criticism of the war reflected general public indignation at the Peace of Aix-la-Chapelle. It seemed incredible to many people—as it did to Shirley—that Great Britain would hand Louisbourg back to France as a condition of the peace and leave the boundary line between the empires an issue for negotiation. Settlers in the Connecticut River Valley and in eastern Maine were terrified by threats of Indian warfare, and Pepperrell and Oliver Partridge, the leading spokesmen in the House for western Massachusetts, petitioned for new defenses in the frontier country.[38] Governor Clinton requested another Indian conference to repair the damage France was doing to Indian relations. The tone of disillusion was sounded by *The Independent Advertiser* when the editor asked: "Who can tell what will be the consequence of this Peace in times to come? Perhaps this goodly land itself—Even this beloved country, may share the same fate with this its conquest—may be the purchase of a future peace."[39]

36. *The Independent Advertiser* (Boston), Dec. 5, 1748; *A Letter to the Freeholders, and Qualified Voters, Relating to the Ensuing Election* (Boston, 1749), 4-11. "Only the wicked governors of men dread what is said of them; the public censure was true, else he [Shirley] had not felt it bitter—Freedom of speech is ever the symptom, as well as the effect, of good government.—Guilt only dreads Liberty of Speech."

37. *Mass. House Journals*, XXVI, 76, 78-79.

38. Pepperrell to Shirley, Nov. 18, 1748, Mass. Archives, XVIII, 288; Shirley to House, Jan. 20, 1749, *ibid.*, 293; Partridge to Shirley, June 6, 1748, *ibid.*, LIII, 342.

39. *The Independent Advertiser* (Boston), Nov. 14, 1748.

The editor might have noted that the Governor's policies were repudiated by his English friends; that his exertion of four years to establish a British frontier on the St. Lawrence River was a sacrifice to European politics. But his efforts now seemed part of the betrayal of colonial interests, and his apparent lack of support from the home government gave the legislature an excuse to go its own way; it cut appropriations for defense, refused to make necessary salary adjustments, and challenged the Governor's power to appoint the attorney general. Some legislators, like James Allen, took advantage of the opportunity of the Governor's weakness to harass him in the columns of *The Independent Advertiser*.[40] While Shirley did not reply publicly, he privately made strenuous efforts to develop new support in the House. By the fall of 1748 he was shifting his political affiliations.

As a preliminary step, he withdrew his support of Kilby, the Massachusetts agent and Waldo's friend, and got the legislature to name Bollan temporary agent. This was a way of reducing Waldo's influence in the administration, but it was also a recognition of the fact that support of Kilby had become a liability because of the agent's controversy with the House. Kilby and his merchant friends had proposed that the British subsidy of £183,649 given Massachusetts as compensation for her expenditures in the Louisbourg campaign be set aside as a fund to establish a hard currency. Although most Americans were outraged by the notion of having Parliament enforce the establishment of a currency, Kilby had the support of many merchants in America and his proposal was admired by British merchants who had influence in the House of Commons. The sanction of the Commons was necessary before Massachusetts could obtain the grant, and the refusal of the Massachusetts legislature to embrace the opportunity for currency reform threatened to block Parliamentary action. The controversy was temporarily resolved when Bollan induced the Commons to grant the money without any restriction on the supposition that it would be used to reform the currency.[41]

40. *Ibid.*, July 25, 1748.
41. Shirley to Newcastle, Jan. 23, 1750, Add. MSS, 32820; Bollan to Willard, Apr. 2, 1748, Mass. Archives, CCLXXXVII, 91. Kilby also angered

Assured of the money under these conditions, and having cultivated favor in the House by espousing its side of the dispute with Kilby, Shirley was in a position to hazard a major change in administration policy. He approved Bollan's promise and took immediate steps to introduce legislation into the General Court that would establish a hard currency in the colony. His daring decision was undoubtedly based on several considerations, but none was so compelling as his loss of political support. One after another of his coalition leaders had left the administration: Waldo, Kilby, and Barnard, as well as some English and local supporters of his defense policies. He was uncertain of Hancock and Pepperrell and their business friends. Besides these hard facts of disintegrating alliances, he was confronted with a currency crisis in the colony that required swift and drastic means for its solution. The British subsidy could form the basis of a hard currency, but the politics of raising the issue in the legislature were especially dangerous and could result in hatreds and divisions as devastating as those that disrupted the Belcher administration in 1741. On the other hand, there were equally great political advantages. Success would win support from merchants in London and Boston, and would particularly please the Pelhams. Even favoring the establishment of a hard currency had some local value, for Shirley could count on the friendship of Thomas Hutchinson, Andrew Oliver, Jacob Wendell, and a host of powerful Boston merchants. Hutchinson, in fact, had a plan for currency reform and was anxious to present it to the legislature.

Shirley cemented his alliance with these Boston merchants when he cautiously announced in his October message to the legislature the need for currency reform.[42] A House majority of Hutchinson and Shirley friends won the appointment of a committee. Its deliberations proceeded slowly, for a mounting

---

the General Court by not insisting on the full payment of the Massachusetts grant. Parliament considered payment on the value of the depreciated currency, but Bollan argued that justice demanded the payment of the full value of the bills when issued. Bollan's position meant a minimum increase of 50% in the grant.

42. *Mass. House Journals*, XXV, 81, 123-28, 139-40.

hostility to the Governor was led by James Allen and his friends. It became so violent that the House expelled Allen; however, the opposition of Allen's friends continued. The Governor's salary was attacked, his defense policies criticized, and his friends denounced. In the midst of this rancor the committee continued its work, and to reinforce his determination to force a decision in this session of the legislature, Shirley presented another address to the General Court. The houses responded by appointing a joint committee of sixteen members, which included such powerful men as Jacob Wendell, William Foye, John Chandler, Robert Hale, Samuel Welles, John Choate, Samuel Watts, and Andrew Oliver. The committee finally drafted a bill. These men, if their opinions and determination can be gauged by those of Welles, were ready to end the paper inflation at all costs. Welles told Roger Wolcott, governor of Connecticut, that "one of the greatest mischiefs that ever befell either your government or ours" was paper money.[43]

When the bill reached the House floor in late December, such old Shirley friends as Choate and Hale backed Hutchinson and his followers, but the bill failed to receive majority assent.[44] Another bill was presented in January. This time pressure from Shirley kept the legislature from further delaying a decision, and the bill finally won legislative approval on January 25, 1749.[45] The victory after sixteen weeks of debate was an embittered one. The act, it seems, was a compromise of various money bills, but was, according to Hutchinson, "as good as could be expected."[46] Hutchinson received most credit and blame for the act; it is clear, however, that the victory was obtained because the bill was accepted as an ad-

43. Welles to Wolcott, Jan. 31, 1749, *Law Papers*, III, 289; Law to Shirley, Mar. 3, 1749, *ibid.*, 294.
44. *Acts and Resolves, Public and Private, of the Province of the Massachusetts Bay* (Boston, 1869-1922), III, 454-62; *Mass. House Journals*, XXV, 148-49, 170, 180; Shipton, *Sibley's Harvard Graduates*, VI, 485; Malcolm Freiberg, "Thomas Hutchinson and the Province Currency," *The New Eng. Qtly.*, 30 (1957), 190-208.
45. *Mass. House Journals*, XXV, 184, 187, 190, 191, 196.
46. Hutchinson to Williams, Feb. 1, 1749, Israel Williams Papers, II, 139, Mass. Hist. Soc.

ministration measure and because it met the political needs of the Governor. The act was very different from Hutchinson's first proposal, providing for complete use of Louisbourg funds and a tax levy of £75,000 to redeem the colony's paper money. The paper money would be redeemed at forty-five shillings old tenor, or eleven shillings threepence middle and new tenor, for one piece of eight. The redemption period would continue for one year, beginning March 31, 1750.[47]

Repercussions from the passage of the act were felt immediately. Shirley and Hutchinson were attacked in the press and threatened with physical harm. In the May elections the opposition showed its strength in the colony's coastal communities by ousting representatives who voted for the bill. Hutchinson, Hale, and forty-three other legislators went down to defeat.[48] Though the friends of the Governor and Hutchinson gathered enough votes to put Hutchinson into the Council, where he soon became a pillar of strength for Shirley, House leadership disintegrated long enough for Waldo, Tyng, and Allen to have themselves appointed to a special committee of investigation. In their new position they began an intensive inquiry into the military accounting practices of Eliakim Hutchinson, John Wheelwright, and others who had helped uncover Waldo's financial dealings.[49]

The committee's investigation was undoubtedly an effort to repel Shirley's offensive against Waldo. In January 1749, the Governor had entrusted his old friend Robert Auchmuty with the task of prosecuting a civil action against Waldo for £12,000. The jury in the Inferior Court of Judicature returned a verdict in favor of Waldo, forcing Auchmuty to appeal the case to the Superior Court, where he easily won an assessment of £500 sterling, court costs, and an order compelling Waldo to file the Massachusetts military accounts with the Governor. Waldo handed over the papers on February 21,

47. *Mass. Acts and Resolves*, III, 430-41; Freiberg, "Thomas Hutchinson and the Province Currency," *New Eng. Qtly.*, 30 (1957), 199.

48. *The Independent Advertiser* (Boston), June 5, 1749.

49. *Mass. House Journals*, XXVI, 81-82; Shipton, *Sibley's Harvard Graduates*, VIII, 158-59; Andrew McFarland Davis, "Threat to Burn Governor Shirley's House," Col. Soc. Mass., *Publications*, 3 (1900), 207-11.

with this saucy note: "You'll find, Sir, if ever you are pleased to look over them that they vary little from those you have already."[50] In the same letter Waldo boldly demanded an additional £14,000 paper currency to take care of some outstanding debts.

Waldo's demand opened another court battle. Both men filed countercharges, and Shirley petitioned for a larger assessment on Waldo's estates than the £500 sterling and court costs. On the morning of April 5, the new trial began. Auchmuty made a brilliant exposition of charges; according to Waldo himself, he spoke "in the most moving manner, that art and dissimulation could invent, charging me with the utmost injustice, unfaithfulness in my trust."[51] Witness after witness presented evidence—Eliakim Hutchinson, Jack Shirley, merchants, and soldiers. Many of the soldiers were surprise witnesses, and their evidence proved to be "most unexpected." Several sensational letters of the Waldo-Shirley correspondence were read into the record—one by Shirley described the harm Waldo was doing to the widows and orphans by taking the money of deceased soldiers.

The climax of the trial was a three-day closing oration by Auchmuty, who, according to Waldo, so impressed the jury that it forgot everything else. The jury reaffirmed the grant of £500 sterling and court costs for Shirley and denied Waldo's claims.[52] The award was firm enough for Shirley to attach Waldo's property, an action so damaging to the latter's businesses that he sought relief by instituting new court cases. Prosecuting the Governor in case after case, he recovered little by little the money he had lost. To stop these tactics, Shirley appealed the cases to the Privy Council in London and prepared to argue them in person. Only the lack of formal permission from the Board of Trade to leave his post held him in Boston, and that permission was granted in late summer.[53]

The news of Shirley's projected trip to England surprised

50. Waldo to Shirley, Feb. 21, 1749, Suffolk Court Records, 65640, doc. 89.
51. Waldo to Kilby, Apr. 24, 1749, Knox Papers, L, 98.
52. Suffolk Court Records, 65640, doc. 64, 65, 86.
53. *Ibid.*, 66972, doc. 3; Shirley to Wentworth, Aug. 28, 1749, Belknap Papers, Lib. Cong.

Waldo and his friends, for they had not anticipated such drastic action. They had, in fact, been laying their plans in London to discredit the Governor, much as Waldo, Frances Shirley, and Dunbar had discredited Belcher in 1739 and 1740. Shirley seemed vulnerable. John Barnard, Kilby's business partner, discovered in 1748 while making the rounds of the public offices that Shirley had "not the least interest with any one person in the administration, the effects of which, he will feel, in a short time."[54]

The question was whether Shirley's presence in London would change his fortunes. He would have to exert every ounce of his strength, for his son William had already been replaced by Benjamin Pemberton, the same official Shirley had removed from the naval office in 1741. His son Thomas had been denied the military patronage of the Pelham administration,[55] and Shirley himself had been unable to prevent the reduction of his regiment at the end of the war or to exchange his commission for an active colonelcy. All around him Shirley saw signs of hostility, but his recent success in establishing a hard currency and his persistent attempt to audit the military accounts along conservative lines of economy and efficiency had possibilities of strength that troubled his enemies.

54. Barnard to Hancock, Sept. ——, 1748, Hancock Papers.
55. Barnard to Hancock, July 8, 1748, ibid. "It seems this young captain was to be introduced to the Duke [of Cumberland], and interest made, that he might go with the Duke to Flanders, but that great man was well apprised of the Governor's management and his youth, [and] he [Thomas] was absolutely refused, and ordered to his post immediately."

VIII

His Majesty's Commissioner

Shirley's effort to arrange his affairs was not easily accomplished. His most difficult task was to construct an effective defense against his numerous and busy opponents. Waldo's committee of investigation was probing the accounts of Eliakim Hutchinson, who had been involved in the impressment riots of 1746, and the insinuations of committeemen were threatening to damage the reputation of his administration. Shirley persuaded Wendell to head another investigation that attacked Waldo's handling of the accounts and then hired an associate of Thomas Hutchinson, Ezekiel Goldthwait, to receive the complaints of soldiers who had not been equably compensated for their services.[1]

But Shirley could not have been satisfied with the results of his counterattack. *The Independent Advertiser,* long hostile to his policies, now turned to his religion, by ridiculing his actions during the ceremony laying the cornerstone of King's Chapel. The Governor, it said, tapped the stone just the number of raps Archbishop Laud gave the door of St. Catherine's Church at that memorable consecration.[2] In another issue the newspaper used a report of Knowles's departure from Jamaica to comment on the return of faithful public servants to the homeland. The writer, perhaps Waldo himself,[3] referred to Shirley's imminent departure for England and warned the Governor that he would "have the difficult and ungrateful task of removing the suspicions of his superiors concerning some parts of his conduct."[4]

1. *Mass. House Journals,* XXVI, 81-83; *The Boston Weekly News-Letter,* June 1, 1749.
2. *The Independent Advertiser* (Boston), Aug. 14, 1749.
3. Waldo to Kilby, Apr. 24, 1749, Knox Papers, L, 98, Mass. Hist. Soc.
4. *The Independent Advertiser* (Boston), Aug. 21, 1749.

The Governor's opposition appeared more vocal than numerous, but it was concentrated along the coast and enjoyed an election victory that momentarily crippled his leadership in the House. It consisted of the Boston representatives, Waldo, Tyng, and Allen, who were his leading adversaries, but joining them were Joseph Heath of Roxbury and Daniel Conant of Beverly, who was Dr. Hale's successor. Sparhawk was also hostile, but Pepperrell carefully maintained his neutrality.[5] Former militia officers like Jonathan Slade, Thomas Kidder, Benjamin Newhall, and James Stevens objected to Shirley's accounting practices. There were such merchants in London as Kilby, Barnard, Partridge, and Palmer, and in Boston a few colonists from other provinces who, for various reasons, had come to the city to protest the Governor's policies. Elisha Williams was the most belligerent of these visitors.[6] Shirley's foes were numerous and dangerous, but they had no great popular backing. John Mascarene, son of the Annapolis Royal commander, believed that a "considerable part of the province" welcomed Shirley's hard money policies, and Thomlinson, a steadfast supporter of a strong currency, was enthusiastic over the legislative decision to provide a sterling backing for Massachusetts money.[7] James Otis, Jr., son of a loyal Shirley supporter, believed that the opposition of Tyng and Allen was motivated by hatred instead of principle.[8] Even *The Independent Advertiser* admitted that the Governor enjoyed vast prestige in the House of Representatives and could easily rally support for his policies.[9]

5. Fairchild, *Messrs. William Pepperrell*, 184-85.
6. Williams to Waldo, June 4, 1750, Amer. Antiq. Soc.; Quincy to Flynt, July 18, 1748, Josiah Quincy Papers, Mass. Hist. Soc. Quincy writes of this opposition: "You will doubtless ere this reaches you hear that Governor S——y has surprisingly lost his interest at this court but by what agency I am at a loss to acquaint you unless his own actions which if they were critically examined into would I believe not only lose him his interest but something that is still dearer to him; however, as I know myself a prejudiced person and that you think me so, I'll leave him to those who will I hope impartially judge, and reward him according to his merits."
7. John Mascarene, Jr., to John Mascarene, Feb. 4, 1749, Mascarene Papers, Mass. Hist. Soc.
8. James Otis, Jr., to James Otis, Sept. 10, 1750, Otis Papers, I, Mass. Hist. Soc.
9. *The Independent Advertiser* (Boston), Nov. 12, 1748; Waldo to Kilby,

Shirley obviously weighed the strength of his support and opposition as he prepared to leave the colony, and he spent the few remaining weeks before his departure regrouping his followers. He sent letters to friends in England announcing plans to visit London, and assured Thomlinson, who had earlier volunteered help, that his regard for him was as great as ever: "My silence has . . . proceeded from . . . a never unceasing round of business, and anxiety, and an endless variety of public correspondence which have long robbed me not only of the enjoyment of my friends whether absent or present, but of every other comfort of life."[10]   Shirley also took steps to guarantee the continuance of his policies during his absence. He persuaded the legislature to send delegates to another Indian conference at Albany, proceed with plans for converting paper money into hard currency, and vote funds for necessary frontier defense.   Then he filled all existing vacancies in the administration.   He gave such old friends as Charles Paxton and Ezekiel Cheever judicial posts and chose as attorney general Edmund Trowbridge, an acquaintance of some years. Other appointments went to Oliver Partridge, Joseph Hawley, and Joseph Richards, friends and supporters of his frontier policies.[11] He also reached an understanding with Hutchinson, Wendell, and Choate that Bollan was to be their nominee for permanent agent, and, perhaps in exchange for the favor, he appointed Ezekiel Goldthwait, to a court position. He promised to look after Massachusetts' interests in settling the accounts and to discuss with authorities in England the relation of the colony's government with the Anglican Church.[12] His reliance upon Thomas Hutchinson in carrying out policies of the governorship was obvious enough for critics to speak of Hutchinson as the Governor's prime minister.[13]

Apr. 24, 1749, Knox Papers, L, 98. Waldo believed that Shirley exercised unfair influence through his control of court appointments and that his popularity with the country people made impartial juries difficult to impanel.

10. Shirley to Thomlinson, June 7, 1749, Shirley MSS, Mass. Hist. Soc.

11. *Boston Gazette*, July 11 and Aug. 15, 1749, Mass. Archives, Council Records, XII, 119, 121.

12. Palmer to Law, Apr. 15, 1749, *Law Papers*, III, 298; Shirley to Willard, July 9, 1750, Mass. Archives, XIII, 117-19.

13. Sparhawk to Waldo, Mar. 8, 1750, *ibid.*, LIII, 493.

Just before his departure Shirley issued a statement of policy. By means of a public letter to Spencer Phips, the lieutenant governor and uncle of his son-in-law, he offered some instructions which clearly indicated to the opposition that Phips would be carrying out his policies. "I wish you all success," the letter read, "but be solicitous that nothing should be done . . . that may render my government uneasy to me upon my return." He warned that appointments should be made only for Phips's incumbency and given only to friends of his administration, that the selection of a permanent agent should be made from persons who have shown no "remarkable disaffection to me," and that the laws against paper currency should be enforced with all possible vigor.[14]

After this public pronouncement in September, Shirley left on the *Boston* for England. While gentlemen from town and legislature gathered on the Long Wharf to wish him good voyage, a farewell salute was fired from Castle William. Without any more ceremony than an editorial blast at Shirley in *The Independent Advertiser*, Waldo embarked on another ship. His decision was so abrupt that he had not taken time to put his personal affairs in order.[15]

I

Unlike many Englishmen who were colonial executives, Shirley was not strongly attracted to London; only once or twice in eighteen years had he mentioned a desire to return home. But he recognized that it was now necessary for him to be there, and he was determined to make the most of the trip. Besides seeing the ministers of state, he welcomed the chance to renew friendships, inspect his estate in Sussex, and walk with his sons through familiar places in London and Cambridge.

These activities were kept secondary to the main purpose

14. *Shirley Correspondence*, I, 489-92.

15. *The Independent Advertiser* (Boston), Sept. 18, 1749; Leblond to Waldo, Dec. 11, 1749, Mass. Archives, CCLXXXVII, 180-82; *The Boston Evening-Post*, Sept. 25, 1749. Just as Shirley was leaving Boston, Bollan arrived with the parliamentary grant. The reception for Bollan was cool in Boston.

of his visit, for his career was at a crisis. However, there was something extraordinary in the way he went about his affairs —an ease that hardly revealed the crisis. He appeared self-confident, even casual, in the way he conducted his business. He did not press his own case directly in early interviews with Newcastle, Pelham, Bedford, and the Earls of Halifax and Lincoln. He discussed New York politics, the Treaty of Aix-la-Chapelle, and the military accounts.[16] Expressing his dismay at the low character of politics in New York, he related his impressions of the de Lancey brothers to Lord Lincoln, Clinton's uncle and patron. Lincoln, noticeably moved, then induced Newcastle and Bedford to help him rescue Clinton.[17] To speak for the client of an influential Whig was an excellent tactic because Shirley was thus able to prepare the way for a discussion of the distressing politics of Massachusetts.

He was also delighted for the opportunity to speak about Nova Scotia to Bedford and the new president of the Board of Trade, Lord Halifax, who were pushing hard for the settlement of Protestants in the colony. Shirley found them appreciative of his recommendations for its development, and he repeated, what he had often written, that Nova Scotian security was bound up with Louisbourg and British control of Canada. To his surprise, Bedford invited him to join the peace commission at Paris, where the boundary line between British and French colonies would be drawn. This negotiation was not his idea of the proper solution of the imperial problem, but he was flattered by the recognition and accepted the offer. Writing his American acquaintances for official descriptions of French encroachments and statements of boundary limits, he correlated their reports with information he had gathered from governmental offices in London. His object was to prove that Britain had vast claims to the American west through exploration and treaty. In his enthusiasm, however, he neglected to secure Newcastle's approval of his Paris appointment, and after

16. Shirley to Clinton, Aug. 1, 1749, and Catherwood to Clinton, May 2, 1750, Clinton Papers; Leonard W. Labaree, "George Clinton," *Dictionary of American Biography*, IV, 225-26.

17. Shirley to Clinton, Nov. 30, 1749, Clinton Papers; Shirley to John Pownall, Nov. 14, 1750, C. O. 323/12, 273.

a few weeks discovered from the gossip of London that Bedford and Newcastle were not on good terms.

Newcastle gave a hint of his feelings during a levee, when he asked the Governor whether there were complaints by the people of Massachusetts against British rule. Taunted by the question, Shirley replied modestly and directly to his patron. There was a certain amount of clamor, he admitted—"No prudence can prevent [it]"—but he thought there was less in Massachusetts than elsewhere in America. He mentioned Waldo and Kilby by name, but did not warmly denounce either. Of Waldo's opposition, he dispassionately commented: "I had entrusted [him] with the payment of one of the late regiments raised in my government . . . and have with great reluctance been obliged to prosecute for several breaches of trust, which he appears to me to have committed with respect to the Crown, the soldiers, and myself, in an action at law. . . . Before this troublesome affair, which a just regard for my own character forced me into, this person on whom I had heaped all the obligations in my power, was perfectly attached to my interest, and nothing but a disappointment in his exorbitant views, and forgetfulness of past favors have instigated him to attempt to do me any ill offices."[18]

When Newcastle continued cool toward his Paris assignment, Shirley wrote again to explain his motives for accepting the appointment. "I . . . assure your Grace that . . . motives of my acceptance were, my hopes that it might give me an easier access to his Majesty's ministers to lay before them the state of Nova Scotia; which from having been long the object of my attention appears to me immediately to affect the safety of all his other Northern Colonies . . .; and that from my acquaintance with the points relative to the . . . limits of his territories . . . , I might be more capable of doing his Majesty service in this negotiation than some other gentleman."[19] Newcastle, in spite of his feelings, agreed to extend Shirley's leave of absence from Massachusetts, which was a major concession considering the patronage value of the governorship.

18. *Shirley Correspondence*, I, 495.
19. *Ibid.*, I, 503-4.

II

Although Newcastle could not forget Shirley's relations with an enemy, he arranged for a swift audit of the military accounts. Newcastle (as well as Bedford and Halifax) was anxious for the peace negotiations to begin, and he scheduled a series of meetings between Shirley and treasury officials so they could examine certain technical details in the accounts. The Duke's arrangement proved to be most fortunate, for Shirley often had opportunities to defend himself when complaints were presented to the Treasury, and his attendance there had the appearance of giving official support to his judgments of the accounts.

But Shirley's foes were not idle. Waldo, Kilby, and the colonial agents remonstrated with the authorities over the items in the accounts which Shirley had reduced. Even Pepperrell, who had also come to London, used his reputation as the military hero of Louisbourg in an attempt to restore certain items. These were days of tax reductions, however, and government economy was popular with officials; the Treasury officials not only approved of Shirley's decisions, but cut back the allowable expenditures even more severely than he thought was justified. A typical comment appended to the New Jersey accounts by the auditors illustrates the general appreciation of his work: "As Mr. Shirley's objections appear to be just and reasonable and founded upon his Majesty's orders, we see no reason to depart there from."[20] Even certain fees of his own were disallowed, and he was forced to petition for them.

Only one item was disallowed in the official Massachusetts accounts—a charge of £3,347 for cannon and military stores that probably should have been paid by the colony. Otherwise, the examiners praised Shirley's work as "being made up with greater exactness and more conformable to his Majesty's orders and the necessary regulations prescribed by Governor

20. Board of Trade to Treasury, Feb. 28, 1750, C. O. 324/13, 160; Elisha Williams to Trumbull, Oct. 16, 1750, Trumbull Papers, Conn. Hist. Soc. Halifax blamed the hostility of the Treasury on the accounting practices of the assemblies themselves (which was Shirley's own position).

Shirley and Admiral Knowles . . . than any other of the colonies."[21] Shirley was delighted to have Waldo's claims rejected, but he was embarrassed by the disallowance of the military stores. He had been careful himself in scrutinizing the accounts, and he expected his judgment to be honored out of respect for his services and those of the colony. The Massachusetts legislature reacted much the same way and instructed Agent Bollan to petition for a reinstatement of the excluded items.

Whatever the justice of these adjustments, Lord Halifax, in his final report on the accounts, stood firm in rejecting the additional claims of the agents, and for this policy Shirley was generally grateful. He incurred criticism; Elisha Williams believed that Shirley "has done a dirty job for a ministry—whose least concern, I believe, is that of doing justice."[22] When Shirley heard a report of the complaint, he defended himself in a personal letter to Williams: "If I have erred on either side, it is in favor of the regiment."[23] For months Richard Partridge also fiercely assailed Shirley's actions, although he eventually had to admit his own failure as colonial agent to influence the ministry: the authorities "seemed to be . . . almost deaf to entreaties." When he was compelled to notify the governor of Rhode Island, William Greene, of a cut of £2,637 in the colony's accounts, or, approximately a 25 per cent reduction, he counseled him to be thankful for what they had received.[24]

Although Shirley was supported by Lord Halifax, his opponents waged a rear guard action. They welcomed Pepperrell to London in 1749, when he arrived on regimental business, and feted him as the hero of Louisbourg. Kilby advertised Pepperrell's availability as Shirley's successor. These regal celebrations did not turn Pepperrell's head. As an astute political observer, he sized up the situation and, though

21. Board of Trade to Treasury, Feb. 28, 1750, C. O. 324/13, 15-17.
22. Elisha Williams to William Williams, May 26, 1750, *Law Papers*, III, 395-96.
23. Shirley to Williams, Feb. 12, 1750, and Williams' comment on letter, *ibid.*, 358-59, 362.
24. Partridge to Law, Feb. 21, 1750, Trumbull Papers, I, Conn. Archives, Hartford, and Mar. 26, 1750, *Law Papers*, III, 383; Partridge to Greene, Nov. 16, 1749, and Mar. 17, 1750, Official Corres., R. I. Archives.

he aspired to be governor, refused to battle Shirley. In Boston Waldo's friends staged a bitter fight to block Bollan's candidacy as permanent Massachusetts agent. Nineteen of the twenty-one members present in the Council voted for Bollan, but his election in the House was only resolved, with the aid of Thomas Hutchinson's friends, after hours of impassioned debate. As one reporter told Waldo: "Many are surprised that Bollan should be chosen. . . . To Mr. Shirley and his prime minister, Thomas Hutchinson, we owe acknowledgments for this."[25]

Despite the hard contest, Shirley interpreted Bollan's election as a victory for his new coalition and for paper money redemption, for Bollan had brought the parliamentary funds to Boston and was on the scene at his election. He also witnessed the start of the process of redeeming the paper money. From afar Shirley supported this redemption by giving his views on paper money to a committee of the House of Commons, which was determined to enact legal curbs for paper money emissions. Parliament eventually passed a bill, perhaps incorporating Shirley's recommendations, that placed restrictions on paper money issues in New England.[26]

Besides appearing before the Commons' committee, Shirley made other profitable uses of his time. He petitioned Newcastle for another regiment to replace the one he lost when it was reduced at the end of the war, asking particularly for Phillips's regiment, then quartered in Nova Scotia. He joined Thomlinson, Apthorp, and Hancock in requesting funds for supplying the Nova Scotia garrisons in 1747 and 1748. He accompanied Pepperrell to the war office, where they petitioned for certain regimental favors. He also acted in his official capacity as head of the Massachusetts government, in one instance visiting the Archbishop of Canterbury in order to determine the truth of a rumor that the Church of England

25. Heath to Waldo, Jan. 29, 1750, and Sparhawk to Waldo, Mar. 8, 1750, Mass. Archives, LXIII, 485, 493; Parsons, *Sir William Pepperrell*, 210-13. Heath noticed that Hutchinson carried "all before him at the Board."
26. Shirley to Willard, Feb. 13, 1750, Mass. Archives, LIV, 2; Freiberg, "Thomas Hutchinson and the Province Currency," *New Eng. Qtly.*, 30 (1957), 203-8; *Boston Evening-Post*, Oct. 15, 1750, and Mar. 25, 1751.

was about to send bishops to America. Many of his Congregational friends were deeply worried about the establishment of Anglican power in the colonies. Shirley wrote Willard that he had warned the prelate: "I thought, if any bishop was sent over, that restrictions on his power . . . were absolutely necessary." He added: "I shall oppose it . . . as far as I have weight here."[27]

The maneuvers of politics held the Governor in London until the summer. Waldo, Kilby, and Partridge had intensified their assaults throughout the spring—Waldo was currently described as "indefatigable in his pursuit" and "fixed" on Shirley's ruin. Their campaign apparently had some effect on Shirley's sanguine nature, for he spoke to Bedford about leaving his position at Boston, and when Clinton asked to be relieved of the New York governorship, he requested transfer to that post. Newcastle did not respond favorably. But despite Shirley's occasional weariness, he stood off his enemies, and they at length realized the hopelessness of further opposition. Within weeks of his departure for the peace conference at Paris, Waldo and Pepperrell returned to New England.[28]

III

When Shirley left London, he had assurances from Newcastle and Bedford that his enemies could do him no harm, and he turned his mind to the issues of the peace conference. From the moment of his appointment, he had acted like a lawyer making a brief, carefully and ceaselessly piling up evidence.[29] For him the halls of diplomacy were the courtroom. Although he had been instructed to settle the outstanding claims of the two countries on the principle of the *status quo ante bel-*

27. Shirley to Willard, July 9, 1750, Mass. Archives, XIII, 177-79; *Shirley Correspondence*, I, 499; Thomlinson to Treasury, Nov. 14, 1749, C. O. 323/12, 33; Shirley to Treasury, Dec. 15, 1749, Treasury I, 335, fol. 136.
28. Williams to ———, May 15, 1750, and Miller to Law, July 11, 1750, *Law Papers*, III, 394-95, 419-20; Fairchild, *Messrs. William Pepperrell*, 185. Miller was perplexed by Shirley's conduct and blamed him for the cuts in Connecticut's accounts. He wondered why Shirley was "so very officious in doing this colony such an injury, a gentleman so wise, so great, so good."
29. Commission, Apr. 14, 1750, Foreign Office 90, 15, 259-62, P.R.O.; Shirley to Willard, Nov. 28, 1749, Mass. Papers, N. Y. Pub. Lib.

lum, Shirley went to the conference determined to enlarge the British empire at the expense of France. Even if he adhered to his instructions, there was much room for expansion: the boundaries of Nova Scotia were uncertain; the neutral islands of St. Lucia, St. Vincent, and Dominica in the West Indies had never been formally incorporated into either empire; and all differences of opinion over territorial claims, prizes, and exchanges of prisoners were left to arbitration.[30] There was no clear-cut British policy, for the ministry was seriously divided about the importance of the colonies to British foreign policy. Bedford and Halifax were expansionists, disinclined to draw fixed boundaries in America, while Newcastle, Pelham, and Hardwicke advocated a peace program based upon limited territorial acquisition and a system of alliances.

Joined equally with Shirley in these negotiations was a middle-aged barrister, William Mildmay, who was already in Paris arranging for an exchange of prisoners. A cousin of the Earl of Fitzwalter, Mildmay was a poor relation who had won the Earl's patronage by cultivating tastes for the theater, the opera, the punch bowl, and the chase. He was clever, intemperate, and abusive. The leader of the Paris delegation was the ambassador, William Anne Keppel, Earl of Albemarle, soldier and spendthrift, who had wasted a fortune on dissipation. Nonetheless, Albemarle had ability as a diplomat and was as impressed with the necessity of speed in these Paris negotiations as were his colleagues in London.[31]

Within a week of Shirley's arrival in Paris, Albemarle took him and Mildmay to Versailles for an audience with Louis XV and arranged a meeting for them with the French commissioners, the Marquis de la Galissoniere and the Etienne de Silhouette. Shirley had once corresponded with Galissoniere,

30. For the basic story of these negotiations I am indebted to Max Savelle, *The Diplomatic History of the Canadian Boundary, 1749-1763* (New Haven, 1940), 21-42; Lawrence H. Gipson, *The British Empire before the American Revolution* (Caldwell, Idaho, and N. Y., 1936-56), V, chap. X.

31. There is substantial biographical material in Mildmay's memorandum and letter books, Clements Lib.; Venn, *Alumni Cantabrigienses,* III, pt. 1, 188; H. Manners Chichester, "William Anne Keppel," *Dictionary of National Biography* (London, 1908-1909), XI, 44-45, Albemarle to Bedford, Sept. 9, 1750, State Papers, 78, 237, 1-2, P.R.O. Hereafter cited S.P.

whose imperialist activities as governor general of Canada he had denounced to the home government. The first meeting of the commissioners was held on September 1 in Galissoniere's apartment. It opened with expressions of peace and good will, but procedural difficulties soon created a tense and hostile atmosphere.[32]

The French wanted a large buffer zone between their settlements and the British, so that each nation would "renounce anything that would give their respective colonists in America the temptation and the means to annoy, attack, or invade each other with ease and success." Recognizing the interrelated nature of the imperial problem, they insisted that claims in Nova Scotia and the West Indies should be discussed concurrently.

The British commissioners were bound by their instructions to center all discussions on the boundary limits of Nova Scotia.[33] Their persistence in forcing the issue deadlocked proceedings, requiring the commissioners to consult the home ministers.[34] Fortunately both governments, aware of the dangers of war, gave the conferees a freer hand, and the commissioners were able to resume the discussions with a minimum of delay.[35] In October, Shirley began presenting his conception of British claims to Nova Scotia. His ideas were even more spacious than the ministry's; Britain's northern region, he said, extended northwest from the mouth of the Kennebec River to the St. Lawrence River and included an area bounded by the river and its gulf that took in present-day New Brunswick, Nova Scotia, Prince Edward Island, Canso, and parts of Maine and Quebec. These "Anciennes limits" of Acadia were based upon the Treaty of Utrecht and, except for Cape Breton Is-

32. Savelle, *The Diplomatic History of the Canadian Boundary*, 34; Instructions, July 19, 1750, C. O. 324/13, 197-208.

33. Newcastle to Albemarle, Aug. 10, 1750, S.P. 78, 236, 294-96; Shirley and Mildmay to Board of Trade, Sept. 2, 1750, Mildmay's letter book; Shirley to Board of Trade, Sept. 4, 1750, C. O. 323/12, 235-36; Bollan to Willard, Aug. 23, 1750, Mass. Papers, N. Y. Pub. Lib.

34. Shirley to Bedford, Sept. 16, 1750, S.P. 78, 237, 34-35.

35. Newcastle to Albemarle, Sept. 10, 1750, *ibid.*, 5-10; Bedford to Albemarle, Oct. 4, 1750, *ibid.*, 82-85.

land, were British territory, though not all had been occupied over the past forty years.[36]

The French commissioners asserted that the ancient limits were not so vast. British Acadia consisted of the peninsula of Nova Scotia, though they would have subtracted from it a strip of land along the northern shore to keep the British from entering the Gulf of the St. Lawrence. The French claims included Canso, all of present-day New Brunswick, and parts of northern Maine.

After a vigorous clash, the commissioners eliminated oral arguments, deciding to present their claims in briefs. This change of procedure, though ultimately approved by Bedford and Newcastle, slowed deliberations and invited the interference of the home authorities. Shirley, who had an inexhaustible capacity for detail, tried to overwhelm the opposition with facts. His statements of claims were a ponderous assortment of documents that might have been filed with a court of inquiry. He explained his research on one minute point to the Board of Trade: "I find errors in two of the dates mentioned in the London edition of the Count d' Estrade's letter of the 13th. March 1662, concerning the taking of Acadia by Sir William Alexander, therein taken notice of to be in 1649 under Charles the First, which was really in 1629. . . . I am now searching to find whether those errors run through all the editions of it now in Paris: If they should, they may be easily rectified by other well known facts."[37]

Shirley's insistence upon documentary accuracy necessitated close preparation on both sides and caused a hardening of views. The Board of Trade reviewed all briefs and did not hesitate to overrule the commissioners, with the result that British replies to French inquiries were rewritten at Whitehall. But much worse, Mildmay and Shirley were not able to agree on the interpretation of their documents; Mildmay did not

36. Savelle, *The Diplomatic History of the Canadian Boundary*, 35-37; Shirley to Board of Trade, Oct. 7, 1750, C. O. 323/12, 249-50; Albemarle to Bedford, Oct. 14, 1750, S.P. 78, 237, 86. These extensive claims were reduced in size by the Board of Trade when it learned of Shirley's presentation, *ibid.*, 238, 301-7.

37. Shirley to Board of Trade, Oct. 7, 1750, C. O. 323/12, 249.

sympathize with Shirley's plans for British expansion and disliked his legalistic approach. He denounced his colleague in letters home as a "slow mule that understands neither French nor English," and he sent the Board of Trade his own briefs.[38]

This rivalry distressed Lord Halifax, and he promptly placed the letters before Secretary of State Bedford, who informed the commissioners that their disputes were "in several places too trivial and immaterial to be . . . observed." He assured them, softening the force of his letter, that he did not want to discourage constructive arguments on policy, and where there was a reasonable difference of opinion, the commissioners could prepare their briefs with the disputed paragraphs in parallel columns.[39]

This further attention to detail bogged down negotiations even more thoroughly and occurred at a time when tensions were increasing in the ministry. Ministerial harmony was disrupted by Bedford's plans to form a separate faction, his desire to force a different line of policy upon the Pelhams, and his closer relations with the royal family, whose influence Newcastle would not share with any associate. When the crown prince died in 1751, Newcastle and Bedford disputed as to the best way to set up a regency for the young prince, the future George III, and their argument occupied the sessions of Parliament through the late winter and spring. Newcastle was determined finally to remove his hated foe from office and only awaited the opportunity.

In the meantime, colonial affairs were worsening. British colonials were expanding their Indian trade into western New York and planning to colonize the Ohio Valley; New Englanders were spreading into Maine and New Hampshire. Frenchmen were planting forts along the Indian trade routes and preparing to contest the British trader's right to push west-

38. Mildmay to Fitzwalter, Nov. 8, 1750, Mildmay's letter book; Bedford to Albemarle, Oct. 4, 1750, S.P. 78, 237, 82-85. Bedford approved Shirley's desire for written statements on the ground that the British government would then have a record of the proceedings.

39. Bedford to Mildmay and Shirley, Feb. 11, 1751, ibid., 49-51; Shirley to Aldworth, Mar. 13, 1751, ibid., 54-55. Shirley denied Mildmay's assertions and insisted that all letters that passed between him and the English ministry were seen by Mildmay.

ward. Forts Niagara, Rouillè (at Toronto), and Duquesne were evidence of French determination to hold the region and get a share of the Indian trade. Shirley's own correspondence pointed up the tension in the empire. Willard told him that the newly strengthened Crown Point was "the Carthage of New England and New York"; the quicker it was destroyed the better the welfare of New England.[40] Bollan wrote Willard that Nova Scotia was in "so extremely dangerous [a condition] that it gives me the greatest concern; I have urged as far as it is possible, the necessity of removing the French without delay."[41] Even Elisha Williams, an enemy of Shirley, reminded him that his post as commissioner put an unusual opportunity into his hands for doing "great service to New England."[42] Similar dispatches filled governmental offices; a crisis was growing in America.

In June 1751, Bedford was forced out of the ministry in a dispute over patronage and was succeeded by the Earl of Holderness, a friend of Newcastle and relative of Mildmay's patron, Fitzwalter. Friends as well as relatives of Mildmay, Holderness and Fitzwalter readily accepted his complaints against Shirley, and Holderness offered to become Mildmay's patron. Mildmay was invited to London for consultation. While in the capital he attended conferences on the peace aims and discussed policy with Newcastle.[43] Shirley, on his part, did not take into account the impression that he was creating in London, nor make any effort to oppose Mildmay's actions. Both commissioners had been warned about acting separately, and Mildmay was open to criticism on this point. Shirley did not deputize any agent to anticipate Mildmay's criticism—not even Bollan and his sons, who were often in London.

This was the time, perhaps, when Shirley became deeply involved with his landlord's daughter. Nothing is known of Julie except that Shirley loved her. Mildmay once said that Paris was no place for a bachelor; one should have either a mistress or a wife. Whether Shirley shared his opinions is

40. Willard to Shirley, Dec. 28, 1752, Mass. Papers, N. Y. Pub. Lib.
41. Bollan to Willard, Aug. 23, 1750, ibid.
42. Williams to Israel Williams, Aug. 20, 1750, N. H. Misc., III Lib. Cong.
43. Mildmay to Holderness, Aug. 14, 1751, S.P. 78, 239, 92-93.

unknown, but he acted on them. Young Julie soon became his wife in a quiet wedding that went unnoticed during that summer. In the eighteenth century, when marriages formed alliances of power, the union of the very dignified and ever-cautious Governor with a woman younger than his older daughters was a political and social blunder.[44]

The summer of 1751 passed rapidly for Shirley and Julie. In the fall the French commissioners, after nine months of preparing an answer to the British brief, presented a bulky volume of "240 folio pages" of documentary proof and arguments to substantiate their own claims to Acadia. Shirley gave the memorial immediately to a secretary for duplication, and without waiting for Mildmay's return from London, started to work comparing citations and evidence. With the advice of Albemarle, he drafted a reply that took nearly two months to complete, and even then had to apologize for the appearance of his formal report: "I am to ask your Lordship's pardon for transmitting so foul a copy of the reply."[45]

While Shirley engaged in these labors, Mildmay returned to his post. He seemed stubborn and self-confident; he refused to have anything to do with the report and asserted that the ministry was opposed to any more briefs. Shirley insisted that his analysis would be invaluable as the basis of a determination of policy.[46] Since his paper was not an official communication, Shirley continued with its preparation, submitting parts of it to his colleague and discussing the general points at length with him. Mildmay permitted him to use the full time of their private secretary and "was pleased to express his approbation of what I had done."[47]

Mildmay gave his version of their relations: "Mr. Shirley did not think fit to consult me in drawing up his reply to the French memorial concerning the limits of Acadia. . . . I will propose to my colleague, what I offered to him long ago, that we mutually assist each other."[48] These were the words of a

44. Henry H. Edes, "Governor Shirley's Second Wife," Col. Soc. Mass., *Publications*, 12 (1911), 46-48.
45. Shirley to Holderness, Dec. 15, 1751, S.P. 78, 239, 142-43.
46. Shirley to Holderness, Nov. 17 and 24, 1751, *ibid.*, 136, 139.
47. Shirley to Holderness, Dec. 29, 1751, *ibid.*, 148-49.
48. Mildmay to Holderness, Jan. 2, 1752, *ibid.*, 153.

MRS. WILLIAM SHIRLEY (FRANCES BARKER)

Portrait by an unknown artist, from the collection of James Gore King.
Courtesy of the Frick Art Reference Library.

SAMUEL WALDO

Portrait by Robert Feke. Courtesy of the Bowdoin College Museum of Fine Arts.

man certain of the attitude of the London authorities and the weakness of his opponent. Shirley was definitely in an inferior position; he could not look to the ambassador for help, for Mildmay and Albemarle were long-time drinking partners. At length realizing the difficult position he was in, Shirley wrote letters to Halifax and other acquaintances in London explaining the situation.[49] He apparently did not dare ask the help of the Pelhams. News of these letters, provided by the alert Mildmay, only nettled Holderness, and in March 1752, the Secretary of State decided, with the approval of Newcastle, to recall Shirley and send him back to Massachusetts.[50]

The rush of business in London delayed his recall until April. It came in a very friendly letter from Holderness: "I have the King's command, to signify to you, an entire approbation of your conduct during your residence at Paris."[51] But Shirley's dismissal implied a rebuke for a view of empire upon which he had set his heart as the only true course for Great Britain. As an advocate of British expansion, he doubted the value to national interest of negotiations that would halt the exploitation of the American west by the creation of imperial boundaries. His work in Paris and London had proved to him, at least, that the peace of Aix-la-Chapelle was a great mistake and re-enforced his conviction that France must be driven from America. Unfortunately, the Pelhams did not hold this opinion. When Shirley read his letter of dismissal, Mildmay was there to record the emotional reaction. Shirley showed no visible feeling; he remained silent, except for the comment that he "was not conscious he had done anything that might give offense." Calm and reserved, he left Paris within a few days, but made sure of appearing friendly to Mildmay and Albemarle, wishing them good luck.[52] Years later when

49. Mildmay to Fitzwalter, Apr. 5, 1752, Mildmay's letter book.
50. His decommission, F.O. 90, 15B, 297. Shirley received £3 per day as commissioner and an extra 20 shillings for a private secretary.
51. Holderness to Shirley, Apr. 23, 1752, S.P. 78, 239, 171-72. Shirley apparently corresponded with Mildmay while he was in England (Mildmay to Fitzwalter, Nov. 22, 1752, Mildmay's letter book).
52. Mildmay and de Cosne to Holderness, Jan. 3, 1753, Mildmay's letter book.

Shirley needed an agent in London he did not hesitate to employ Mildmay.

Mildmay was pleased to be rid of a colleague whom he had accused of deadlocking negotiations for two years. He struck boldly for the policy of containment, for drawing boundaries of empire in America and establishing neutral zones between the empires. In the end he failed to win French cooperation, and events in America proved that the rivalry for empire could not be avoided.

Returning to London, Shirley discussed Massachusetts politics with the Board of Trade and made some observation on his experiences in Paris. He was warmly welcomed by Lord Halifax, an expansionist like himself, and was put to work with Charles Townshend, a member of the Board, completing the British answer to the same French memorial that he had dealt with in Paris. Through the summer and fall he was busy and could not tell friends in Boston with any certainty how long he would be needed by the Board, but in December the memorial was finished. It was generally credited to Townshend, who was probably responsible for its final form;[53] yet Shirley was among those praised, even by his former colleague at Paris, and he did not hesitate to reveal his pleasure: "I flatter myself that in the opinion of all his Majesty's ministers the English right . . . to the ancient limits of the province . . . is asserted in the clearest and most convincing manner."[54]

Throughout the winter of 1752-53 Shirley tried to put off the day of his departure. He petitioned for a change of governorships; he wanted to replace Governor Clinton. But Shirley encountered the unexpected opposition of Lord Halifax, who desired the position for a sick brother-in-law that needed an easy post. Shirley attempted to speak with Newcastle, but the Duke, disturbed over Shirley's marriage and his imperial views, refused to grant him an interview.[55] Never before in his life had Shirley been involved in an affair so

53. Mildmay to Fitzwalter, Dec. 2, 1752, *ibid.*; Gray to Otis, June 23, 1752, Otis Papers.

54. *Shirley Correspondence*, II, 10; Bollan to Willard, July 20, 1752, Mass. Archives, CCLXXXVII, 306-14.

55. *Shirley Correspondence*, II, 4-7.

peculiarly embarrassing as his marriage to Julie. The father of seven living children, he was about to bring home to Boston a young French bride. If he could delay the day of departure, or avoid it altogether, he would have been happier. Unfortunately his differences of opinion with Newcastle doomed him to the scrutiny of Boston.

Thomas Hancock was already expressing the reaction of many Bostonians when he told Kilby that "Governor Shirley's marrying in France is a shocking affair. . . . I am amazed. Lord, what will become of his family and what shall we do if he should come here."[56] Conversations with Bollan, his sons, and friends at last convinced Shirley that Julie should not come to America—at least, not immediately. By the last of May 1753, after transacting some odds and ends of official and family business, he journeyed to Portsmouth, ready to take the *Port-Mahon*, for the six-week voyage to Boston. He never saw Julie again.[57]

56. Hancock to Kilby, June 11, 1753, Hancock Papers, IV.
57. There is a family tradition that Julie and Shirley lived together in the Bahamas and, perhaps, in Massachusetts during the days of Shirley's retirement. She is also said to have married again after his death in 1771.

IX

The Empire in Crisis

AFTER FOUR years away, Shirley's home-coming in August 1753 was widely acclaimed. During his first days in the colony, when large crowds clustered around Province House, the Governor frequently appeared on its balcony. Standing before the governor's mansion, a delegation of the inhabitants of Pulling Point requested, and received, permission to rename their village Point Shirley.[1] The Governor was delighted with the receptions in his honor and the spirit, if not the quality, of the popular poetry written to commemorate these events:

> The Commons cheerfully imbibe,
> What to your Senate you prescribe;
> Their Views and yours the same.[2]

His return to Boston had given heart to citizens frightened by French refortification of the frontier; many remembered the seizure of Louisbourg in 1745 and looked to his leadership in removing French encroachments. Orators described the rivalry of Britain and France in terms of the classical battle between Rome and Carthage; Cato's *delenda est Carthago* was well known, and the fear was that France was turning Crown Point into a modern day Carthage. "Unless it be demobilized," Willard had already told Shirley, Crown Point "will be a constant scourage to [us] . . . in times of war, being a place of retreat and shelter for the enemy, after their depreciations upon the English frontiers."[3]

1. *The Boston Weekly News-Letter*, Sept. 13, 1753.
2. *Ibid.*, Sept. 26, 1754; *The Boston Evening-Post*, Aug. 13, 1753.
3. Willard to Shirley, Dec. 28, 1752, Mass. Papers, 125, N. Y. Pub. Lib. During these celebrations Shirley met hundreds of people. Their names were easily forgotten in the confusion and hurry of events. But he, always the politician, tried to remember their names. In a letter to Samuel Mather, Aug.

Through these festive days no public incident reminded Shirley of his marital embarrassment, and no one recalled the bitter days of 1748 when paper money redemption was a political issue. *The Independent Advertiser* was dead, as was also Dr. William Douglass; Waldo, Hale, and Choate were retired; Wendell, Oliver, and Hutchinson welcomed him to the governor's chair. Waldo and Pepperrell suspected that he was awaiting an opportunity to exchange his post for another, but they were careful to keep their opinions to themselves. When the General Court convened on September 5, its members went as a group to Province House to present their salutations of welcome. After their spokesmen had delivered their greetings, they invited the Governor to address them at the Court House and escorted him royally to the council chamber. Shirley assured them that at the Paris peace conference their boundary claims were supported with the "clearest proofs and . . . vouchers of the most authentic and highest nature."[4] The fourteen-day session reflected the general political condition of the province. A bill was enacted hastening the redemption of paper money by allowing holders of outstanding bills to use them to pay taxes;, another supplied the treasury with £10,000; still another "encouraged the killing of wolves, bears, wildcats and catamounts within the province." A series of resolutions instructed House committees to confer with the Governor on frontier defense and the boundary controversy with New York. There were two portentous signs of political disturbance: in one division of the House, Shirley's former majority was badly split; and in the legislative haste to end the session no salary bill was passed.

During the fall Shirley often joined legislative committees as they considered reports on frontier defense and inspected forts in the Boston area. The condition of the bastions troubled him. Many of the cannon were "old and honey-

27, 1753, he asked for help: "I shall be much obliged to you, if you will give yourself the trouble to cast your eye over the inclosed (which to the best of my memory), contains a list of the clergy, who did me the favor of waiting upon me in company with yourself."

4. *Mass. House Journals*, XXX, 63-65; Pepperrell to Spooner, Dec. 27, 1753, Misc. bound MSS, XII, Mass. Hist. Soc.

combed," more dangerous to those that discharged them than to a potential enemy; the supply of arms and powder was as inadequate as the garrison was inexperienced. "I would propose," Shirley reported in December to the legislature, "to have all the cannon . . . from their age, unsizeableness, and being honeycombed . . . cast into guns of 4 pound ball, . . . Also that the carriage wheels, which are at present of wood . . . should be made of cast iron. . . . I would further propose fortifying the inland garrisons . . . with two cohorn mortars each."[5]

Shirley's speech was examined by committees dominated by friends of Allen and Sparhawk, who were still hostile. These committees showed opposition by reducing the funds for Forts Massachusetts, Number 4, and Dummer—the very defenses that would hold off the initial blows of an enemy striking from Crown Point. When the legislature passed a bill embodying these recommendations, Shirley protested and emphasized his position by vetoing it. A committee thereupon visited the Governor's office. Speaking for the committee, Pepperrell observed that the legislature wished to avoid assuming responsibility for Nova Scotian defense and for garrisoning forts in New Hampshire and New York. In the past the colony had utilized her resources unselfishly while neighboring colonies were contributing little or nothing. Her sacrifices appeared unappreciated. The home government not only had abandoned Louisbourg at the close of the war, but had not fully reimbursed her for the 1746 campaign. In the future Massachusetts desired to keep her defense expenditures within manageable bounds of taxes and resources, but she was always ready, he hastened to add, to consult with other colonial legislatures on mutual security.[6]

Pepperrell was, in effect, not denying Shirley's contention that the colony needed to improve its defenses, but was assailing the Governor's imperialist position of 1745-48: the position that Massachusetts could be better defended by eliminating the source of the trouble—Crown Point, Louisbourg, and Que-

5. *Mass. House Journals*, XXX, 98; *The Boston Weekly News-Letter*, Dec. 6, 1753.
6. *Mass. Archives*, LXXIV, 161-63; *Doc. Hist. of Maine*, XII, 236-41.

bec. Pepperrell was also attacking a directive of August 1753 from the secretary of state which ordered the governors to correspond with each other and to repel any aggression on the colonies through mutual assistance. He was serving notice on Shirley that Massachusetts would look out for herself and that fortifications in other colonies must be maintained by the colonies concerned. Forts Dummer and Number 4, though essential frontier posts, were not an obligation of Massachusetts, since they were in New Hampshire territory; nor were the forts of Nova Scotia and New York her responsibility. Pepperrell was taking an unnatural position, for he personally accepted the necessity of adequate military expenditures. He was undoubtedly the spokesman of members who would vote money for local defense, but who wanted to avoid committing themselves to large expenditures for regional defense—unless all the colonies paid their way.

In the face of this opposition, Shirley followed the committee's advice and suggested to the Board of Trade that, before hostilities with France became any more serious, the Board should unify the colonies. The union could be a kind of defensive alliance, financed by proportionate assessments upon each colony, with the regulation of forts, Indian relations, and military forces entrusted to commissioners. To such an arrangement, Shirley pledged Massachusetts's support: "[I have] the utmost reason to think that the people of the province are most readily disposed to do their part in promoting so necessary an union and to exert the same spirit which they have hitherto done in his Majesty's service."[7]

I

Shirley's setback on the issue of defense was the second in a series of defeats. In January 1754 the House of Representatives elected two months prior to his return split forty-four to forty-one over the issue of the Governor's salary.[8] Shirley had first raised the question on December 5, when he

7. *Shirley Correspondence*, II, 30-31.
8. *Mass. House Journals*, XXX, 152-53.

asked the House to be especially generous in voting his annual salary. He believed the lawmakers should consider the benefits the colony had received because of his long period of service in London and Paris: "During my residence in *England,* I had the interests of the province as much at Heart and employed my attention, in serving them, as much as I could have done, if I had continued in the province."[9] Committees of the House considered his message and recommended £1,400 local currency for salary and past services. This was no more than fifty pounds above the usual grant for salary and expenses.[10]

When the bill finally reached his desk, Shirley wanted to veto it, but he weighed the consequences. He was not certain of support from the Board of Trade, and the grant could easily be delayed for months while he battled the legislature. He sent, instead, a blunt message to both houses that reviewed his services at Louisbourg in 1745 and discussed his visit to London:

I mentioned to you my service during my absence in the years 1750, 1751, and 1752, and I am not without hopes that the good effects of it may be soon felt by the province more sensibly than it is at present. . . . I had not views of recompence from you when I engaged in it; but I was detained in it much longer than I expected. The charges of my family left in the province, were going on all the while, and you were making a considerable saving out of the ordinary salary to a governor; and I thought I had a good foundation to mention these things to you, and that they deserved your consideration.[11]

His message brought a sharp reply from a committee appointed by the House. Chairman Allen, having his revenge for the legislative battles of 1748 and 1749, notified Shirley that he was overpaid by the King and already rewarded for his service as colonel of a British regiment.[12] On January 11 and 16 the Governor answered with two unusually long and somewhat abusive addresses. First he flatly denied any rela-

9. *Ibid.,* 100.
10. *Ibid.,* 132; *Mass. Acts and Resolves,* III, 717, chap. XXV, 1753-1754.
11. *Mass. House Journals,* XXX, 150-51.
12. *Ibid.,* 152-53, 164-65.

tion between the King's grant of his colonelcy and his services at Louisbourg, and then restated his arguments. His continued insistence upon compensation for past services was motivated, in part, by the slighting action of the legislature in allowing Pepperrell £140 for damages to his business during the stay at Louisbourg in 1745 and 1746. Shirley was angry, too, because Sparhawk was a member of the opposition and had undoubtedly been instrumental in getting the grant for his father-in-law, Pepperrell. But Shirley's messages only won him a commendation for his services in London.[13]

Unable to control the House of Representatives, Shirley resorted to a governor's most potent weapon: the use of political patronage. After four years' absence from Massachusetts, he reviewed Phips's appointees and filled up the accumulated vacancies.[14] Some nominations were ready for the Council in September 1753, and he submitted a longer list in February 1754. Among those he nominated in September were four members of the Council—Danforth, Cheever, Foxcroft, and Royall—who were favored with judicial posts. In February, he made their colleagues Leonard and Watts justices of the peace. Almost the entire Dwight family of western Massachusetts received legislative and civil honors, and their kinsmen, the Williamses, were given military posts. Within a few months, Shirley allowed Israel Williams to succeed to the full power and authority of the late John Stoddard and become his chief lieutenant in organizing the western defenses.[15]

While winning powerful friends, Shirley was sensitive to the feelings of people removed from office. In naming Ephraim Williams, the half-cousin of Israel, as commandant of Fort Massachusetts, he replaced Captain Elisha Chapin. But he wrote Israel: "I should be sorry to do anything which may look like a slight upon the present commander, Captain Chapin, of whose courage I have a good opinion. . . . I shall be very glad if he will serve as lieutenant under Major Wil-

13. *Ibid.*, 164, 166, 172-76, 182-85, 187.
14. Shirley to Clinton, Nov. 9, 1752, Clinton Papers.
15. *The Boston Evening-Post*, Aug. 30, Sept. 13, 1753, and Jan. 28, 1754.

liams; and will give him the first proper promotion which shall happen in my power. You will be pleased to let Captain Chapin know this."[16]

Shirley also looked to family alliances that would help him recover political power. Seeking suitable husbands for his three unmarried daughters, he found for headstrong but attractive Catherina Maria, John Erving, Jr., the son of a wealthy merchant and landowner. The Ervings were related in marriage to the Bowdoins, Royalls, and Fluckners and belonged to Trinity Church, the second largest Anglican church in the city. John and Catherina Maria were married in April 1754, and John, Sr., became a member of the Council in May. The Governor's new son-in-law was readily given contracts for colonial defense, much to the annoyance of Thomas Hancock who struggled to maintain a monopoly of military supply.[17]

II

The May elections of 1754 were most important to Shirley. With only a minority of the House of Representatives favorable to him since his return to the colony, his power was crippled. Shirley was too careful a politician to leave a record of his manipulations during these elections, but even a casual inspection of events shows some interesting maneuvers.

The elections were held in unusual excitement. Just before the 1753-54 legislature ended, Shirley received reports of French troop movements in Maine. Threats of this sort alarmed the legislature, many of whose members were connected with trade and land companies that would be ruined by a French invasion. The wealthy Boston merchants who comprised the Kennebec Proprietors were particularly aroused. They rushed to Shirley with a plan for protecting their interests. Apparently all agreed that a small expeditionary force should be organized immediately and the costs of any new forts in the exposed country should be assumed by the land company. Shirley readily took up their cause. With the con-

16. Shirley to Israel Williams, Sept. 26, 1754, and Chapin to Ephraim Williams, Jan. 29, 1755, Perry, *Origins in Williamstown*, 255-56.
17. *The Boston Weekly News-Letter*, May 30, 1754.

sent of the Council he mobilized six militia companies and drafted some reinforcements for the garrison posts. Their captains were alerted for military action, and Captain William Lithgow of Fort Richmond was instructed to keep patrols moving along the rivers.[18] The opposition of Allen and Sparhawk vanished as the legislature prepared bills providing for the expedition.

Military operations on an expanded scale were envisaged when the Board of Trade announced a special conference of the northern colonies at Albany to discuss policies of defense and Indian relations. The crisis with France was intensifying, and the need for rebuilding frontier defenses was urgent. Shirley's earlier plea for military preparations was vindicated by these events. Now his request for Massachusetts's participation in the Albany conference, at a time when militiamen were getting ready to go to Maine, brought assurances from John Osborn, chairman of the legislative committee, "that we are ready to do everything that can be expected from us. . . . We think ourselves happy that we have a gentleman at the head of the province who is so perfectly acquainted with his Majesty's just title to the countries encroached upon by the French. . . . We pray your Excellency likewise to order a sufficient force up to the Carrying-Place [of the Kennebec] to remove any French that may be settled there. . . . Your Excellency must be sensible that an union of the several governments . . . has long been desired by this province."[19]

The legislature provided everything that Shirley needed for the Maine expedition, voted to send delegates to the Albany conference, and then asked to be dissolved. The weeks following the dissolution were hectic. With the election in mind and the expedition to be planned, Shirley toiled day and night. He issued orders to recruit 500 men, raise supplies for four months, and commission ships to carry the expedition to Falmouth and then up the Kennebec River. As commander,

18. Shirley to Muggeridge and others, Mar. 6, 7, and 18, 1754, *Doc. Hist. of Maine,* XII, 242-43, 245-46; *Mass. Acts and Resolves,* II, 746.

19. *Mass. House Journals,* XXX, 273-74; *The Boston Weekly News-Letter,* Apr. 25, 1754; William Goold, "Fort Halifax: its Projectors, Builders, and Garrison," Maine Hist. Soc., *Collections,* 8 (1881), 199-289.

he chose John Winslow, equally known for his skinny legs and his military judgment, a person of tested military experience and a popular leader of men. Winslow had seen service in the Caribbean campaigns of the 1740's and was then a gentleman farmer at Marshfield. With Winslow appointed, the Governor urged Benning Wentworth of New Hampshire to check the information about French encroachments. Wentworth conducted a thorough investigation and concluded that the French were invading British territory.[20]

Whether it was the military crisis or political maneuvering that was responsible, Shirley gained strength in the May elections. The voters restored John Choate and Robert Hale to office after years of absence and returned many of the Governor's earlier supporters. Forty-eight new members took their seats in a House of one hundred. The only change in the Council was the seating of John Erving, Sr., in place of John Quincy, which left it with substantially the same members as in 1749.[21] Leadership in the House of Representatives changed more gradually than the turnover of membership would indicate, but Allen and his friends were no longer in complete control. Hale and Choate assumed their former places of prominence, sharing duties with Chambers Russell, John Tasker, and James Otis. Three of the four representatives from Boston were regular members of Shirley's working majority. It is interesting to note that these leaders came from coastal towns, indicating a restoration of his power in this area.

The new legislature was faced with two important issues: military preparedness and raising a revenue. The expedition into Maine was upon everyone's mind because French penetration of the back country of Maine would deprive the colony of its frontier inheritance. Land companies like the Kennebec Proprietors already had pre-empted large districts for future towns. To stop this enemy invasion now became the principal business of the defense committees. Their plans for men and supplies were enlarged as they realized the magnitude of the

20. Wentworth to Shirley, Apr. 26, May 17, and June 7, 1754, Mass. Archives, V, 188-96.
21. Mass. House Journals, XXXI, 4-6.

crisis, and the General Court approved the increase, but not without serving notice that defense expenditures could not be made on the same scale elsewhere in the colony. Though money was voted for Castle William, appropriations for forts in western Massachusetts were denied.[22]

These cuts in expenditures were necessary, for the colonial treasury was running a deficit, trade was sluggish, and the tax load was heavy. In his opening address to the legislature, Shirley asked for the imposition of more taxes in order to preserve public credit, but he did not anticipate the radical departure in taxation that the House finance committee, with Dr. Hale as chairman, presented on the floor. The bill provided for an assessment on all liquor produced in the province, even upon the output of stills in private homes. Every producer was required to keep records of production and to file them with the farmers of taxes.[23] This bill inspired a fierce debate lasting more than two weeks which split political groups and pitted House and Council against each other. Shirley's own friends were badly divided: Hale favored the measure, while Choate joined Allen and Sparhawk in opposition.[24] So bitter did the argument become that Shirley was forced to end the deadlock, promising to withhold his assent to the bill until the legislators had an opportunity to consult with their constituents. It is interesting that he believed that the bill violated the "natural rights of every private family." His responsibility to his office, he declared, led him to compel the legislature to seek popular approval of the bill.[25]

With action on the bill postponed until October, the legislature finished its business by passing economy measures. Shirley was voted his salary of £1,300, £100 less than the previous year; the legislators accompanying the militia to Maine were refused expense allowances; and some additional reductions were made in the defense establishments. Though the session ended early because Shirley was eager to join the

22. *Ibid.*, 34, 39; Mass. Archives, LXXIV, 161-65, CVIII, 662-63, CIX, 10.
23. *Mass. House Journals*, XXXI, 14, 20.
24. *Ibid.*, 38.
25. *Ibid.*, 47; *Mass. Acts and Resolves*, III, 820-21.

Maine expedition, he was careful to see that the legislative committee appointed to attend the Albany Congress was instructed to seek "a general, firm and perpetual union [of the colonies]."[26]

By the twenty-fifth of June, Shirley was in Falmouth, where he reviewed the troops and talked with a delegation of the Norridgewock Indians. Conferences with them and with the Penobscots prepared the way for the expedition to march through their hunting grounds. Before these meetings were over, however, John Winslow began his reconnaissance of the interior, tramping through the heavy grass and dense thickets until he came to the headwaters of the Kennebec River. Though he and his men found no Frenchmen, they were pleased with what they saw of the region, and many of the soldiers expressed a desire to return as settlers. Besides looking for the French, Winslow began construction of two forts to provide protection for future colonists.

The ease with which this rich country passed under Massachusetts's control delighted Shirley, and he rushed his talkative son Jack off to Boston with a dispatch describing the large grass lands, the acres of cleared fields, and the "extremely good" soil. Shirley would have been happier if some French camps had been found; yet he believed that the money and effort of sending the expedition into Maine had been expended wisely. The new forts, especially Halifax at Taconnet, were better situated to defend the frontier settlements than the older ones in the region. The colony could now dismantle such interior posts as Richmond.[27]

The Massachusetts people felt no misgivings about the expedition; few acts of Shirley's career were more popular. His welcome at Boston exceeded by far the welcome he had received on his return from Europe and reminded him of the victory celebration of Louisbourg nine years before. As his procession moved through the town, "the vessels in the harbor,

26. *Mass. House Journals*, XXXI, 22-23, 38, 47; Mass. Archives, IV, 468-69.
27. Shirley to Robinson, May 23, 1754, C. O. 5/14, 349-53; Joseph Williamson, "Materials for a History of Fort Halifax," Maine Hist. Soc., *Collections*, 7 (1876), 167-98.

the wharves, streets, balconies and windows of the houses, by which his Excellency passed, were crowded with spectators; and there was the greatest concourse and acclamation of the people, that was ever known in Boston, upon this occasion."[28] The proprietors of the Kennebec Company were jubilant. On behalf of his associates, Charles Apthorp presented Shirley with some shares in the company. Robert Temple, one of the proprietors, married Shirley's daughter Harriet—which, considering the motives of many eighteenth-century marriages, may not have been unrelated to Shirley's success.[29]

III

The expedition had a snowballing effect in bringing popularity to the administration. The newspapers were full of poetry celebrating the expedition's success, clergymen referred to its exploits in their sermons, and pamphleteers recalled the need of effective defense against the expansion of popery. The expedition also attracted proponents of better defense to the administration, and Shirley promised them further support if they would in turn back other projected measures of the government. His friends from western Massachusetts were particularly concerned about the condition of local forts, and he assured Israel Williams and Oliver Partridge of his help. When the October legislative sessions opened, Wendell and Otis took the leadership in drawing up a suitable defense bill and in getting funds voted to implement it.[30]

The major bill of the session, however, was the controversial plan to tax liquor production. After his return from Maine, Shirley received many petitions about the bill from both sides, and he was obliged to be careful not to alienate influential groups; however he managed to find a broad position that was both defensible and popular. He deferred action on the bill

28. *Boston Gazette*, Sept. 8, 1754; Shirley to Willard, Sept. 3, 1754, *Doc. Hist. of Maine*, XII, 308-10.
29. *The Boston Weekly News-Letter*, Sept. 5 and 12, 1754. Shirley was given 8 of the outstanding 190 shares. Thomas Hancock, Sylvester Gardiner, and William Bowdoin were also shareholders.
30. *Mass. House Journals*, XXXI, 121-22; Israel Williams to Shirley, Sept. 12, 1754, Perry, *Origins in Williamstown*, 289-90.

until fall and urged the legislators, in the meantime, to consult their constituents before the final vote was taken. If the legislature finally passed the bill, he promised to sign it.[31] The selectmen of Boston were the first to praise his stand. They believed the measure to be a radical departure in taxation and dangerous to the liberties of the people. They welcomed the opportunity to debate its merits and instruct their representatives. "The noble pattern your Excellency has in this affair . . . convinces us of the tender regard you have for the liberties of the people."[32]

Though the bill was given rough treatment by its enemies, a heavily revised version was passed in record time. The bill was sponsored in the House by William Brattle, and he, Robert Hale, and James Otis, the Governor's loyal friends, were apparently responsible for making it acceptable to a majority of the representatives. Shirley gave it his support by delivering the votes of his friends and later signed it into law.[33] Further, he asked the Board of Trade to approve it:[34] "I am persuaded that a disallowance of this act would greatly shock the minds of the Representatives and disserve his Majesty's government."[35]

His behavior in the excise controversy won Shirley the respect and admiration of the legislature. To show its gratitude a grant of £200 was voted for his expenses in the Louisbourg campaign of 1745, reversing the decision of the 1753-54 legislature.[36]

IV

Another vital issue debated in the October session was a plan for colonial union submitted by the Albany Congress.

31. Mass. Acts and Resolves, III, 782-90.
32. Ibid., 825; Malcolm Freiberg, "How to become a Colonial Governor: Thomas Hutchinson of Massachusetts," The Review of Politics, 21 (1959), 649.
33. Mass. House Journals, XXXI, 150-60; Thomas Thumb, The Monster of Monsters ([Boston], 1754), 4-8; Mass. Archives, CXIX, 688-702.
34. Mass. Acts and Resolves, III, 826-30. The bill was finally approved by the Board of Trade on July 1, 1755.
35. Ibid., 828; Observations on the Bill, Entitled "An Act for Granting to His Majesty an Excise . . ." (Boston, 1754).
36. Mass. House Journals, XXXI, 165-66; T. B. Akins, ed., Selections from the Public Documents of the Province of Nova Scotia (Halifax, 1869), 382-83; Shirley to House, Dec. 20, 1754, Mass. Archives, CIX, 6.

CASTLE WILLIAM, BOSTON

Sketch by Joseph Frederick W. Des Barres, from the *Atlantic Neptune* (London, 1780). Courtesy of the Henry E. Huntington Library and Art Gallery.

A View of the Landing of the New England Forces in the Expedition Against Cape

The urgency of union was becoming increasingly evident through the summer and fall. In frontier Virginia a military force under George Washington was attacked and forced to capitulate. In New York the Iroquois were uneasy, and, though the Albany Congress relieved some of the tension, the Indian superintendent, William Johnson, was worried about French troop movements in the frontier regions of northern New York. In Nova Scotia the borderland on the Bay of Fundy was imperiled by two French forts and the infiltration of French spies. The seriousness of Anglo-French relations in America was recognized by the Board of Trade when it instructed the governors to correspond regularly with each other and to consult on mutual problems of defense.[37]

In spite of Shirley's involvement in the Maine expedition and matters of taxation, he was deeply concerned about the proceedings of the Albany Congress. The Massachusetts commissioners had been instructed to support a general plan of union, but for some unknown reason they advocated a partial union of the colonies. They seem to have had two unions in mind, one for the northern colonies and one for the southern, and it is certain that they wanted their colony and its governor to head any confederation involving Massachusetts. Their plan may have been Shirley's idea of union or, at least, the idea of his closest associates. In fact two of the commissioners, Hutchinson and Partridge, were his most intimate advisors, and since no important correspondence passed between them and the Governor during the sessions at Albany, they apparently continued to have his full confidence. The commissioners as well as the Governor were primarily concerned about providing better military preparedness, and they wanted to assure Massachusetts initiative and leadership in planning for it. Shirley, however, was also concerned about maintaining a strong imperial connection. He had privately drawn up a plan of union that provided for a meeting of the governors and delegates from their councils. In a crisis these leaders would determine the number of troops for the army, build fortifications, and direct military operations. Funds for

37. *Shirley Correspondence*, II, 62-68, 71-72, 97-98.

defense would be drawn from the British Treasury, which, in turn, would be supplied by a parliamentary tax on the colonies. Shirley refused to give out any more details of his plan, preferring to let the Albany Plan of Union stand as the basic recommendation for the General Court to consider. Apparently he had no strong convictions about the structure of the union, except that some form of union was necessary and that safeguards should be provided in it for British authority. As he wrote the governor of Pennsylvania, Robert Hunter Morris, "the best advice I can give you is to lose no time for promoting the plan of a union of the colonies for their mutual defense. . . . I am laboring this point, *totis viribus*."[38]

Despite Shirley's reluctance to state his own views, he laid the Albany Plan before the General Court on October 18, 1754, with the earnest recommendation that the legislature give it deliberate and prompt consideration. The Plan, so different from his own, provided for a British president general, a popularly elected council, authority over Indian affairs, frontier settlement, and colonial defense. As a super-colonial administration, it would tax, maintain a military force, and legislate within the scope of its authority for the general welfare of American subjects of the crown. However, its actions were always to be supervised by the home authorities. Four days after Shirley's address, the Massachusetts legislature took the Plan under advisement, appointing a joint committee of administration leaders to study it.[39] With Thomas Hubbard as chairman, hearings were conducted until early December, when the Council gave the bill first consideration. After a favorable vote, discussion was opened in the House, where, although a majority seemed receptive to ideas of union, debate quickly turned hostile to the Albany Plan itself. Antagonism was inspired by a letter from Agent Bollan who cautioned the legislature that an English scheme of union was being ad-

38. Samuel Hazard *et al.*, eds., *Pennsylvania Archives* (Phila. and Harrisburg, 1852-1949), 1st Ser., II, 181; Robert C. Newbold, *The Albany Congress and Plan of Union of 1754* (New York, 1755), 141-46.
39. Mass. Archives, LXXXIII, 231-32, 239, 246-47; *Mass. House Journals*, XXXI, 152-53. Lawrence H. Gipson, "The Drafting of the Albany Plan of Union," *Pennsylvania History*, 26 (1959), 297-301.

vanced as a means of extending British control over the colonies. He urged the legislature to anticipate the British plan by presenting its own, but Bollan's letter had the effect of making the House uneasy about any plan of union. Further committee consideration, however, was authorized; an alternative plan was soon advanced that projected a temporary union of New York and New England for defense and Indian relations. There followed three votes for various plans of union, which indicated lack of agreement on even a general plan. In a recorded vote of forty-one to thirty-seven on December 14, however, the representatives expressed willingness to allow a joint committee to reconsider the plans.[40]

The new committee re-examined the proposals for union. Ten days of discussion brought new recommendations and another debate in the House. This time a vote of forty-eight to thirty-one put off further consideration, and four days later the House instructed Agent Bollan to oppose any plan of union on the grounds that it would be "inconsistent with the fundamental rights of the colonies."[41]

Through these votes Shirley remained silent, perhaps because his majority was in danger of splitting. John Choate, Enoch Kidder, and William Brattle had joined Allen and Sparhawk in opposition to union. Shirley must also have been distressed by Bollan's criticism of the parliamentary plan, for he had been close to his son-in-law and relied upon their friendship in dealing with the home government. Moreover, the fact remains that Shirley was not overly sanguine about the success of the Albany Plan, nor the advisability of using it as the basis of union, and had from the beginning of the debates looked to Parliament for help in forming a suitable plan. His evaluation of these proceedings for the secretary of state indicates this attitude: "The commissioners have failed for want of sufficient powers to perfect an union among the Colonies at their Congress, yet they have made a great progress

40. Mass. Archives, IV, 272-73, VI, 169-83; Shirley to Robinson, Dec. 24, 1754, O'Callaghan, ed., *N. Y. Col. Docs.*, VI, 930-33.
41. Bollan to Hubbard, Sept. 19, 1754, Mass. Papers, 169-73, N. Y. Pub. Lib.

in concerting the proper measures for effecting one and discovering the absolute necessity of its being done without delay. . . . Their . . . determinations upon this point seem to have paved the way clearly for his Majesty's ordering a plan of an union to be formed at home . . . by act of Parliament."[42]

Although Shirley never made clear the kind of colonial union he wanted, in general he favored a plan that would change colonial government as little as possible. However, he would make it possible for the British governors and their councils to come together for consultation and planning on matters of intercolonial significance and, if adjudged necessary, to wage war on an enemy. When he discussed his ideas with Benjamin Franklin, who was in Boston during the legislative debates, he was apparently convinced that these minimum conditions in his plan were all that could be expected from political authorities in England and America. Franklin complained that Shirley's suggested union would not provide any popular representation in considering such matters as war and spending tax funds. Shirley readily agreed, but argued that true representation was possible only by giving the colonies appropriate membership in Parliament. Though Shirley was not ready to force a vote on union in Massachusetts, he was the only American governor to induce his legislature to consider the matter, and he was the only leader to press the idea upon the home government.[43] His weakness was his inability to formalize his ideas into a plan of action and to gain the backing of the British government.

Shirley may have felt that union was too much to expect in this period of imperial crisis. Two events deeply impressed on him the need of immediate military preparedness, and these events occurred at a critical moment during the legisla-

42. *Shirley Correspondence,* II, 113; Shirley to Robinson, Jan. 24, 1755, Parkman Trans., XL, 128; Council Resolution, Jan. 1, 1755, Mass. Archives, VI, 183.

43. Other governors, like Robert Dinwiddie of Virginia, later urged colonial union. Shirley to Robinson, June 20, 1755, O'Callaghan, ed., *N. Y. Col. Docs.,* VI, 958; John Bigelow, ed., *The Complete Works of Benjamin Franklin* (Letter-Press ed., New York, 1887-1888), II, 376-87; Lawrence H. Gipson, "Thomas Hutchinson and the Framing of the Albany Plan of Union, 1754," *The Pennsylvania Magazine of History and Biography,* 74 (1950), 5-35.

tive debates. From the war office he learned that his old regiment was reactivated and that he was expected to recruit the
necessary number of men by spring. From his son William,
whose letter was in the same packet, he was told of secret
plans to send a British army under Major General Edward
Braddock to the Virginia frontier. William would accompany
Braddock as secretary. From a different packet Shirley read
a report from Governor Charles Lawrence of Nova Scotia
describing French encroachments on the Bay of Fundy. Lawrence, like himself, believed that sending a counter expedition
into this disputed country was absolutely necessary and recommended appropriate action in the spring.[44]

With military preparations increasing, Shirley felt the enthusiasm of 1745 returning. Each week new dispatches tested
his energy and skill. He was fast becoming the King's most
important governor; his opinions were being sought and his
cooperation requested. "I have had for several days an inevitable load of business on my hands. . . . It is now near
eleven at night, and I have been writing hard ever since seven
in the morning to dispatch a London ship waiting for my letters, and can scarce[ly] hold my pen in my hand."[45] Some
Bostonians observed his preoccupation and courteously remained away from his office.[46] One man not fully acquainted
with his work reported to a friend: "Mr. Shirley I hear is closely
confined to his politics, so that some extraordinary affair is
thought to be in agitation. He has stopped the vessels bound
to Halifax. . . . His son is appointed a captain."[47]

An air of crisis had drawn visitors to the capital. Officers
from Nova Scotia held long meetings with the Governor and
began to purchase war materials. Franklin was constantly in
conversation with the Governor; his ideas for colonial union
became the basis for prolonged deliberations. On hand, too,
was Thomas Pownall, a young gentleman from London who
was the brother of the secretary of the Board of Trade and a

44. Shirley to Robinson, Dec. 8, 1754, Parkman Trans., XL, 43, and Dec.
14, 1754, C. O. 5/46, 65-67.
45. Akins, ed., *Public Documents of Nova Scotia*, 389-90.
46. Perry, *Origins in Williamstown*, 293.
47. *William Johnson Papers*, I, 438.

friend of Lord Halifax. A self-important person, the scholarly Pownall lent mystery to his movements by giving out stories that he was soon to be the head of the new American union.[48]

The year 1755 seemed to hold much for Shirley and Massachusetts. The challenge of great issues captivated the Governor's imagination, and war was causing politics and business to flourish.

48. Pownall to Morris, Dec. 9, 1754, Julian P. Boyd, ed., *The Susquehannah Papers* (Wilkes-Barre, 1930-1933), I, 187.

X

Limited Warfare

LIGHTS IN Province House were burning longer than usual during the December evenings of 1754 as Shirley and his advisors initiated measures to combat the encroachments of France. Their policy was to shun hostilities if possible, but the frontier was violated everywhere, and the uncertainties of the Anglo-French boundary made it necessary for Britain to assert herself in the disputed country.[1] A clash with France seemed unavoidable. Shirley's letters from the new secretary of state, Sir Thomas Robinson, who had succeeded Lord Holderness, cautioned against offensive warfare and approved of force only if it were employed to restore boundaries with French Canada. But Robinson assured the Governor that the Massachusetts expedition into Maine was the kind of undertaking that was expected, and congratulated Shirley for anticipating the wishes of the ministry. Robinson urged him, moreover, to consult with Governor Lawrence of Nova Scotia and take advantage of French weaknesses in the northern region to restore boundaries. This vague instruction left the resourceful Shirley some freedom of decision, and he soon discovered that he and Lawrence were agreed on a course of action.[2]

Governor Lawrence, who complained repeatedly about the insecurity of Nova Scotia, with its population of French speaking Acadians, welcomed an opportunity of stopping French infiltration. He planned an expedition into the border country

1. Shirley to Lawrence, Aug. 20, 1754, Cumberland Papers, Royal Archives, Windsor Castle; "Considerations relating to measures to be taken with regard to affairs in North America," Nov. 1754, *ibid.*; Walpole to Newcastle, May 18, 1754, Add. MSS, 32735, fol. 285.

2. These letters are in Akins, ed., *Public Documents of Nova Scotia*, 376-90.

of French Acadia and sent two experienced officers, Robert Monckton and George Scott, to solicit help from Shirley. Arriving in December, they explained Lawrence's plans and showed Shirley a secret map of Fort Beausejour, the key fortress of this area, drawn by a French traitor. Their information increased Shirley's enthusiasm for the expedition; he saw it as a practical way of fulfilling Robinson's wishes. The plans, however, provided for an offensive which expanded considerably the Secretary's instructions and required more troops, supplies, and money than either Shirley or Lawrence could provide without support from the home government. Hence, Shirley wrote the Secretary of State for authorization to undertake the campaign, insisting that "the longer this service is put off, the more difficult it grows on every account. . . . And it seems equally certain that the longer it is delayed the French works will grow still stronger, and France [will] part with them with greater reluctance."[3]

Without waiting for a reply, Shirley and Lawrence decided to prepare for the expedition in anticipation of British support. Shirley had general knowledge of Braddock's plans for a Virginia campaign, and he probably thought that Robinson and Braddock would approve the Nova Scotia expedition as an extension of the general military operations. At any rate, the governors took matters into their own hands. Lawrence used his power to draw bills on the British Treasury, and Shirley engaged Apthorp, Hancock, and Eliakim Hutchinson to purchase supplies while he sent letters to local officials of the Massachusetts government asking their help in recruiting men for the expedition. Military purchases taxed even the active Boston market; but the military agents did their best to collect large quantities of powder, clothing, and medicines, and they rented warehouses on the docks in which to store their purchases until shipment. Hancock personally advanced nearly £20,000 in gold and war materiel.[4] Since so much materiel was needed, Shirley found an excuse to bring his son-in-

3. *Ibid.*, 386, 395. See also John Bartlet Brebner, *New England's Outpost* (New York, 1927), 198-99.
4. Baxter, *The House of Hancock*, 131; Shirley to House, Jan. 10, 1755, Mass. Archives, CIX, 18.

law John Erving, Jr., into the contracting business. Hancock, who wanted to preserve his near monopoly of army purchasing, countered by attempting to bring Kilby into the war preparations.[5] Shirley opposed the maneuver.[6]

These political matters absorbed most of the Governor's time, and by necessity the military details of the mobilization were left to Winslow, Lawrence, and Monckton. However, Shirley undoubtedly remembered the difficulty in extending enlistments in 1744, and on his recommendation the period of military service was extended from half a year to a year.[7] He also raised the bounties to encourage enlistments. Most of the plans were on schedule in February, though he had not received approval for the expedition, and certain supplies had not been provided from London.[8] But Lawrence was in Boston; the military leaders were working harmoniously; and Braddock, who could give the necessary approval for the expedition, was expected daily in America.

I

About the same time Shirley received Lawrence's plans for a northern campaign, Pepperrell and he were ordered by the home government to recruit men for their reactivated regiments. The troops were to be ready to aid Braddock in the summer campaign. For reasons not clear to Shirley from Robinson's letter, he was instructed to enlist men in New York and colonies to the south. No funds were provided for recruitment, and none of his regimental officers was in America. Since Shirley himself was forbidden by his instructions as governor to leave Massachusetts, he was compelled to make the best of a difficult situation.[9]

5. Hancock to Kilby, Mar. 17, 1755, Hancock Papers, IV.
6. Hancock to Kilby, June 16, 1755, *ibid.;* Mass. Archives, CIX, 18, 20, 27; and XXI, 235-37, 246-47, 258-59.
7. Shirley to Robinson, Dec. 8, 1754, Jan. 24 and Feb. 18, 1755, Parkman Trans., XL, 55, 128, 180; Shirley to House, Jan. 10 and Feb. 26, 1755, Mass. Archives, CIX, 18, 46-47.
8. Shirley to Keppell, May 20, 1755, Admiralty Records, I, 480, 4, 173. These armaments had not been all delivered in May when the expedition left Boston.
9. *Shirley Correspondence,* II, 107-9; Pepperrell to Wendell, Feb. 19,

Turning to Governor Robert Hunter Morris of Pennsylvania for help, he sent his son Jack to the Quaker province. The price of Morris's assistance was patronage for his two nephews, Staats Long and Lewis Morris, and a share of the provisioning profits for himself.[10] It was a high price to pay, but Morris's support was immediately helpful. His contacts in the neighboring colonies of New York and New Jersey made it possible for Jack Shirley and Long to enlist several hundred men in a few weeks. Perhaps even more important were the cordial relations established between the Morrises and Shirleys. "Many thanks to you for all your kindness to Jack," Shirley wrote Morris. "Give me leave," Morris replied, "to do friend Jack a piece of justice by saying, that no officer ever managed with more prudence or good sense than he has done upon this service; he has kept his men in great order, avoiding all disputes with the people, Quakers, magistrates, and others."[11]

Shirley was delighted with the progress of recruiting; even in New York a large number of men were raised for his regiment, and he was able to side-step a dispute with the de Lanceys, who were now in control of the government. They were hostile to Massachusetts because of the almost constant rivalry between the colonies over trade, boundaries, and Indian relations. They were also offended by Shirley's friendship with former Governor Clinton. Their antagonism was more apparent now, for James de Lancey was acting governor of the colony, and Oliver was aspiring to be the leading merchant contractor. Governor Morris's recruiting activities in their province scarcely challenged their powers, but he worked through agents that were rivals of the de Lanceys, who were thus deprived of the kind of patronage that Shirley had been obliged to give Morris.

Pepperrell did not have such able help, and though he tried to work out agreements with Wentworth and other New England governors, his regiment filled slowly. He was further

---

1755, Wendell Papers. Pepperrell used the Wendell connections in Boston, New York, and Albany to help in his recruiting.

10. *Pa. Archives*, 1st Ser., II, 233, 262-64.

11. *Ibid.*, II, 263; Pitcher to Robinson, Feb. 13, 1755, C. O. 5/46, 703-5. Shirley's Memorial, 1757, Add. MSS, 33055, fol. 240.

handicapped by the Nova Scotia expedition that drew upon the manpower of New England. In addition, Shirley had decided in late January that the northern colonies could do more to help Braddock than they were required to do. He planned another expedition that would enter the Lake George country of New York and march to a site near the French fort at Crown Point, and there establish a British fort to command the area. This was a modification of his plan of 1748, which proposed the destruction of the French fort as a preliminary step in the invasion of Canada. Limited warfare to which he was formally restricted in 1755 would not allow a direct assault upon Crown Point, but Shirley wanted British forces to be nearby when war broke out. He hoped to have this expedition ready when Braddock landed in America, and to offer it as New England's contribution to the containment of France.

These ideas Shirley presented to the legislature on February 13. Although some legislators desired a pledge of financial aid from the ministry, and others worried about help from the neighboring colonies, a spontaneous response assured him of support; in fact, the plan was expanded during the course of debate to include a direct assault upon Crown Point. In thorough sympathy with the idea, Shirley again wrote home for permission, but, in the meantime, accepted the authorization of the legislature to plan an attack. An enlistment of 1,200 men was approved, and the legislature promised to supply the materiel if the neighboring colonies joined the enterprise and contributed their share. This condition put a heavy burden upon Shirley and his associates; they had to win the approval of six legislatures before they were assured of final authority to levy men in Massachusetts.[12]

Choate and Welles spent several days in Connecticut, consulting with the legislature, which finally pledged 1,000 men and its full cooperation.[13] In New Hampshire Shirley expected that the legislature would be reluctant to vote men,

12. Shirley's address, Feb. 13, 1755, Curwin Papers, IV, Amer. Antiq. Soc.
13. Partridge to Williams, Feb. 11, 1755, Williams MSS, Mass. Hist. Soc.; Choate and Welles to Willard, Mar. 14, 1755, Curwin Papers, IV; Sanders to Wendell, Mar. 8, 1755, Sanders' Letter Book, Boston Pub. Lib.

and he tried to form plans with Governor Wentworth before the arrival of his spokesman Robert Hale. Shirley's frank advice to Dr. Hale gives an unusual insight into his persuasive methods: "I believe it would be of service to alarm the New Hampshire government by hinting to them in a proper manner, as thoroughly as you shall judge prudent, that if they refuse to join with us in this scheme, there will probably be an end of their scheme of land jobbing with the townships, they have late gotten from the Massachusetts government." The crown, he said, would rather hand the lands back to Massachusetts than have the "defense of their new frontier a dead charge upon it."[14]

Although Wentworth was overly cautious, Hale was publicly received "with candour and attention," and he lobbied privately with friends and foes of the Governor. He believed that the winning argument was his assertion that the expedition was an attack upon popish "idolitry."[15] New Hampshire eventually contributed 500 men.

Soliciting aid from New York was an even more delicate task. James de Lancey was still acting governor, and Shirley took the precaution of sending as his envoy the young Englishman Thomas Pownall, friend of both the de Lanceys and Lord Halifax.[16] To assist Pownall in the negotiations, Shirley notified de Lancey of his intention to back William Johnson, an influential resident of New York, as leader of the Crown Point expedition: "The gentleman I have thought . . . [would command our forces] is Colonel William Johnson . . . [;] the great influence he hath for several years maintained over the Indians of the Six Nations, is the circumstance which determines me in my choice, preferably to any gentleman in my own government though there are not wanting there officers of rank and experience out of whom I could have nominated one."[17] Although it

14. Shirley to Hale, Mar. 16, 1755, Curwin Papers; *Shirley Correspondence,* II, 142.
15. Hale to Shirley, Apr. 13, 1755, Mass. Archives, LIV, 409.
16. *Pa. Archives,* 1st Ser., II, 260-61.
17. *Shirley Correspondence,* II, 136; Pepperrell to Kenwood, Sept. 3, 1756, Pepperrell MSS, II, 198. Pepperrell was angry that Shirley passed over him for Johnson: "Governor Shirley would not let me go against the French last year and this, and now I think I am too old; affairs have been managed here

could be expected that de Lancey would be induced to co-operate if one of New York's prominent officials was the leader of the expedition, Johnson was in fact independent of the de Lancey power. As Admiral Warren's relative and former Governor Clinton's friend, he had carved a place for himself in Indian affairs that had brought him wealth and influence.

Johnson proved reluctant to serve; he suggested that there were better qualified men. Surprised by the answer, Shirley pressed for an unequivocal acceptance of the commission: "I am very glad to find that there is no exception to your engaging in the service, for you have mentioned none to me that ought to have any weight."[18] Johnson finally accepted. With this matter settled, ideas were exchanged on the strategy and plans for the mobilization. By this time Shirley had received letters from Robinson, Braddock, and Halifax and had discovered that the plans he had formed with Lawrence and the northern governors were in general harmony with British ministerial thinking, and would undoubtedly be approved. Braddock was ordered to drive the French from frontier Virginia and then from New York and Nova Scotia. Shirley's son had advised him well. The only problem that troubled the Governor was Braddock's plan to begin the year's campaign in frontier Virginia; he thought that a better object of assault was Fort Niagara, in western New York. The capture of Niagara, he conceived, would sever French communications with settlements in the Ohio Valley, and her colonials, facing isolation, would be "glad to accept . . . safe passage back to Montreal."[19] Fort Duquesne could then be taken without bloodshed. Shirley felt so strongly about Fort Niagara as an object of Braddock's attention that he wrote a long letter to Robinson outlining his ideas for containing France. The pattern of attack he suggested was generally what he had been planning all winter and spring, except that he would now have Braddock lead an expedition to Fort Niagara.

---

but poorly and now we are in miserable circumstances. No money and lost many of our young men and strength."

18. *William Johnson Papers*, I, 461.

19. *Shirley Correspondence*, II, 147-48; *William Johnson Papers*, I, 456-59; de Lancey to Robinson, Apr. 3, 1755, C. O. 5/14, 497-98.

II

The time for speculation was over. Braddock had arrived in America, and it became known that he intended to attack Fort Duquesne first, as preliminary to assaulting Fort Niagara. Except for Secretary of State Robinson, who was shocked by the aggressive appearance of the American mobilization, other members of the ministry were enthusiastic over what Shirley, Lawrence, and the northern governors had already accomplished. In a letter to the Duke of Newcastle, Halifax wrote: "Your Grace will observe that the province of New England alone has raised . . . 7100 men. . . . I yesterday told your Grace that everything in that quarter of the world more than answered our expectations, and I hope we shall soon have news of success."[20]

When the Paris negotiations had proved a failure, Newcastle reluctantly came to accept the need for containing French aggression. He hoped to avoid total war, however, and counted upon an impressive show of force to compel France to accept a compromise. To that end, he not only approved Shirley's activities, but authorized Admiral Edward Boscawen to intercept in North American waters any reinforcements for the French colonial army. The Duke likewise decided to appoint a permanent governor for New York. Many people aspired for the post, but he found no candidate that satisfied his colleagues. They had generally agreed, however, in their criticism of James de Lancey's ability and reputation, and Newcastle was anxious to find someone who would strengthen the administration of the colony during this crucial period and who would cooperate with New England. He chose finally a seasoned navy man, Sir Charles Hardy, who promised to be in New York by the summer at the latest. News of this appointment undoubtedly pleased Shirley, who had little regard for the de Lanceys, and he may have anticipated better cooperation between New York and Massachusetts in frontier defense.[21]

20. Halifax to Newcastle, May 15, 1755, Add. MSS, 32854, fol. 524; Robinson to Hardwicke(?), May 12, 1755, ibid., fol. 501.
21. Newcastle to Walpole, June 29, 1755, Add. MSS, 32735, fol. 597; Newcastle to Holderness, May 16, 1755, ibid., 32854, fol. 544.

Newcastle and his colleagues settled down to await word of victory from Braddock. The General was not so sanguine as the ministry; from his arrival in Virginia, he had encountered problems of military organization that were complicated by local jealousies and insubordination. He was perplexed by the vast area of America and the military requirements of the expedition, and began to realize the naiveté of military planners at home.[22]

About three weeks after his landing, Braddock called a conference of the governors for early April at Annapolis, Maryland. The letter did not reach Shirley until approximately March 18,[23] and it came at a most disadvantageous time; Lawrence was completing the Nova Scotia mobilization and needed help in procuring vessels; the New England mobilization was just getting underway, and the legislature was in its final days of the 1754-55 session. Nevertheless, determined to attend the conference, Shirley left Boston about March 28. From Philadelphia he was accompanied by Governor Morris of Pennsylvania and a group of gentlemen that included young Pownall. They arrived at Alexandria, Virginia, on the evening of April 13.

Meeting with Shirley and Morris were their fellow governors from Virginia, Maryland, and New York; Commodore August Keppell and William Johnson; and a score of lesser officials and officers, including William Shirley, Jr. Though all of them had corresponded, this conference was the first opportunity most had to meet one another. Shirley and Braddock got along cordially from the beginning. About the same age as Shirley, the General was stout and short, blunt in his conversation, and quick to win friends. He was deeply impressed with Shirley: "I have the greatest opinion of his integrity," he wrote the Secretary of State.[24]

The plans for the year, which were nearly settled by the time of Shirley's arrival, were what he might have anticipated

22. Braddock to Robinson, Mar. 18, 1755, 34, 73, 23-27, War Office, P.R.O.
23. Because of the late date of the conference, the place of the meeting was changed to Alexandria, Braddock to Robinson, Apr. 15, 1755, *ibid.*, 28-31.
24. Braddock to Robinson, Apr. 19, 1755, C. O. 5/46, 19-27.

with Braddock surrounded by Virginians and their governor, Robert Dinwiddie. All the regular troops, except Shirley's and Pepperrell's, were to be used against Fort Duquesne, and the Virginia frontier was designated as a major battle area. Shirley undoubtedly questioned the value of this campaign (as he had earlier to the Secretary of State), and he succeeded in persuading Braddock to give him command of the two American regiments and whatever colonials he could recruit for an expedition to Fort Niagara. Braddock planned to meet him there in late summer after Fort Duquesne was captured. Braddock also approved without reservation the Crown Point and Nova Scotia expeditions, instructing Governor Lawrence to "proceed . . . without delay" from Boston.[25]

Braddock's most surprising action was to name Shirley commander of the Niagara expedition and second in command of British forces in North America. It was a tribute to Shirley's leadership and an honor that he deserved for all the work of the past winter. Undoubtedly, too, it reflected his personal charm, for some days later George Washington wrote to a friend: "I have had the honor to be introduced to . . . Mr. Shirley, whose character and appearance has perfectly charmed me, as I think every word and every action discovers the gentleman and great politician."[26] There is no report of Shirley's reaction to the appointment. He had never led an army, and had no experience in planning a campaign that involved such vast problems of organization and supply as this one. Perhaps he felt it politically unwise to refuse an opportunity that involved considerable honor and patronage. Once before he had forsaken the role of a general, only to see others applauded for what he considered his just reward.

Lesser matters of policy were settled at the conference. Braddock gave Johnson a special commission as Indian superintendent, and the governors confirmed his leadership of the

25. Minutes of the Alexandria Conference, Apr. 14, 1755, *ibid.*, 31-35; Lawrence to Shirley, June 15, 1755, Mass. Archives, V, 398-401. Lawrence replied to Shirley that he did not doubt for a moment that Braddock would approve the Nova Scotian expedition.

26. J. C. Fitzpatrick, ed., *The Writings of George Washington* (Washington, 1931-1944), I, 116-17.

Crown Point expedition. It should be emphasized that Johnson served directly under the governors, owing no obedience to Braddock and receiving no British aid for his expedition. Shirley was given, in addition to his responsibility as commander of the Niagara expedition, some general responsibility over military operations in New York, including some supervisory authority over Johnson's Indian affairs. Shirley was also permitted to draw bills on the British Treasury for his own expedition, to aid Johnson's superintendency, and to construct a small navy on the Great Lakes.[27]

The campaign was to take this essential pattern: Braddock would attack and defeat the French at Fort Duquesne; the victorious army would make its way to Fort Niagara later in the summer. Simultaneously, Shirley's regiments would converge upon Niagara, while Johnson attacked Crown Point. By that time Governor Lawrence's troops would have finished operations in French Acadia, and Admiral Boscawen would be blockading the Gulf of the St. Lawrence.

In many ways the Alexandria conference was a curious affair. Such essential matters as manpower, supply, and geography were apparently passed over lightly—or at least not given the serious attention they deserved. The manpower problem was especially crucial. Without a pool of at least eight thousand men, the campaigns at Crown Point and Niagara were impossible. The most optimistic estimate put the available number at six thousand men, and most of them were raw recruits, lately from the fields, shops, and colleges of the north. The two northern expeditions were without the benefit of British army contracting, and they were bidding on the same market for available supplies. Other logistical factors were no less important. The Niagara campaign, for example, required a 200 mile march and water transport for an equal distance.[28] Without proven experience in the woods, even veteran soldiers would find the road westward brutally hard.[29]

27. Keppell to Shirley, Apr. 15, 1755, Admiralty Records, I, 480, 95-96.
28. Alexander to Livingston, Oct. 4, 1755, Sterling Papers, I, N. Y. Hist. Soc.; Robert Livingston to Wendell, Mar. 12 and Apr. 18, 1755, Livingston Papers.
29. Lawrence H. Gipson, *The Great War for the Empire: The Years of Defeat, 1754-1757* (New York, 1946), 182-84.

More amazing is Braddock's failure to allow for Shirley's inexperience. The Governor had no professional staff to advise him and help in managing his affairs, not even such elementary officials as a secretary, aide-de-camp, quartermaster, and paymaster. His orders from Braddock gave him only the vaguest control over Johnson, who was designated both his subordinate and his equal in the New York theater of operations. Since the men were on good terms and firmly committed to the Crown Point and Niagara expeditions, Braddock probably did not think exact definitions of authority were necessary. But he apparently did nothing to win the cooperation of James de Lancey, whose bitterness toward Shirley was obvious to the conferees. No doubt, Braddock expected that Governor Hardy would soon be in charge of New York.

III

When the conference ended, Shirley and Governor Morris traveled together to New York, where the Pennsylvania executive helped arrange certain business matters for Shirley that would normally have been done by the local governor. Though de Lancey arrived at New York about the same time as his colleagues, he immediately secluded himself. Shirley negotiated with Peter Van Burgh Livingston, Lewis Morris, and William Alexander, choosing them and their partners as his military agents. Morris was already associated in business with John Erving, Jr., who thus became the Boston partner of this New York firm. With Erving's association Apthorp and Hancock were tied into military procurement; Livingston's and Alexander's partners were William Bayard, William Richards, and John Beekman; Morris's were John Mifflin, Reese Meredith, and Samuel Smith. Outside of this group, but closely involved in their transactions, were John and Jacob Wendell, whose relatives in Albany were already in the provisioning business. Many of these men, in turn, were agents of such merchants as Kilby, Thomlinson, and Trecotick.[30] Shirley's contractors were

30. Sanders to Wendell, Mar. 8, 1755, Sanders' Letter Book; Alexander to Gambier, Oct. 13, 1755, Sterling Papers, I; Livingston and Alexander to Oliver Wendell, Apr. 28, 1755, Livingston Papers.

particularly well situated to buy on the most important markets—London, Boston, New York, and Philadelphia. One exception to Shirley's otherwise excellent business relations was the exclusion of the de Lanceys, who bitterly resented this Massachusetts intrusion into New York affairs.[31] Since most of the contracting was ultimately handled in New York, Shirley chose Alexander as his secretary. Alexander, as Livingston's brother-in-law and the heir of a wealthy New York merchant and official, knew local politics intimately and was exceptionally well qualified to manage the Governor's affairs in New York.

After placing these men in charge of his supply arrangements, Shirley hurried to Boston where he saw the last troops embarking for Nova Scotia. He announced the appointment of Jack as his private secretary and captain in his regiment; his son also became his liaison officer in regimental matters around Boston. He looked into the details of the Crown Point mobilization, found recruitment lagging, and issued orders to the militia colonels to assist. The annual elections were at hand, and he consulted Hale, Choate, and others, whose administrative tasks took them outside the colony, about their successors as representatives.

These problems were more than he could easily handle, and he was obliged to leave military affairs in New York almost entirely to Alexander. Working with Morris, Livingston, and Erving, his secretary purchased food, powder, muskets, and other equipment. By May 17, Alexander reported: "Most of the articles your Excellency ordered us to procure are purchased, or tradesmen employed to make them. We have bought 300 barrels [of] pork and 300 barrels [of] beef, 500 of which are already gone to Albany with the cordage. . . . About 100,000 weight of bread we have ordered to be bought at Philadelphia . . . as we found our bakers advanced the price so high it would come cheaper from thence."[32]

Later in May, Shirley was assured that further progress was

31. Lewis Morris to John Shirley, May 24, 1755, Sterling Papers, I; Alexander to Robert Hunter Morris, July 6, 1755, *ibid.*
32. *Pa. Archives*, 1st Ser., II, 314.

being made. Factors along the water route to Lake Ontario were preparing for the movement of supplies and men, building warehouses, and constructing hundreds of bateaux to carry the provisions on the shallow streams. "I have viewed," Alexander wrote, "all the grounds about Schenectady fit for encampments, and three places which I think the most convenient I shall have plans of, ready to lay before your Excellency at New York. . . . A number of people are at work in the Wood Creek and on the Carrying Place, to mend the passage there."[33]

Such an enterprise required vast expenditures of money and detailed accounting. Knowing the difficulties that Treasury auditors could cause, Shirley warned Alexander to obtain proper vouchers. By return post his secretary promised that all accounts would be paid "in the presence of one or two witnesses, who shall swear to the bona fide payment of them." Such efficiency pleased the Governor. "My father," Jack wrote, "is more and more pleased with Billy Alexander, every letter he receives from him."[34]

But in New York opposition to Shirley's projects was developing. Acting Governor de Lancey and his brother Oliver withheld governmental authority from Shirley's purchasing agents, refused to lend necessary arms and cannon, and aroused the merchants over loss of contracts to their Boston and Philadelphia rivals. Bayard became disaffected; he denounced Shirley's contracts as a "gross mistake" and threatened to boycott the merchant alliance. Although Alexander promised Shirley to endeavor "to cultivate a good understanding," the difficulties had only begun.[35]

An open break in Shirley's relations with the de Lanceys occurred when Oliver de Lancey went on a recruiting trip into Connecticut, and Shirley moved to prevent New York from raiding Connecticut's supply of men. Whether Shirley was justified in stopping the move is problematical, but de Lancey

33. *Ibid.*, II, 351-52.
34. *Ibid.*, II, 333; Alexander to Shirley, May 27 and June 9, 1755, Sterling Papers, I.
35. Alexander to John Shirley, June 9, 1755, *ibid.*

created such a furor that Alexander had difficulty keeping the rivalry between the governors from destroying both New York campaigns.[36] Shirley was undoubtedly tactless in handling the de Lanceys, but he was increasingly provoked by their methods. Even the small matter of procuring additional cannon forced him to write futile letters for a month. He finally said in exasperation: "As to the six 18 pounders and 4 small brass field pieces . . . , I understand they were sent out of Albany, where they have laid these last ten years, and I don't see how the loan of them now can have weakened the city of New York."[37]

Shirley counted upon Braddock's support, but admitted to Morris that he was worried: "The D——ys have thrown all imaginable obstructions in my way, and I perceive an open quarrel with the G——r is unavoidable."[38] He relied heavily upon Johnson's loyalty and the popularity of the campaigns to keep the de Lanceys in line, underestimating the malice of the New Yorkers and failing to sense Johnson's growing distrust.[39] Johnson was irritated by his proposal to redistribute the available forces. His colonials numbered nearly forty-two hundred while Shirley's regiments had not more than sixteen hundred men. To insure a successful expedition, Shirley believed that a minimum of one thousand additional troops was necessary for the Niagara expedition, and he asked Johnson to give him the men. Without waiting for consent, which he readily anticipated, Shirley petitioned the colonial legislatures for permission to change the campaign plans to allow for this redistribution of troops.[40]

In making this change, Shirley had no other purpose than to assure the success of the Niagara campaign and obey

36. Morris to Peters, May 1, 1755, Peters coll., Pa. Hist. Soc.; *Pa. Archives*, 1st Ser., II, 326-28; *William Johnson Papers*, I, 534-35.

37. *Shirley Correspondence*, II, 183-84; James de Lancey to Shirley, June 17, 1755, Mass. Archives, IV, 494.

38. *Pa. Archives*, 1st Ser., II, 331.

39. Johnson to Eyre, June 19, 1755, *William Johnson Papers*, I, 613-14; Banyar to Johnson, June 19, 1755, *ibid.*, 611.

40. *Mass. House Journals*, XXXII, pt. 1, 34, 73-75; Wentworth to Shirley, June 7, 1755, Public Records, XV, 7, Division of Public Records, Historical and Museum Commission, Harrisburg, Pa.

Braddock's orders. He was in the peculiar position of interfering with a campaign that he had promoted and repeatedly
affirmed was the most important expedition in which New
England could engage. But the Niagara campaign was a part
of Braddock's campaign, and the fort's capture would block
French reinforcements in that area. Success there would
make it possible to help Johnson at the close of the year. If
the Crown Point attack went badly, he believed Johnson had
sufficient men to cover a retreat and was close enough to the
settled area to get help.

There was some rivalry, too, between their staffs. The
mobilizations were separate affairs, though Shirley himself was
involved in both. The contractors purchased separately, often
competing for the same supplies and facilities. Johnson's army
lacked adequate funds, suffered from scarcities of arms and
ammunition, and was divided into units representing each of
the participating colonies. Shirley was not without feeling
for his colleague and assisted him in Boston and New York,
but he was often in a poor position to show his regard for
Johnson.[41] Tension increased when men from Massachusetts,
in the perpetual boundary quarrel with New York, invaded
Robert Livingston's lands and destroyed the foundry that was
making iron products for the armies. Later, Shirley momentarily forgot the dignity of his position and replied by letter
to one of Johnson's staff members in harsh tones that offended
the correspondent and Johnson himself. With so much fuel
for argument and complaint, it is little wonder that hints from
the de Lanceys were effective in arousing suspicions.[42]

IV

The weeks before his departure for Fort Niagara were busy
ones for Shirley. The May elections brought fifty-four new
representatives and a reorganization of House leadership.
With Hale, Choate, and Welles performing other govern-

41. *Mass. House Journals*, XXXII, pt. 1, 84-86. John Erving, Sr., was
re-elected to the Council and was a most active member of that body during
this June session.
42. Hancock to Kilby, June 26, 1755, Hancock Papers, IV.

mental tasks, Shirley looked to James Otis and Chambers Russell for help. His political position was for the moment secure; opposition was at a minimum. Sparhawk was its leader, reflecting the bitter disappointment of his father-in-law, Pepperrell, who had wanted to lead another campaign, but neither man dared openly oppose the Governor.[43] Hancock again tried to make Kilby colonial agent, but was defeated. The spirit of the people was high, and Hancock himself well expressed their feelings: "I wish the French Dogs may be followed to their headquarters and dens at Canada and wholly rooted out."[44]

The June session of the legislature was taken up with measures for frontier defense, new taxes, and salary grants to Shirley and members of the government. Bills were also passed to aid Johnson. Confident of legislative backing, Shirley put himself at Johnson's disposal: "Nothing shall be wanting in me to obtain a suitable provision of every kind of stores necessary for the service."[45]

Time passed rapidly. The Governor became increasingly uneasy because the details of the mobilization kept him in Boston longer than he had expected, and he was disturbed by military news. His regiment, according to Jack, was rebellious. Whippings had brought some men around, but more than a hundred were nearly impossible to manage.[46] Braddock was finding his march most laborious and had been delayed in Virginia more than a month by supply difficulties, while Boscawen was unable to intercept the French fleet bringing reinforcements to Canada.

One success sparked the northern campaign. Governor Lawrence and his generals had captured Fort Beausejour and were preparing to attack several lesser forts. Though Law-

43. Pepperrell to Kenwood, Feb. 2, 1757, Pepperrell MSS, II, 213. "I never have been consulted nor my advice asked by General Shirley nor any of the commanding officers of this war. I choose to be silent."

44. Hancock to Kilby, June 16, 1755, Hancock Papers, IV; Robert Livingston to Wendell, Apr. 18, 1755, Livingston Papers.

45. *William Johnson Papers*, I, 599.

46. Shirley to Winslow, June 25, 1755, Nova Scotia Hist. Soc., *Collections,* IV, 198-99; Lawrence to Shirley, June 15, 1755, C. O. 5/398-401; *Pa. Archives*, 1st Ser., II, 332-33.

rence had done an admirable job, the *Boston Gazette* was quick to remind its readers that these victories were the result of the untiring labor of Governor Shirley and the men of New England.[47] To his fellow soldiers of the north, Shirley sent his congratulations and promised that his own army, with those of Braddock and Johnson, would complete the victory.

In early July he joined his troops at Albany. The Niagara campaign had begun.

47. *Boston Gazette*, July 14, 1755. The victory in Nova Scotia was just the beginning of a prosperous undertaking for Apthorp and Hancock. They were soon busy supplying transportation for the hundreds of Acadians who were moved out of this northern country. There is little evidence to indicate Shirley's feeling towards this deportation. Francis Parkman, in a letter to Abbe Henri-Raymond Casgrain, Oct. 23, 1887 (Mass. Hist. Soc.), believed that Shirley and Lawrence were the chief authors of the deportation. Parkman's current biographer, Professor Wilbur Jacobs, also holds this view. Shirley, to be sure, was strongly Protestant in his feelings and very distrustful of the Acadians.

XI

Niagara Campaign

In ALBANY nearly five thousand soldiers lodged in barns in all corners of the city.[1] Walking on muddy streets and crowding into hot taverns, these young men waited for the start of the campaigns. They watched the wagoners stop their carts at the docks and saw the ships load food, arms, and cannon; they looked down the Hudson River for the ship that was bringing Major General Shirley to Albany.

Shirley's journey from Providence, Rhode Island, which had taken more than a week, included several days in New York City, where he and James de Lancey negotiated terms for the use of local cannon in Johnson's campaign. Though he secured some cannon, the meeting itself did nothing to dispel the suspicion and antagonism existing between himself and de Lancey. Alexander noticed that Shirley had achieved his object with the "utmost difficulty" and that de Lancey's brother and some other merchants were openly hostile.[2] Leaving this bickering behind him, Shirley stepped ashore in Albany, dressed in the uniform of a general, and prepared to lead his army over the 400 miles to Fort Niagara.

With Jack at his side, Shirley went to his headquarters—a roomy house, with a cellar of imported wines, meats, cheeses, and dried fruits. He had little time to enjoy them as he turned to problems of supply and manpower that were aggravated

1. Marsh to Williams, July 7, 1755, Williams Papers, Mass. Hist. Soc.; Shirley to Committee of War, July 14, 1755, Mass. Archives, LIV, 493; Louis Effingham de Forest, ed., *The Journals and Papers of Seth Pomeroy* (New York, 1926), 128-29; *Read's Weekly Journal*, Aug. 23, 1755.

2. Alexander to Robert Hunter Morris, July 6, 1755, Sterling Papers, I. Selections from the Sterling Papers are published in New Jersey Historical Society, *Proceedings*, 1st Ser., 5 (1906-7), 180-96; 6 (1909-10), 41-48, 56-64, 93-96; 7 (1912-13), 38-48.

by the delay of his arrival. Good relations with Johnson would do much to solve his problems, he knew, and as one of his first acts in Albany, Shirley invited the Indian leader to dinner. Despite his enviable reputation in handling the Mohawk, this vigorous man of forty was inexperienced in commanding thousands of soldiers and managing matters of supply.[3] Sensitive and insecure, he felt trapped in the generalship. Though Shirley promised him help, he worried about the number of troops and provisions, the Indian auxiliaries and their treatment. He had six colonies to deal with; their agents, militiamen, and legislatures demanded tactful handling and patience. On these matters Shirley had solid advice to give, but he too was perplexed by shortages of men and supplies. The longtime rivalry between Massachusetts and New York contributed to the short tempers of the staffs of the two armies.[4] Shirley was amazed by the complexities of military problems, complaining to Willard that there "is no end of petty objections and imaginary inconveniences, in opposition to the most beneficial schemes."[5]

The dinner meeting did nothing to solve the problems confronting the two commanders. Tensions remained; in fact, they were heightened by Shirley's continued attempt to distribute the available manpower more evenly. Since Johnson's army was larger by 2,300 men than his own, he wanted to absorb the New Jersey contingent of 500 men and requested Johnson's aid in enlisting Indian auxiliaries. His expedition to Niagara, he argued, had to travel over three times the distance, into more exposed and dangerous country, and with longer lines of supply than the Crown Point expedition. He contended further that the New Jersey regiment had not been originally granted to Johnson and, therefore, should be transferred to strengthen his undermanned British regiments.

Shirley was finally successful in detaching these men, but he incurred the ill will of Johnson, who delayed answering his

3. *William Johnson Papers,* I, 677-80, 687, 721-22, 733-39.
4. Shirley to Willard, July 8, 1755, Mass. Archives, LIV, 485; Alexander to Livingston, July 22, 1755, Sterling Papers, I. Alexander noticed a "great deal of grumbling and want of activity in our agents."
5. Shirley to Willard, July 28, 1755, Mass. Archives, LIV, 517.

request for Indian auxiliaries until Shirley was ready to leave
Albany. The help of the Indians had become essential to the
safety of his expedition when it was apparent that Braddock
would not arrive at Niagara as soon as they expected. Although Johnson agreed with Shirley about the importance
of the Niagara campaign, he believed the Indians were unnecessary. "I am of the opinion," he finally wrote, "that an
attack upon Niagara and securing that important pass is now
more than ever necessary, and that no delay be suffered which
can possibly be avoided. . . . I continue to think [it] does not
require the assistance of any considerable number of Indians
as the operations will be chiefly conducted by water."[6] Johnson held to this opinion, and by one pretext after another
avoided raising the auxiliaries. Though he held his commission
from Braddock, he refused to obey the orders of the General's
second-in-command, thus forcing Shirley to hire agents to
bargain with the Indians. Johnson then denounced the agents
and permitted his assistants to spread opposition to them. He
delayed communicating the requests of Shirley's officers, who
needed Indian consent to build warehouses and armed posts
in Iroquois country, asserting an independence in Indian affairs that seemed ridiculous even to his friends, who cautioned
him against challenging Shirley's right to parley with the
Indians.[7]

Johnson's unreasonable conduct seriously disturbed Shirley. He had no time to appeal the issue to Braddock before
his departure from Albany. The season was far advanced, and
he apparently hoped that the anticipated victory would rec-
oncile their differences. However, the strain had a visible
effect upon Shirley. "He appears cheerful," one observer
noted, "but something lies heavily on his mind."[8] Another
blamed his age; he was sixty-one, and the exhausting work was
probably too much for him. Much of the tension registered in
his face must have also been caused by the demands of a

6. *William Johnson Papers*, I, 790. Shirley's answer to an earlier denial of
Indian auxiliaries is interesting: "Your opinion that there is no occasion for
any Indians to join me 'till my arrival at Oswego is singular." *Ibid.*, I, 734-35.
7. *Ibid.*, I, 794-97.
8. Shirley to Willard, July 8, 1755, Mass. Archives, LIV, 485.

virtually new profession. Shirley was an experienced and energetic leader, and he tried to learn the art of military administration, but he had spent so much of his life in court rooms and civil offices that it was impossible for him to develop quickly the aptitudes of a major general. He was involved in a strange role for a man of his age and training. One of his critics questioned his failure to review the troops regularly and, when he did, his habit of calling them "my children."[9]

Just as he was leaving Albany for the march west he received ominous dispatches from Pennsylvania; the details were not clear, but apparently Braddock had been injured in battle. Shirley swore his subordinates to secrecy until he confirmed the information. Battle plans remained unchanged. Men and supplies kept moving westward to Oswego, an Indian trading post 200 miles distant on Lake Ontario, where ships were being readied for the lake voyage to Fort Niagara. On July 24 Shirley moved his headquarters to Schenectady, staying there three days in order to supervise the loading of the ammunition and provisions; then he pushed upstream on the wide Mohawk River. Against its gentle current the army made fifty-six miles to Little Falls in two days. At the falls the bateaux were unloaded, hauled by horses over marshy grounds to the upper river, and then reloaded with the provisions brought there by horse-drawn wagons. The men worked day and night, whipping the tired animals as the wagon wheels sank in the mud.[10]

Because water levels were low, hundreds of men were forced to pry and shove the bateaux through mud and water. At the Great Carrying Place all provisions were again loaded on wagons and hauled over crooked, rocky roads to a small stream that was even less navigable than the upper Mohawk River. Again the bateaux were floated; again the sweating

9. Perry, *Origins in Williamstown*, 311; Alexander to Livingston, July 22, 1755, Sterling Papers, I.
10. Alexander to Livingston, Aug. 4, 1755, and Livingston to Alexander, Aug. 5, 1755, Sterling Papers, I. Jack Shirley to Robert Hunter Morris, July 20, 1755, *Pa. Archives*, 2nd Ser., II, 381-82. The hauling of these provisions was "fatiguing beyond conception."

soldiers and workmen struggled with the heavy boats. Low water forced Shirley to split his supply corps into many parties, and finally the bateauxmen, wagoners, and supervisors were strung out over an ever lengthening supply route, and Shirley's advanced party was left with just enough provisions to make the march to Oswego.

From his temporary headquarters in a log building prepared for him by Captain William Williams, who had opened the road to Wood Creek early in June, Shirley was within earshot of all this activity. Here it was that he received official eye-witness reports of Braddock's ambush in a Pennsylvania forest and the wholesale casualties suffered in his defeat. For Shirley the defeat was a personal tragedy; the dead included Braddock and William Shirley, Jr. The death of his eldest son and the responsibility of serving as commander-in-chief of all the British forces seemed too much to bear, and one associate observed that "the old man went off with a heavy heart."[11]

As Braddock's successor, he had inherited the heroic task of leading the 1755 campaign to success. He asked the governors for additional levies for the Crown Point expedition and ordered his own army to leave for the west. Uncertain of military strategy, he pondered over whether to order Braddock's troops to continue their march to Fort Duquesne or join his expedition; or, indeed, whether he should attempt to go to Fort Niagara now that Braddock was defeated. The general military situation was threatening. Dispatches from Admiral Boscawen indicated that the French fleet he had failed to capture off Louisbourg had brought huge reinforcements to Canada. Shirley received further word from Johnson that no Indian auxiliaries would be supplied.[12] Braddock's defeat and reminders from friends that he too could be ambushed were sufficient to convince him that he must have Indian guides

11. Perry, *Origins in Williamstown*, 326.
12. Shirley to Johnson, Aug. 4, 1755, photostat coll., Mass. Hist. Soc. Shirley was still pleading for Indian auxiliaries: "You observe to me that my proceedings will have a bad consequence for the common cause; is not the expedition to Niagara part of that cause, or does it wholly center in the expedition to Crown Point?"

and scouts. Taking a detachment of soldiers, he visited an Indian village nearby, where he was welcomed, but was forced to negotiate for several days before he could hire any men. Though he paid dearly in time and money, he obtained Indian auxiliaries.[13]

As his forces pressed toward Oswego, they were aware of French and Indian parties moving in the woods near their camps. Extra sentries were posted, and small parties of scouts regularly searched the thickets along the rivers. Every possible precaution was taken, but Shirley was understandably apprehensive after Braddock's defeat. "There is the greatest reason," he wrote Johnson, "to expect that they [the French] will use their utmost efforts to harass and cut us off in our passage before our arrival at Oswego, as they did General Braddock on his march to Fort Duquesne."[14]

Within hearing of the work gangs and the rattling wagons, Shirley wrote to Secretary of State Robinson re-emphasizing the importance of driving France from the continent. Since Braddock's defeat, however, he had changed his mind about the purpose of his expedition; he thought that Oswego should first be fortified before he went on to Niagara, for it was the only English trading post on the Great Lakes. "It is as much the key of these lakes and the southern and western country lying round them, to the English, as Nova Scotia is of the sea coast and eastern parts of North America; and the loss of it to the French . . . must not only make them absolute masters of the navigation of all these lakes, and trade upon them, . . . but let them into the heart of the country inhabited by the Six Nations." Shirley then looked beyond the immediate problem of fortifying Oswego to the strategy of containment. He recommended a campaign from Oswego that would remove French forts from the Great Lakes region and put Indian trade into British hands. With French forts reduced, Britain would secure "the whole southern country behind the Appalachian

13. Morris told him that "I imagine they will move from the Ohio to oppose you at Niagara," Papers of the Governors, Pa. Archives, 4th Ser., II, 435; New York Council Minutes, Aug. 1, 1755, C. O. 5/46, 123.

14. Shirley to Johnson, Aug. 4, 1755, Photostat coll., Mass. Hist. Soc.; Bradstreet to Shirley, Aug. 17, 1755, Loudoun Papers, 634, Huntington Lib.

or Alleghenny Mountains to the Crown of Great Britain, and have a further effect, to render Canada itself, of little or no value to the French, as the cost of maintaining it, after the loss of their trade with the Indians[,] . . . would greatly exceed any advantages which the French can reap from the possession of a country so barren and of so difficult a navigation."[15]

With his men moving down Wood Creek and into Lake Oneida, Shirley transferred his camp to the Oneida Carrying Place. Then by fast canoe over the hazardous waters of the Oswego River he went ahead of the slow moving army, arriving at Oswego on August 18. It was a crumbling fort with a tiny garrison, a dusty, ill-kept town, where traders did business with Indians and halfbreeds. The post was in desperate need of attention. Shirley first turned to the problem of procuring a supply of food. Provisions were short, and he knew that hungry men could not repair the fort and resist an enemy attack. If the French were to besiege Oswego, he believed that the fort could be easily starved into submission, and he hastened to order Williams at Wood Creek to send stores. He assigned Marcus Petri to guard the road between Schenectady and Wood Creek and James Stevenson to supervise the warehousemen at Schenectady and Albany.

Despite these efforts, the shortage of food and clothing became acute, and Alexander had to rush orders for 300 barrels of pork, 100 barrels of rum, and extra shirts, shoes, stockings, and breeches for the men—a thousand pairs of breeches, red in color and made "of some good strong woollen stuff."[16] Williams procured flour and rum from Schenectady and bought all the available beans, squash, green corn, and fish from the Indians. The unexpected shortages were partly due to the strikes and desertions of the bateauxmen, who were demanding payment of their wages, but more to the faulty leadership of the contracting merchants. Petri, Stevenson, and Williams were often careless and irresponsible, and Lewis Morris was

<hr>

15. Shirley to Robinson, Aug. 12 and 15, 1755, C. O. 5/46, 127-28, 139-53 (Quotation on 135); Shirley to Newcastle, Aug. 11, 1755, Add. MSS, 33029, fol. 198; Shirley to Fox, Aug. 15, 1755, Loudoun Papers, 632.

16. Alexander to Livingston, Aug. 4, 1755, Sterling Papers, I.

especially negligent; he left business at Albany to subordinates while he traveled to Philadelphia. Even his associates, Livingston and Erving, were critical of his conduct, insisting that Morris's presence was necessary at Albany to coordinate the work of the subcontractors and keep them posted on supply problems in the hub city.[17]

The contractors were also guilty of failure to respond to an emergency created by administrative technicalities. For some reason the deputy paymaster at Boston, Abraham Mortier, refused to honor drafts from Morris and Livingston, demanding Shirley's signed orders before he would transfer funds to them from Shirley's account. Instead of treating the situation as critical, Erving, Morris, and Livingston argued for weeks with Mortier, while credit dried up and the contractors themselves went into debt. Mortier's distance from New York caused further delay, because the negotiations were carried on by correspondence. In the near isolation of Oswego, Shirley could not understand why the paymaster was not providing the funds for military necessities. With bateaux-men and wagoners leaving their jobs, he pressed Alexander for an answer and ordered troops out to protect abandoned supplies.[18] When letters from the contractors finally arrived, Shirley promptly signed the required papers, but then took matters into his hands by ordering Williams to bring stalled bateaux from Wood Creek and elsewhere farther east.

While awaiting the supplies, he turned his attention to the refortification of Oswego. Although in letters to his superiors he had described the trading center as a key to frontier defense, he could not bring himself to make its defense the major purpose of his expedition. Fort Niagara's capture again figured in his plans. This objective spared him neither time nor money to erect costly battlements at Oswego, but his staff officers assured him that at least makeshift defenses were nec-

17. Livingston to Alexander, Aug. 29, 1755, *ibid.*
18. The Sterling Papers have letters from Livingston, Morris, Stevenson, and others explaining the difficulties in raising funds for the army. Shirley to Fox, Aug. 12, 1755, Loudoun Papers, 624. Theodore Thayer, "The Army Contractors for the Niagara Campaign, 1755-1756," *Wm. and Mary Qtly.*, 3rd Ser., 14 (1957), 31-46.

essary because Oswego would become their most advanced base of supply if they went on to Fort Niagara. Accepting these recommendations, he put the soldiers to work constructing several forts. Through haste and inexperience mistakes were made in constructing Fort Oswego. An army engineer in 1756 reported that the new hornwork and the raveling in front of the fort were badly laid out. "The flanks of the half bastions do not defend the opposite faces, the wings are enfiladed from end to end, the terreplain [are] seen almost throughout, the north wing towards the Lake [is] quite open, with only a small cliff of earth and rock where anybody may run up and down."[19] The soldiers, however, had to overcome great difficulties: timber was green; saws, nails, and shovels were scarce; and heavy rain turned the camp into a swamp. Days passed without progress as the season advanced. The supply of provisions was critically short.

I

Camp life depressed morale. For Shirley there were few physical hardships, but the strain of commanding a weakened and demoralized garrison was great. Each day a few men deserted; some were caught by patrols; but a larger number managed to escape. Those captured were put in chains until court-martialed and then stripped and punished with the lash. These public beatings made only momentary impression, and more drastic action was necessary. After the trial of five deserters on September 3, Shirley ordered the army to the parade grounds. The convicted men, dressed in white shirts and breeches, were marched before a firing squad, where they were allowed a brief prayer and then blindfolded. The squad took aim, but just before the shots rang out, Shirley signaled a halt. Three of the doomed men were pardoned; minutes later the remaining two were shot. A few days later twenty-one men deserted.[20]

19. Patrick MacKellar's journal, entries for May 25, 1756, Stanley Pargellis, ed., *Military Affairs in North America, 1748-1765* (New York, 1936), 190.

20. Entries for Sept. 3 and 15, 1755, *Journals of the Hon. William Hervey* (Suffolk Green Books, No. 14, Bury St. Edmunds, 1906), 14-15.

The bitter moments of camp life were often captured by Jack Shirley in his letters to Governor Morris. In one, written shortly before midnight on September 11, he scribbled:

We have just received fresh intelligence . . . that the French have about 1200 men . . . and . . . they were coming here. I suppose they [will] wait for us to go to Niagara first. Our bateauxmen desert us in large numbers, as do the soldiers who are dissatisfied at our being obliged to allow them no more than half a pound of bread and no rum. We lost 21 of the latter last night, 15 of them are Schuyler's. Had we but provisions we might, I am satisfied, with our fleet and train, save the French the trouble of coming hither. . . . We have now only 8 days bread, pork and beef enough, but no rum or peas. . . . Excuse blots and blunders; I hope my next epistle will give you a better account of us.[21]

Despite these shortages, which extended to the very paper being used in official correspondence, Shirley still planned to take his troops to Fort Niagara and, if successful there, to attack Fort Frontenac at the other end of the lake. Although assault upon Niagara was exceedingly dangerous, it was approved by a council of war on September 18. Jack's letters caught the daring of the enterprise:

We shall find the whale boats of vast service to us, but I fear what bateaux we are forced to take with us must be left by the way, if they are not overset, for the least puff of wind so ruffles this lake, that one of our bateaux cannot I think well live in it. . . . We shall add to our 600 men seventy or eighty Indians and some few Albany men. Many of the latter we are forced to make bateauxmen of to fetch provisions hither from the German flatts. . . . For want of provisions it will be impossible to leave a garrison this winter at Niagara in case we succeed. We must knock it down and visit it early in the spring. . . . All I am uneasy about is our provisions. Our men have been upon half allowance of bread these three weeks past, and no rum given to them. We have many ill of fluxes, and some of the dry bellyache.[22]

Though the officers had agreed to leave for Niagara on the 26th, they grumbled about the long voyage.[23] Shirley called another council of war in which the officers recommended that

21. *Pa. Archives*, 1st Ser., II, 404.
22. *Ibid.*, II, 424-25.
23. *Ibid.*, II, 425

the campaign should be delayed until spring, when greater numbers of men, vessels, provisions, and muskets would be available.[24] Jack's letter to Morris about the change of plans was his last from Oswego. He had contracted dysentery and was too weak to write. He responded slowly to treatment and was carried back to Albany on a stretcher.

Before Shirley left Oswego for the winter he decided to quarter his regiments there and at Wood Creek rather than return them to Albany, so they would be readly available for action in 1756. In anticipation of letters from Secretary Robinson which would outline the strategy for 1756, he invited the northern governors to a meeting at New York where plans could be concerted for the next campaign. Though uncertain of his own part in future campaigns, he wanted to put his ideas before the ministry, and he wrote many long letters interpreting political developments in the colonies. He remained convinced that Britain should concentrate its energies upon French encroachments in the Great Lakes region. "I think," he told the Secretary of State, "there is abundant reason to be persuaded that this place [Oswego] will be the principal object of the French the next spring, and that Fort Frontenac should be that of the English."[25]

To prepare for this new campaign, he ordered the Albany supply route to be fortified. He sent John Oisher to build larger storehouses at the Lake Oneida Carrying Place, where an elaborate stockade, with a picket fence nine feet high, and barracks for a detachment of soldiers were already being constructed. At Wood Creek he had Marcus Petri building another armed house in which thirty men were to be quartered during the winter. He then ordered various officers to examine the roads, bridges, and carriage places and to repair and improve them whenever it was advisable.[26]

Since Oswego had only forty days supply of bread, sixty

24. Ibid., II, 427-31; Shirley to Robinson, Sept. 19 and 23, 1755, C. O. 5/46, 141-47, 171-87; Alexander to Livingston, Oct. 4, 1755, Sterling Papers, I.

25. Shirley to Robinson, Oct. 10, 1755, C. O. 5/46, 128-29.

26. Alexander to ———, Oct. 17, 1755, ibid., 216; Order to Williams, Oct. 29, 1755, ibid., 230-31.

days of meat, and twenty-one days of rum left in the store-houses in October, more provisions were absolutely necessary for the health and safety of the men. Shirley instructed Williams to haul food there before the winter snow closed the roads. Apparently there were ample provisions along the route, and Williams had only to transport them to Oswego. The order was repeated when Shirley arrived at Albany, for he had heard through his aide-de-camp James Kinneer that Williams had not obeyed the previous command. "It is now his Excellency's orders," Kinneer wrote Williams, "that you don't leave your command at the Carrying Place until you shall have sent off to Oswego, a sufficient quantity of provisions for the garrison for the winter."[27] Unfortunately, neither Williams, James Mercer, the commandant at Oswego, Petri, nor the contractors at Schenectady exerted themselves before winter closed the area. Isolated at Oswego, the men lived on reduced rations until March. Much has been made of the deaths and illnesses of the Oswego troops, but it is clear that Shirley had left orders to provision them. In November he sent two distinct orders to Williams; and in January, when he heard of their plight, he prepared to open the road as soon as possible.[28]

II

During his stay at Oswego, Shirley had never forgotten the campaign against Crown Point. In his correspondence with Phips, Willard, and members of the Massachusetts legislature, he strongly supported the expedition.[29] Save for his personal participation, which was impossible, he could not have given more encouragement to Johnson and his men than he did.

27. Kinneer to Williams, Nov. 16, 1755, Williams Papers, I, 143; Emerson to Osborn, Dec. 14, 1755, Mass. Archives, LV, 144-45. "I don't think Albany was ever before so full of provisions as at present." Perhaps blame may still be placed upon Shirley for continuing Williams in the service. There were many letters sent to him from Aug. to Nov. 1755, ordering various things. In performing these tasks Williams does not appear to have been efficient. Shirley, of course, may have been bound to keep him for political reasons.
28. Shirley to Williams, Sept. 11, 1755, C. O. 5/46, 443-44; Alexander to Williams, Sept. 16, 1755, Williams Papers, I, 133; Williams to Alexander, Sept. 17, 1755, ibid., I, 134.
29. Shirley to Johnson, Sept. 24, 1755, C. O. 5/46, 237-41; *William Johnson Papers*, I, 841-86; *Shirley Correspondence*, II, 289-301.

Johnson, however, remained bitter toward him, becoming even more hostile as the campaign progressed. His feelings may have been caused by poor health—he suffered from sleepless nights and hypertension—or his fear of losing control of the Indian trade. Perhaps the constant pressure from the de Lanceys and their friends alienated him from Shirley. Whatever the reason, Johnson imagined that Shirley was intent on destroying his influence over the Iroquois and was plotting against him. In this frame of mind he wrote numerous letters to friends, acquaintances, and the ministry. His military campaign became of secondary importance as he enlarged upon the significance of his commission from Braddock, in which he was given the management of the Indians; he was soon asserting an independence as Indian commissioner that challenged Shirley's military authority as Braddock's successor. His ideas became so inflated that his friend Thomas Pownall warned him to emphasize less the aspect of "independence" and more the interference of Shirley's agents in Indian affairs.[30]

Johnson's military operation began on August 9. After some days on the road, he heard rumors of troop activity at Crown Point and, like Shirley, feared an ambush. Slowing the forward progress of his march, he spent valuable time petitioning the northern governors for reinforcements. By August 29 he was at the mountain ridge overlooking Lake George, and hours later he supervised the construction of a fortified camp near the water. He had soldiers bring up food, arms, and cannon from the upper Hudson River, some fifteen miles to the south, and because of enemy activity he kept scouts searching the forests. This work continued until September 7, when scouts spotted a French force of three or four thousand men moving through the woods. Johnson sent Ephraim Williams

30. See my *Thomas Pownall: British Defender of American Liberty* (Glendale, Calif., 1951), chap. III. Pownall to Johnson, Nov. 11, 1755, *William Johnson Papers*, II, 289; *Shirley Correspondence*, II, 243-48—"From Governor Shirley's late behavior and his letters to me I am under no doubt that he is become my inveterate enemy and that the whole weight of his power and abilities will be exerted to blast if he can my character." If letters of this sort were written by Shirley, they are missing or destroyed.

with 1,000 men to slow its advance while he readied camp defenses for the attack. Instead of surprising the enemy, Williams's forces were ambushed and scattered, and Williams himself was fatally wounded.

The French commander, the Baron Dieskau, quickly pressed his advantage with an assault on Johnson's fortifications, but met hot artillery fire. British batteries were so well protected behind the heavy pines and rocks that the Canadian militia and Indians fled, leaving the French regulars to cover their retreat. By dark they were game enough to renew battle, but again the British fought back boldly and courageously, jumping out of their fortifications to pursue their enemy.[31] In the heat of these skirmishes Johnson was painfully wounded in the thigh, and the French commander, also seriously injured, was captured.

Although Johnson could not join the joyful celebrations of victory, he welcomed letters of praise from Pownall, the de Lanceys, and Banyar, who dramatized the dispute between him and Shirley into something resembling Sir Lancelot's battle with the dragon. Johnson was aware that his good fortune in war had advanced him toward the baronetage he coveted,[32] but he was bedridden and in terrible pain: "I was seized with an inflamation in my head which gave me inexpressible torment. I have been bled, blistered, and purged, which, with want of sleep and appetite, confines me to the bed."[33] His judgment was affected, and his actions became eccentric. Instead of pushing on to Crown Point, he sent his secretary on a tour of New England governments to get advice as to his next move against the French, and he abused members of his staff when they pressed for action. Unable himself to lead the army, he refused to allow Phineas Lyman, his second-in-command, to take over. Inaction consumed valuable time. In October, the weather turned unfavorable, and the rain affected

31. Callaghan, ed., *N. Y. Col. Docs.*, II, 678-80; *William Johnson Papers*, II, 24-32.

32. Arthur Pound and Richard E. Day, *Johnson of the Mohawks* (New York, 1930), chap. XXII.

33. *William Johnson Papers*, II, 169.

roads and supplies. As conditions worsened, the men rebelled, and Johnson lost faith in himself.[34]

This idleness irritated Shirley, who wanted Johnson to follow up his victory at the lake with an attack upon Crown Point. It was ridiculous, Shirley believed, to solicit advice from the New England governments when Johnson had a clear mandate to assault Crown Point. Writing with a comprehension of the difficulties, he calmly reproached Johnson for delaying the campaign. Though he withheld comment in his letters to the ministry, he could easily have blasted Johnson's reputation or, at least, have made the Indian leader appear ridiculous. The most he did was counter many of Johnson's complaints about shortages of supplies and manpower.[35]

III

As the fall deepened, the outlook for Shirley's early return to Boston grew less promising. The most important business, the conference of governors at New York, had to be postponed until December. Albany was again the center of activity, crowded and muddy, filled with hundreds of sick soldiers, including Shirley's dying son Jack. The wounded suffered because the New York government had neglected medical arrangements, and as in most other matters, Whitehall had also left the army to shift for itself. With "doctor bills pretty extravagant" and the cost of rooms equally outrageous, Shirley billeted the sick with local householders and trusted that the Treasury would approve the expenditures.[36]

But this was only one of many emergencies. Orderly payment for military purchases proved an impossibility, despite the warrants Shirley had signed. Part of the trouble was the complex manner of converting British sterling into colonial currency. The northern deputy paymaster, Abraham Mortier, was stationed in Boston, where he conducted most of his financial

34. *Ibid.*, II, 180-85.
35. Shirley to Willard, Oct. 15, 1755, Mass. Archives, LV, 27-29; Shirley to Fox, Nov. 5, 1755, W.O. 34, 73, 38-41.
36. Emerson to Osborn, Oct. 14 and Nov. 7, 1755, Mass. Archives, LV, 21, 73-75. Shirley to Hardy, Nov. 8, 1755, W.O. 1, 4, 19; Pownall to Johnson, Nov. 2, 1755, Emmet coll., N. Y. Pub. Lib.

business. While this was profitable for Shirley's Boston friends, it proved burdensome for the army; British money had to be converted into Massachusetts commercial paper, which was then converted into New York currency. The endless amount of red tape allowed for much graft and serious delays in payment of bills.[37] Shirley found himself victimized by the commercial interests he had always supported. The ministry had done nothing to provide him with the usual equipage and contingency funds, which, for Braddock, amounted to £3,000. He was meeting these expenses himself or was juggling the accounts to raise the money.

More bewildering was the problem of Johnson's army. Because it was stalled at Lake George, supply and morale became critical issues as the weeks passed; but these were overshadowed in November by rumors of an impending French attack. The alarm brought rapid mobilization of transport facilities at Albany, and Shirley convened a special advisory council which attempted to push Johnson into making a counterattack. At Lake George the picture was different. When the French did not appear, Johnson abandoned the campaign, and the bored New Englanders, company after company, pulled up stakes and walked home. There would not have been any force at the Lake to hold the fortifications had not Shirley and the New England commissioners persuaded nearly six hundred men to stay as garrison soldiers.[38]

Meanwhile Governor Morris wrote Shirley about the raids of enemy Indians on the Pennsylvania frontier. So great had the slaughter become that frontiersmen were retreating toward Philadelphia. Morris's appeals to the Pennsylvania assembly had brought little response, and he turned to Shirley for assistance. Handicapped by a lack of funds and men, not to mention authority, Shirley could do nothing more than lend some barrels of powder and quarter a few troops in the colony.[39]

37. Emerson to Osborn, Oct. 14, 1755, Mass. Archives, LV, 21; Alexander to Williams, Sept. 11, 1755, C. O. 5/46, 455-56.
38. Hardy to ———, Nov. 20, 1755, Add. MSS, 33029, fol. 238. Massachusetts provided 185 men. *New-York Mercury,* Nov. 24, 1755.
39. *Pa. Archives,* 1st Ser., II, 535, 537-38, 569-70.

On the heels of these crises, Shirley chaired the governor's conference at New York, where Sir Charles Hardy was the host. The new governor had visited Albany since his arrival in the colony and had been fed a poisoned diet by the de Lanceys and Pownall. Letting appearances of confusion at Albany deceive him, he had sent home a hostile appraisal of Shirley's ability and the military situation. His views, together with those already sent by Pownall and Johnson, required a thorough refutation. Shirley, however, was unaware of this mischief; he sensed some hostility as he faced the governors at the conference table, but his mind would not be deflected from the 1756 campaign. The theme of his letters since early summer had been the war—the strategy and the future of the conflict with France—when he should have been countering the activities of his enemies. Apparently he did not write directly to Newcastle, Halifax, Townshend, Bedford, Bollan, or Thomlinson concerning his career as governor and military commander. This was strange conduct for Shirley, who was so well versed in patronage politics.

Shirley undoubtedly counted on his heroic efforts of 1755 as his defense. He looked back on the mobilization with pride. Although he shared honors with Lawrence and Johnson, the victories in Nova Scotia and New York had been successful only through the magic of his leadership. He had given much to his country: nine months of the hardest exertion of his life and the lives of two sons—Jack had died in November. He was also proud of his government, which had surpassed all others in sending its men into battle. The more than seven thousand Massachusetts recruits were the backbone of the Nova Scotia and Crown Point ventures and the strength of the American regular regiments. What other governor could boast such support from his people?

In facing his critics Shirley chose a bold course. Old friends who remembered him in the spring, hesitant in the newly fitted uniform of a major general, could only wonder now at the way he presided over the conference. More deeply serious than ever before, he spread out in front of his audience a plan for the sudden expansion of the imperial domain. He outlined a massive offensive against French forts in the Great Lakes; control of these lakes would give Britain possession of the continent. Thus he recommended an attack on Forts Frontenac, La Galette, Niagara, and other fortified places, to be launched from Oswego in early April 1756. He also proposed that Braddock's work be finished by attacks on Forts Duquesne and Frederic (Crown Point). To round out the campaign, he believed an ascent of the Kennebec River, with assaults on French settlements on the Chaudiere and a feint at Quebec, would keep French forces near the capital. Shirley had not entirely thrown off the pretense that these military engagements were directed against French encroachments, but his audience understood the purpose of his campaign was to take the Ohio Valley and force the submission of Quebec.

The plan of operations was well received, though changes were suggested in the allotment of men and in the employment of Indian auxiliaries. Governor Hardy, however, took strong exception to Shirley's plan to attack other forts besides Niagara in the Great Lakes region. His opinion was echoed in New York City by Shirley's enemies, who denied that the commander was right in proposing an assault upon lands that properly belonged to France. But Shirley countered the criticism by insisting that the territory they would seize was British territory awarded Great Britain by the treaties of Ryswick and Utrecht; and who would know better than he, the King's former commissioner to Versailles.[40]

Despite the opposition Shirley had his way at the conference and sent his plan home for approval. His critics concentrated their attack upon him in the newspapers, and several governors, particularly Robert Dinwiddie, urged the home government to appoint a professional military man. Though Shirley's friends engaged these critics in debate, Shirley was too busy for these matters, as he turned to other business. He asked Governor Morris to appoint several trust-

40. Shirley was not alone in advocating this expansion. In the Hardwicke Papers (Add. MSS, 35909, fol. 208) there is a plan that projected an all out attack upon Canada. Even Belcher lent his influence to a sweeping assault upon the enemy—"The sacred pages tell us we must lay the ax to the root," *ibid.*, fol. 215. Shirley to Robinson, Dec. 19, 1755, W.O. 34, 73, 73-74; *Shirley Correspondence*, II, 350-54.

worthy merchants of Philadelphia to approve the Braddock accounts. They were to review the expenditures and allow whatever they considered reasonable. He then studied his relations with Johnson. Fortunately, even before the conference had convened, Johnson had resigned his army commission, but he kept the highly prized superintendency, which he asserted was established directly by the home government. Shirley realized that Johnson would be no help if Indian auxiliaries were required in 1756, and he attempted to exercise his military authority over Indian affairs by sending Johnson a new commission to replace the one given the Indian leader by Braddock. Johnson withheld his answer for some time,[41] then replied in an obscure vein: "I have this long time been told there was a commission from his Majesty for me, and that it was sent by the late General Braddock, but I never received any, nor pay for the one I had of him."[42] This was, indeed, a serious admission considering the opposition he had raised against Shirley. With no more solid basis for a commission than wishful thinking, he had set in motion a campaign of bitterness. The admission was more than Shirley could take, and he reported their disagreement to Henry Fox, the new secretary of state: "The construction, which Colonel Johnson made of his Indian commission was, that it excluded me from employing any person whatever to engage any Indians to go with me to Niagara. . . . One instance among others of this is, that he forbid Captain Staats, who told him that he should carry some Stockbridge Indians to Niagara in the expedition under my command, to presume to take one of them into it."[43]

When Johnson visited New York in late December for a

41. *William Johnson Papers,* II, 396-97.
42. *Ibid.,* IX, 331; II, 403, 409-12; Minutes of the Alexandria Conference, Apr. 14, 1755, W.O., 73, 33-34. The minutes of this Council do not indicate that Johnson was given charge of Indian affairs to the exclusion of regular army officers. His position would appear to be that of an agent responsible to the commander-in-chief. Braddock's instructions of Nov. 25, 1754, item eight, refers to Johnson by name when Braddock was ordered to maintain good relations with the Indians. But Johnson was not given exclusive power as he was claiming (see W.O. 34, 71, 34-38). This was also the position of the Board of Trade (Memorandum, Nov. 27, 1755, C. O. 5/1129, 42) which referred to Johnson "as sole superintendent of Indian affairs under commission from the late General Braddock."
43. Shirley to Robinson, Dec. 20, 1755, W.O. 34, 73, 58.

celebration in honor of his military victory on Lake George, Shirley had an opportunity to meet him. To the surprise of everyone, their conference was amiable. Shirley, with his usual charm and tact, maneuvered Johnson on to friendly ground, and a compromise was arranged. The results of their parley, as Shirley interpreted them, were then reported to Secretary Fox: "Colonel Johnson hath given me an assurance . . . that he will follow my instructions in the execution of his trust relative to the Indians, which I have already settled and delivered to him."[44]

Their cordial relations, however genuine, did not decrease the plotting of the de Lancey brothers. They had waited too long to be disappointed. Their plans encompassed Shirley's removal as commander-in-chief, Johnson's appointment as Indian superintendent, and Livingston's dismissal as military contractor. At the base of their opposition was the financial and political rivalry of Massachusetts and New York business interests. With the war growing hotter, their expectations of profits from a change of military leadership were great.[45] So well did they succeed in laying their plans that a prominent man like Governor Hardy, who had the best interests of the empire at heart, fell into their scheme without realizing their selfishness.[46] They were able to win the ambitious Pownall over to their cause by treating him as a person of considerable prominence, and his return home to England in February 1756 was heralded as an important event for the colonies.[47]

By that time Shirley was homeward bound to Boston. For seven months he had worn the red uniform of a general; and though he was returning to Boston, he could not leave his military responsibilities behind. The aging governor, tired, worried, and thinner, was happy to be home among friends, but the uncertainty of his future disturbed him.

44. Shirley to Fox, Jan. 12, 1756, W.O. 1, 4, 49-51; *Shirley Correspondence,* II, 373-77.

45. Hardy to Board of Trade, Dec. 18, 1755, O'Callaghan, ed., *N. Y. Col. Docs.,* VI, 1023; Johnson to Hardy, Sept. 16, 1755, *ibid.,* 1013-15.

46. Hardy to Halifax, Nov. 27, 1755, Pargellis, *Military Affairs in North America,* 149-53.

47. Pownall does not seem to have known the motives of Shirley's opponents. His own eyes were on political patronage in England where he hoped to establish himself as an expert on colonial affairs. *The Boston Weekly News-Letter,* Feb. 5, 1756.

XII

Patronage Lost

THE YEAR 1756 marked a turning point in the French and Indian War, and in the life of William Shirley. For twenty-six years the Governor had managed to win the Duke of Newcastle's patronage. Sometimes he had waited for the Duke's favor, often he had altered his ambitions to suit Newcastle's plans, but he was always successful in getting something. He had a spectacular record in gaining patronage and as remarkable a one in extending patronage to the merchants of Massachusetts; war had given him and Newcastle rich prizes to distribute. Their partnership had weathered the difficulties of time extraordinarily well. Now, however, the Newcastle ministry was faced with a military situation in America where victory was essential for the future stability of the regime. No longer was the American conflict considered a battle of containment. Politicians in England were putting pressure upon Newcastle to end that pretense and turn back the tide of French encroachments. For this important task, Shirley was a liability to the ministry. He was party to a quarrel with Johnson, whose cooperation was essential in Indian affairs; he was involved in the intercolonial rivalry of New York and Massachusetts; he was abused and denounced by powerful colonial leaders.[1]

Although Shirley had taken precautions to defend his military program, he had not realized that he desperately needed the help of an able spokesman with the home government. The loss of his sons William and Jack had forced him to turn

1. Belcher to Hardwicke, Dec. 8, 1755, Add. MSS, 35909, fol. 215; *Pa. Archives*, 1st Ser., II, 537-38, 569-70; Shirley to Fox, Jan. 12 and 13, 1756; W.O. 1, 4, pt. 1, 42-52, 65-68; Johnson to Robinson, Jan. 17, 1756, C. O. 5/ 46, 398-402; *Boston Gazette*, Feb. 2 and 9, 1756.

to John Rutherfurd of New York, a member of the New York
Council, captain in the British army, and an observer of the
Crown Point expedition who understood the politics of cam-
paigning in America far better than the politics of patronage
in England. To assist Rutherfurd, Shirley relied upon help
from Thomlinson, Bollan, and Newcastle. He did not know
that Newcastle had agreed to replace him as military commander and turn over the supply of American forces to certain
British and New York merchants, with Kilby as a prominent
leader of the group.[2]

Though Shirley was unaware of his changing relations
with the Duke, he nevertheless sized up his military career as
a temporary one and prepared for his successor. His tasks
in the meantime were to anticipate future military needs, unify
the army, and make the best political use of an interim position. One of his first duties was to incorporate the officers of
Braddock's army into his own. He had great difficulty during the summer and fall of 1755 securing the cooperation of
these officers;[3] as a nonprofessional soldier he was unable to
command their loyalty and respect. But with the arrival of
his commission from London, there was no doubt of his authority to issue commands. He placed the blunt spoken Sir
John St. Clair in charge of army supplies at Albany, where he
had already ordered Robert Leake to supervise transport and
housing. He gave John Bradstreet the responsibility for transportation between Albany and Oswego, with supervision over
Petri and Stevenson. To avoid the rivalry between contractors
for the British and colonial armies, he urged the Massachusetts
legislature to transfer supply of its troops from the Albany merchants to a special legislative committee and agreed to the
appointment of John Choate as its chairman. Besides this
appointment, Shirley had the sorrowful duty of selecting a new
personal secretary to replace his son Jack. Though he wanted
Alexander to assume these duties, "Billy" was too burdened

2. Baxter, *The House of Hancock*, 136; Treasury proceedings, Mar. 11,
1756, Add. MSS, 35909, fol. 223; Baker-Kilby contract, Mar. 26, 1756, *ibid.*,
fol. 233.
3. St. Clair to ———, Feb. 23, 1756, C. O. 5/46, 426; Warrent for St.
Clair, Feb. 24, 1756, Sterling Papers, II.

with other work. Shirley then chose James Bradford, a talented young man of good family and political connections.[4]

Shirley's arrival in Boston momentarily interrupted this military business. He was afforded the unusual honor of a legislative escort from Province House to the State House, where he was asked to survey the military situation for the legislature. Pepperrell saluted him warmly: "We attribute the preservation of the fort at *Oswego*, and the continuance of his Majesty's possession of the Lake *Ontario*, and the country adjacent, next under GOD, to the care and vigilance of your Excellency."[5]

Though the Governor's response on this occasion was not recorded, he later sent a statement of his 1756 plans to the legislature. In explaining the military situation he took great care to stress the defensive nature of the campaign, which was undertaken, he said, to anticipate future French aggression: "We have . . . great reason, *Gentlemen*, to think it happy that the *French* have been hitherto frustrated in these enterprises . . . . But as we have at the same time the utmost reason to expect . . . that France will endeavour soon to land more regular troops in *North-America*, and exert the whole strength of *Canada* this year, from their encroachments at *Crown-Point*, Fort *Cadaraqui*, and *Niagara*, against our western frontiers, it highly behoves us to lose no time in making the necessary preparations."[6]

The 1756 battle plans were not entirely satisfactory to the legislature. Limited warfare and military spending had the twin disadvantages of inconclusiveness and high taxes. Boston's commercial interests valued the increased war trade, and the majority leadership in the legislature supported an aggressive attack upon Canada. They subscribed to the message of a Boston correspondent of *Read's Weekly Journal* when he asserted that the "chief things we want here are money and a liberty to act. [If] these things are granted . . . , there would

4. Shirley's orders for Livingston and Morris, Jan. 14, 1756, Loudoun Papers, 780; Supplementary contracts, *ibid.*, 486; Shirley to Bradstreet, Mar. 17, 1756, C. O. 5/47, 115-19.
5. *Mass. House Journals*, XXXII, pt. 2, 305.
6. *Ibid.*, 497.

not be a Frenchman, or an Indian in America, near enough to annoy us."[7] But they wanted England to foot the bill. They desired a subsidy that would make the prosecution of the war easy, and for the present they urged Shirley to finance their mobilization. The idea apparently came from Bollan, who had heard rumors in England of a British subsidy and believed that Shirley was authorized to assume some of the burden of the colonial mobilization. Although Shirley assured the legislators that he had no power to divert his military funds in this way, their continual insistence forced him to weigh the value of a colonial army against a violation of his military instructions, and he finally granted their request to draw £30,000 from his funds. Once the precedent was set, other colonies were quick to petition for loans.[8]

Some legislators, worried about the employment of troops to garrison posts in Nova Scotia and New York, raised the question of the colony's good faith in keeping the men from their families.[9] Other legislators were concerned over leadership of the colonial army in the forthcoming campaign. Shirley proposed to send Americans against Crown Point, but no one wanted them placed under Johnson. His record at Lake George was so bitterly criticized in the Boston papers that Shirley himself urged moderation: "I have never been fond of any unnecessary restraints upon the press, but pieces of this sort . . . should at all times be discouraged."[10]

For commander of the new expedition Winslow and Pepperrell were high on Shirley's list of candidates. He finally named Winslow to the post, probably because Pepperrell was lame and aging. In drawing up Winslow's commission, he made certain that as governor he would have control of the commander; he did not intend to fight another Johnson.[11]

7. *Read's Weekly Journal*, Aug. 23, 1755; Shirley to House, Feb. 7, 1756, Mass. Archives, CIX, 210-11.
8. Shirley to House, Feb. 14, 1756, Mass. Archives, CIX, 218-19; James Otis to James Otis, Jr., Feb. 29, 1756, Otis MSS, I, 132; War Records, VI, 29, Conn. Archives.
9. Shirley to Lawrence, Feb. ——, 1756, Akins, ed., *Public Documents of Nova Scotia*, 421-28; *Mass. House Journals*, XXXII, pt. 2, 315-16.
10. Mass. Archives, CIX, 244.
11. Proceedings of the General Court, Feb. 16 to Mar. 4, 1756, Loudoun

For the manpower of the expedition, he promised to help Winslow raise 7,500 men from the northern colonies. Whether that many men could be recruited depended on the good will of the local officials and the continued enthusiasm of the people. A good sign for the future was the better spirit in New York. Governor Hardy, despite his apparent friendship for the de Lanceys, favored the national interest and promised his fullest cooperation.[12]

Shirley placed the responsibility for the Crown Point expedition upon the northern colonies, while he amassed regular troops at Oswego for the various assaults in the Great Lakes region. Though separate military organizations, the attacking forces would cooperate in buying supplies and using the Albany warehouses. He hoped that southern colonies would take over the attack on Fort Duquesne, and he asked the governors of Maryland, Pennsylvania, and Virginia to support an expedition into the Ohio Valley. The response was discouraging. Shirley tried to inspire confidence by appointing a southern governor, Horatio Sharpe of Maryland, as leader of the expedition, but he found Sharpe lacking in vision and unwilling to lead an army unless he had guarantees of funds, arms, and men. Shirley had nothing to offer except encouragement and example—which were not enough for the southern governors, who had never enjoyed the support of their people that Shirley had experienced in Massachusetts.[13]

In contrast with the south, the north was full of activity. Lawrence, the energetic and resourceful governor of Nova Scotia, was strengthening the colony. He was using the New England troops raised in 1755 to garrison the forts and remove Acadians from strategic defense areas. However, the troops' enlistment period would soon end, and complications had arisen. Lawrence wanted to hold them until the regular

Papers, 759; Shirley to Fox, Mar. 8, 1756, W.O. 34, 73, 149-50; Pepperrell to Fox, 1756, C. O. 5/46, 430-31. Apparently Pepperrell was chosen first to lead the Crown Point campaign, but then was removed because of his health.

12. Hardy to Shirley, Mar. 21, 1756, Mass. Archives, IV, 549-50; Shirley to Hardy, Mar. 17, 1756, ibid., 547-48.

13. Pa. Archives, 1st Ser., II, 587-92; Shirley to Sharpe, Mar. 5, 1756, W.O. 1, 4, pt. 1, 109-10.

regiments replacing them were filled to full strength; in fact, he suggested forcing men from the New England irregulars into the regular army. News of this proposal reached an alarmed Massachusetts legislature which quickly conveyed its feelings to Shirley. He, in turn, had to warn Lawrence that the New Englanders should be returned home because, to do otherwise, "would be a violation of his Majesty's faith with the soldier."[14] Shirley, nevertheless, realized that Lawrence needed men, and he was able to turn the crisis only by adopting the unpopular expedient of permitting army recruiting officers to enlist indentured servants. This was done at the risk of riots in Philadelphia and over the protests of Governor Morris.

With the release of the New England veterans, the legislature relaxed its pressure on Shirley, and he gave his full energy to readying the British army for the Great Lake campaign. He put provisioning again into the hands of Livingston, Morris, and Erving. Their work was simplified by his decision to transfer the responsibilities of transportation to the army. St. Clair and Bradstreet undertook these duties.[15]

Part of the provisioning arrangements were concerned with items for Shirley's military table. Letters from Alexander, ordering these materials for the table, show that the General had no intention of allowing frontier conditions to disturb his diet. They account too for his increasing tendency to put on weight, despite the exertion of military life: "The list I mentioned in my last is now enclosed: coffee, chocolate, sugar, anchovies, capers, olives, pepper, mustard, oil, vinegar, and other spices, hams, beef, tongue, port, rice, butter, cheese, flour, bisket, raisens, figs, currants, prunes, ketchup, soap, Indian sweetmeats, limes, lemons, Jamaica rum, Madeira, twenty dozen, English beer, etc. . . . The General's table should always be set for fourteen persons."[16]

14. Shirley to Lawrence, Mar. 13, 1756, Akins, ed., *Public Documents of Nova Scotia*, 429-31; Shirley to Morris, Feb. 20 (two letters), 23, and 29, 1756, *Pa. Archives*, 1st Ser., II, 578, 579, 582, 587.

15. St. Clair to ———, Feb. 23, 1756, C. O. 5/46, 426.

16. Livingston Rutherfurd, *Family Records and Events* (New York, 1894), 65, 67.

The most serious military problems concerned Indian activity along the Oswego route and the difficulty of supplying the British garrison at that post. In late winter forts along the route were assaulted, their occupants butchered, and their bodies burned. William Johnson investigated the disasters for Shirley, but little could be done except to reprimand William Williams for constructing a defective fort and not maintaining proper defenses in the area.[17] News of the massacre aroused Shirley's interest in the welfare of the soldiers garrisoned at Oswego. The long winter of isolation had eroded morale, and shortages of food had increased the normally high death rate of garrisoned soldiers. The reports of death and disease made it apparent to Shirley that Williams had ignored his repeated orders of October and November to furnish supplies. Despite orders to the contrary, he had left his post and had not returned to duty until February. He remained insensitive to the crisis at Oswego until Mercer, the garrison's commander, made heroic efforts to drag supplies through the wet snow from various forts along the carriage route, and Governor Hardy organized a relief party.[18]

Shirley sent Bradstreet and Johnson to strengthen defenses along the carriage route and ordered an engineer to Oswego to inspect the fortifications. Through April and May, supplies, laborers, and armaments were rushed to prepare the fort for the coming campaign. In addition, three ranger companies were formed in May to assist Johnson's Indian auxiliaries. These, together with some regular troops, convoyed forces and guaranteed the safety of the route. By May 15, one of de Lancey's friends, Daniel Claus, pronounced Oswego "in a tolerable situation" and "shall do well enough this summer if the French don't plague our provision bateaux too much."[19]

17. Johnson to William Williams, Mar. 12, 1756, Williams Papers; Shirley to Lawrence, Mar. 13, 1756, Akins, ed., *Public Documents of Nova Scotia*, 428-37; Emerson to Osborn, Mar. 18, 1756, Shirley to House, Apr. 1, 1756, LV, 147, CIX, 255, Mass. Archives; *William Johnson Papers*, IX, 434. Apparently Williams had totally forgotten his duty during these winter months. His first letter on his return does not even mention Oswego and reveals that his trip was a "merry one."

18. Mercer to Williams, Mar. 14, 1756, C. O. 5/46, 236; Hardy to Johnson, Mar. 12, 1756, Loudoun Papers, 911.

19. *William Johnson Papers*, II, 435-62 and IX, 395-445; Williams to

I

While the American mobilization was taking form, the English ministry pondered the 1756 campaign. Little had been done since Shirley's appointment as Braddock's successor. Questions of domestic politics, strategy, diplomacy, and economy delayed military decision. Lord Hardwicke, like Lords Halifax and Newcastle, favored an enlarged assault upon French bases and believed "the reduction of Montreal and Quebec" should be the ultimate objective, but Newcastle was undecided about the importance of these engagements if a general European war should break out. King George II also entered the debate by raising the question of Hanoverian defense. Since he was the elector of that country, he saw British (and Hanoverian) security in the maintenance of European alliances and not in a war of conquest in America.[20]

As the debate continued, letters from America flooded the home offices. The criticisms of Shirley's conduct convinced the leading ministers that a change of command was absolutely necessary. Lord Halifax, in particular, believed the reports of his friend Thomas Pownall and exerted his influence upon the Secretary of State.[21] Other events also conspired against Shirley. British intelligence officers had discovered letters passing between the former French ambassador and someone in Pennsylvania who had inside knowledge of military planning.[22] A few officials suspected Shirley of writing these letters, for he was married to a Frenchwoman and had contacts in Paris; others concluded he was at least careless with official secrets. The Duke of Cumberland, the King's son, favored bringing him home in chains; Henry Fox considered him a blunderer who should be relieved of all responsibility. Lord Halifax, under the influence of the Pownall brothers,

Shirley, Apr. 12, 1756, Williams Papers, I, 176; Read's testimony, Sept. 15, 1756, C. O. 5/47, 755-59.

20. Hardwicke Papers, Add. MSS, 35909, fol. 208.

21. William S. Johnson to Samuel Johnson, Jan. 9, 1756, Johnson Papers, Conn. Hist. Soc.; Hardy to Halifax, Nov. 27, 1755, Cumberland Papers, Box 46, fol. 101.

22. Halifax to Hardy, Mar. 19, 1756, Loudoun Papers, 950; Nicholas B. Wainwright, *George Croghan: Wilderness Diplomat* (Chapel Hill, 1959), 106-9.

was angry and bewildered. All he knew of Shirley's prior conduct contradicted these accusations, but he would not un-
equivocally defend him. He explained the investigation of
the intercepted letters to Governor Hardy: "I greatly dislike
his [Shirley's] present behavior . . . fomenting disputes, promoting ineffectual inquiries, and countenancing a paper war
against your province. . . . Orders are given for his return to
England as soon as possible, and the reason given for it, is,
that he may be consulted on several matters relative to the
King's service in America."[23]

Though an investigation of many months had turned up
nothing, the treasonous correspondence reinforced the ministry's decision to recall Shirley. It chose a new commander
and formulated new war plans. The details of campaign took
an inordinate amount of time, but resulted in the full establishment of an American military command. The new general, John Campbell, the Earl of Loudoun, was given a staff
of two generals (James Abercromby and Daniel Webb), regular troops, and substantial money. A generous provision contract was also provided which, among other things, took paper
work from his hands.[24] The completion of their military arrangements held Loudoun and his assistants in England until
late spring, though Webb was expected to relieve Shirley of
his command while Loudoun was concluding business in England. Apparently there was considerable argument about the
financial details of the campaign: the firms to contract supplies, the margin of profits, and the management of military
funds. Shirley's own procedures were thoroughly analyzed
and generally defended. When Thomas Pownall arrived in
London, however, he proceeded to denounce Shirley's contractors, and so damaging were his assertions, according to an
observer, that John Rutherfurd was helpless in defending

23. Halifax to Hardy, Mar. 31, 1756, Loudoun Papers, 987. "No suspicion
at all attends Mr. Shirley, but many particulars of the last year's transactions
are highly disapproved."
24. Stanley Pargellis, *Lord Loudoun in North America* (New Haven,
1933), chap. II. Mr. Pargellis has a harsher interpretation of Shirley for
this period. His older, though scholarly work should be compared with
Mr. Lawrence H. Gipson's recent analysis, *The British Empire Before the
American Revolution*, VI, chaps. VI and VII.

them. In the end, the firm of Baker-Kilby won the contract,
and, worse still for Shirley's merchant allies, military business
was transferred to New York, where Oliver de Lancey and his
associates became local agents for the Baker-Kilby company.[25]
These negotiations not only kept Loudoun in the capital
longer than he had expected, but held Webb there too; during the interval Shirley remained in charge of military affairs
in America.

II

Shirley's agents gave him the first reports of these transactions in April. He had been informed that a change in his
position was pending and that he would be transferred to the
governorship of Jamaica, but he did not realize the full significance of what was happening in London until late April. The
news hurt him deeply, though he was determined to push the
"preparations for both expeditions [Crown Point and the Great
Lakes] with as much vigour as I was doing it before."[26] Governor Morris, in consoling him, warned that "your adversaries
. . . will take a pride in impeding any operations."[27] Certainly
they rejoiced. The de Lanceys spread the great news of his
recall; Hancock applied to Kilby for a contract; and Shirley's
enemies converged on New York in order to wait upon the
new commander.[28]

The delayed arrival of the British generals was used as an
excuse for colonial authorities to slow their preparations. Even
Massachusetts postponed sending her men and materiel to Albany. Soldier morale was low, and the townsmen of Albany,
ever mindful of imperial politics, did not fire a salute when
Shirley arrived in the town.[29] In spite of his own feelings, he
conscientiously worked to finish the job. He ordered more
rangers to guard the supply route to Oswego; he reconsidered
Indian relations in the light of the recent massacres; he hastened additional provisions westward to the Oswego garrison.

25. De Lancey to Abercromby, July 1, 1756, Loudoun Papers, 1273;
Abercromby to Loudoun, July 5, 1756, *ibid.*, 1288.
26. Shirley to Morris, Apr. 18, 1756, *Pa. Archives*, 1st Ser., II, 630.
27. Shirley to Morris, Apr. 25, 1756, *ibid.*, 644.
28. *William Johnson Papers*, II, 441.
29. *Ibid.*, II, 471.

For the Crown Point expedition, he obtained cannon and shot
from Castle William and surveyed military discipline. Since
desertions from the regular army were heavy, he sanctioned
whippings and hangings to tighten authority. He gave his
attention to deficiencies in the colonial levies, which were 1,200
short of their estimated strength, with 500 of that shortage
attributed to Massachusetts. In trying to remedy this situation, he hurried messages to his fellow governors and exhorted
Secretary Willard to hasten the colony's recruits to Albany.
He seemed to emphasize his absolute sincerity: "I look upon
our success in this expedition to be so essential to the welfare
of the province that my heart is extremely engaged in it."[30]

The mobilization continued to absorb Shirley's energy as
he labored on without real authority and haunted by his disgrace. By May 25, he had become so depressed about the delay in Loudoun's arrival that he convened a military council.
He was concerned about the security of Oswego and was convinced that two military expeditions at this time were impractical because of deficiencies in both the colonial and regular regiments. The Crown Point expedition needed help from
British regulars.[31] Without hesitation the military council
concurred in his recommendations. He would use the available British forces to support the Crown Point expedition and
would do everything he could to keep the Oswego route open.
The merger of colonial and regular troops raised a touchy issue
of military discipline, but he relied upon Winslow's good
judgment to avoid an incident.

Four days after the council adjourned, Shirley had a copy
of its transactions in the hands of Governor Hardy, and together with this document he sent a letter asking for the
Governor's cooperation in managing the campaign.[32] A few
days later Hardy received as a house guest Daniel Webb, who
was long awaited as Shirley's interim successor. It is reasonable to assume that Webb was shown these reports and prob-

30. Mass. Archives, LV, 156-57; Shirley to Adams, May 15, 1756, W.O.
34, 76, 23.
31. Council of War, May 25, 1756, W.O. 1, 4, 76-81; C. O. 5/46, 537-46.
32. Shirley to Hardy, May 27, 1756, Loudoun Papers, 1183.

ably given the Governor's analysis of their contents. Webb did not leave New York City, but awaited the arrival of General Abercromby, Loudoun's second-in-command; they then traveled together to Albany.

They arrived on the hot afternoon of June 25. Virtually the last act of Shirley's command that day had been the court martial and execution of a notorious deserter. The white-clad body was still hanging when Abercromby took formal command of the troops. Abercromby asked Shirley to prepare a written survey of the military situation, which he did in a lengthy letter on the 27th and in a shorter one dated the 28th. Both later became subjects of controversy. Though the regimental lists were incomplete, Shirley turned them over to the new commander and promised a report on Oswego's fortifications from James Mackellar, the engineer. On the 29th he attended a military council meeting in which the Crown Point expedition was fully discussed. Abercromby concurred in his plans, permitting the regulars to take supporting positions in the campaign. Except for the intense heat that made camp life nearly unbearable, these terminal arrangements went off smoothly for Shirley, although Abercromby was inclined to deprecate, as a military man would, the value of a civilian's reports and services.[33]

Between June 29 and July 22, when Loudoun arrived in New York, military affairs deteriorated. The carriage route between Albany and Oswego was pierced several times by enemy forces. An attack on July 2 or 3 by a French army of 500 men aroused Albany and was the probable reason for a military council on July 16, which considered a report from Mackellar on Oswego's fortifications and a letter from Colonel Mercer of the Oswego garrison.[34] These reports generally supported Shirley's earlier statement at the time of his retirement that the garrison could not put up a successful fight if the town was attacked: "It is likewise probable from their [the

33. Abercromby to Loudoun, June 25, 1756, *ibid.*, 1263.
34. Craven to Shirley, June 28, 1756, *ibid.*; Choate to Osborn, July 12, 1756, Mass. Archives, LV, 374; Mercer to Shirley, July 22, 1756, C. O. 5/47, 167-69.

regiment's] sickness, fatigue of duty through frequent alarms, and their being posted at different places, they may not be so well disciplined as might otherwise have been expected."[35] His warning standing by itself was clear enough, but there was repeated evidence of a serious military crisis, and still no action was taken. On July 22 Mercer again stressed the danger of attack; on August 3 Abercromby summarized the latest reports from Oswego by saying that the post was in a "bad state."[36] Even the *New-York Mercury,* on August 2, had in its possession information that warned of an impending attack on Oswego by 1,200 French and Indians.[37] In short, the crisis at Lake Ontario was well known to everyone from the time Abercromby took over as acting commander-in-chief.

While this crisis was developing, Shirley left for New York City, where he had promised to meet Lord Loudoun.[38] Loudoun's ship did not arrive for three weeks, and Shirley busied himself putting his accounts in order. There were many bills outstanding; he had been short of funds all spring due to his loans to the colonial governments, and the contractors had been obliged to extend credit for £15,000.[39] There was additional confusion over the advance purchasing of supplies for the British army. Other merchants were now in charge, and the stores purchased by Shirley's contractors were held in warehouses pending an agreement with the new agents, who were represented by Oliver de Lancey, the local correspondent of Baker-Kilby. De Lancey, not unexpectedly, rejoiced in using his power. He refused to accept any general purchase of the supplies, but he had them studiously examined, caustically criticized, and hesitantly purchased, with the result that the Albany regiments were starved for weeks.[40] It added to Shir-

35. Shirley to Abercromby, June 27, 1756, W.O. 1, 4, 129-43 and June 28, 1756, Loudoun Papers, 1258.

36. Abercromby to Loudoun, Aug. 3, 1756, C. O. 5/47, 53-58.

37. *The New-York Mercury,* Aug. 2, 1756.

38. Shirley to Morris, July 5, 1756, *Pa. Archives,* 1st Ser., II, 693; Shirley to Fox, July 4, 1756, C. O. 5/46, 557-62.

39. Memorial of Livingston and Morris, Dec. 15, 1756, Sterling Papers, II.

40. Bradstreet to Shirley, July 24, 1756, W.O. 1, 4, 188; Choate to Committee of War, June 14, 1756, Mass. Archives, LV, 321; Shirley to Admiralty, Sept. 7, 1756, Admiralty Records, I, 3818, 373-75; Deposition of John Murray, Sept. 4, 1756, C. O. 5/46, 337-38.

ley's embarrassment that de Lancey found many barrels of salt pork and dried peas of inferior quality and challenged the prices of other supplies. At Shirley's request, Governor Hardy appointed a committee of merchants to review some of his military accounts. Though their report was encouraging, Shirley knew that the laborious work of passing the accounts through the Treasury lay ahead of him. Uncertain whether he could stand the strain without assistance, he planned to take William Alexander with him to England.

Recall was hard for him to face when rumors persisted that he was going home in disgrace. Secretary Fox had promised him the governorship of Jamaica, the best patronage in America, but no commission had arrived and nothing more was said of it. In a letter to the governor of Rhode Island, Shirley tried to put a good face on his recall: "I have the pleasure of being acquainted . . . that the disposition his Majesty has thought proper to make of the command of his forces in North America, is not owing to any dissatisfaction with my services; but on the contrary, it is the King's intention to give me a new mark of his royal favor." He solicited letters of commendation from Governors Sharpe and Morris, and the kindly Morris responded with words of warm praise that, as Shirley admitted, gave him "great consolation."[41]

Early in the morning of July 23, Shirley watched Lord Loudoun enter New York City amid a display of pageantry and excitement that contrasted sharply with his own declining fortunes. Their meeting later in the day was cordial, but Loudoun asked so many questions that there was little time for any social pleasantries.[42] Shirley saw friends of the de Lanceys everywhere. In Loudoun's personal staff was Thomas Pownall, the "Secretary Extraordinary," who was acting in the role of political advisor and was rumored to be the next governor of Massachusetts.[43]

Shirley had long trained himself to disguise his feelings, and few people knew his sorrow on this occasion. Benjamin

41. *Shirley Correspondence*, II, 483-85.
42. Shirley to Loudon, July 23, 1756, Loudoun Papers, 1335, 1336, 1337, and July 26, 1756, *ibid.*, 1363.
43. See my *Thomas Pownall: British Defender of American Liberty*, 74-75.

Franklin, who studied him during these trying hours, described his reaction: "I was at the entertainment given by the city of New York to Lord Loudoun on his taking upon him the command. Shirley, though thereby superseded, was present also. There was a great company of officers, citizens, and strangers, and some chairs having been borrowed in the neighborhood, there was one among them very low, which fell to the lot of Mr. Shirley. Perceiving it as I sat by him, I said: 'they have given you, Sir, too low a seat.' 'No matter,' said he, 'Mr. Franklin, I find a low seat the easiest.' "[44]

After Loudoun left for Albany, Shirley returned to Boston, expecting to stay a few weeks while his private affairs were put in order and then sail for England. He must have been cheered by the reception that greeted him in one of his darkest hours. An informal celebration brought thousands of people into the streets, and Castle William sounded its familiar salute. His official residence was again filled with the procession of clergy, educators, business people, and legislators; and he, ever gracious, let it be known that he was soon to be honored by the King with a greater preferment.[45]

III

Not long after Shirley's return to Boston, French forces seized Oswego. Abigail Dwight, writing to her brother, tried to put into words the feeling of Bostonians: "Our wisdom is become folly, our councils confusion—light darkness—our country and its cause sinking. . . . Surely it should now be the whole business of the whole country, and every individual to espouse the common cause with all the warmth, life, activity, resolution, that ever fired a Roman breast—to save themselves, their posterity, and precious liberties of Protestants."[46]

44. Bigelow, ed., *The Works of Benjamin Franklin*, I, 302.
45. Fox to Shirley, Mar. 13, 1756 (two letters), Loudoun Papers, 915 and W.O. 34, 71, 64-66. Fox promised Shirley the Jamaican governorship, but instructed him to remain at Boston until Loudoun's arrival in America.
46. Abigail Dwight to Joseph(?) Dwight, Sept. 28, 1756, Sedgwick Papers, II.

Another observer noted that many people reacted as if the occasion were "something like the end of the world."[47]

The fall of Oswego was a blow to Loudoun, who apparently had not anticipated a serious crisis. Though there were sufficient danger signs everywhere—even members of his official family were aware of the peril of French attack—he had not believed that the fort would collapse so soon.[48] He had initiated precautionary measures to strengthen the post, but they were taken too late. His attention had been upon other matters. Surrounded as he was by Pownall, Kilby, and the de Lanceys, he was enmeshed in problems of military organization, finance, and discipline. Everywhere he turned he was annoyed by Shirley's policies, which violated the usual military way of doing things. His sense of procedure was offended time and time again, until he suspected Shirley of intentionally muddling military affairs.[49] The Oswego disaster convinced Loudoun, without much evidence except his belief in proper military conduct, that Shirley had done nothing but confuse the North American command. He decided to investigate and send whatever documentary evidence he could find to the ministry. In August, September, and October he and his staff took depositions and gathered their evidence. Loudoun boasted to Halifax, "I think I shall be able to send as much in relation to Oswego alone as will hang him, as an officer."[50]

Shirley was dismayed by the fall of Oswego. Many of the men killed and captured were soldiers of his regiment; many were from Pepperrell's regiment of New Englanders. He also saw his plans for 1756 threatened by the paralysis of the high command and urged Winslow to proceed at once with the colonial campaign against Crown Point. But Loudoun was extremely hesitant about the fighting qualities of militiamen and put off the Crown Point campaign from week to week until one Bostonian wrote in anguish: "I hear nothing from the army

47. Choate to Osborn, Aug. 23, 1756, Mass. Archives, LV, 334.
48. Pownall to Halifax, Aug. 7, 1756, Personal Papers, Lib. Cong.; Abercromby to Loudoun, Aug. 3, 1756, C. O. 5/47, 27-29.
49. Loudoun to Fox, Aug. 16, 1756, C. O. 5/47, 15; Loudoun to Barrington, Aug. 20, 1756, W.O. 1, 4, pt. 2, 181-82.
50. Loudoun to Halifax, Oct. 3, 1756, Loudoun Papers, 1956.

when they are likely to go forward, or whether at all. . . .
Many are of [the] opinion that nothing will be done this summer but hope they may be mistaken."[51] Instead of making a
firm decision, Loudoun kept Winslow traveling back and forth
between Lake George and Albany until the lateness of the
season ruled out the campaign.[52]

Shirley tried to turn the tide of gloom and despair, but
was bluntly told to mind his own business and leave the colony
to his successor.[53] Though none was then appointed, Pownall advertised himself as Shirley's successor, and Loudoun
had the temerity to address the official military correspondence
to the "Governor of Massachusetts," naming no individual
and implying that Shirley was no longer acting in that capacity.[54] Shirley and Loudoun clashed on almost every significant issue—the granting of military commissions, contracting,
provisioning, and the causes of Oswego's capture. Loudoun
was particularly incensed over Shirley's last-minute appointments as military commander, claiming that his power had
ceased in January. Shirley answered that such a position was
at best ridiculous, because a "great hurt must certainly have
happened to his Majesty's service, if all preparations for the
ensuing campaign had been stopped from the time of your
Lordship's commission."[55]

Nor was Shirley content to debate issues with the commander. He took depositions which supported his position
that the confusion at Albany and New York was due to
Oliver de Lancey and the other contractors.[56] He even secured
evidence that British forces arrived too late to save Oswego
because they were held too long near Albany while de Lancey
inspected the Livingston-Morris supplies.[57] His evidence was

---

51. Winslow to Fox, Dec. 30, 1756, C. O. 5/46, 455-58.
52. Choate to Osborn, Aug. 30, 1756, *ibid.*, 441-42.
53. Loudoun to Shirley, Sept. 6, 1756, W.O. 1, 4, 333-34.
54. Loudoun to Shirley, Aug. 29, 1756, *ibid.*, 221-22.
55. Shirley to Loudoun, Sept. 12, 1756, C. O. 5/46, 623-27; Shirley to
Barrington, Sept. 15, 1756, W.O. 1, 4, 353-56.
56. Shirley to Admiralty, Sept. 7, 1756, Admiralty Records, I, 3818, 373-76;
Shirley to Barrington, Sept. 16, 1756, W.O. 1, 4, 357-64; Shirley to Halifax,
Sept. 5, 1756, Mass. Papers, N. Y. Pub. Lib.
57. Bradstreet to Shirley, July 24, 1756, C. O. 5/46, 348; Deposition of
John Murray, Sept. 4, 1756, *ibid.*, 337-39.

especially damaging to the reputations of Abercromby and Webb, and it was reinforced by their anxiety to explain it away. In one letter to Loudoun, Shirley warned the commander-in-chief that he would never know the truth of military operations while he was surrounded by prejudiced men.[58]

While these arguments continued, Shirley put his personal and public affairs in order: he raised more men for Winslow's army, secured stand-by instructions for the mobilization of 1,000 militiamen in the event of an invasion, and filled fifty-nine vacancies in the civil administration. His conduct throughout his stay in Boston was generally discreet. He did not arouse any unusual opposition to Loudoun—though he had opportunities to do so[59]—and he took the trouble to explain the circumstances of his recall as clearly to the legislature as he himself understood them. He participated in farewell receptions and accepted the praise and acclaim of the people. From Loudoun's letters, however, he extracted the extravagant charges made against him and answered them, with copies and covering letters for the secretaries of state and war.[60] By October he was ready to sail for London. Within days of his departure, Pownall embarked from New York to press the commander-in-chief's charges against him and secure the Massachusetts governorship.

IV

When Shirley arrived in the capital, he found politics drastically changed. His friend and patron Newcastle, after

58. Shirley to Loudoun, Sept. 4, 1756, *Shirley Correspondence*, II, 536-41 and Sept. 12, 1756, C. O. 5/46, 653-55.

59. Shirley to Loudoun, Sept. 3, 1756, *Shirley Correspondence*, II, 528-31; Shirley to Halifax, Sept. 5, 1756, Mass. Papers, N. Y. Pub. Lib.; *Mass. House Journals*, XXXIII, pt. 1, 130-31, 138-39, 141. Not all legislation went off smoothly. John Tyng, friend of Waldo and successor of Allen, criticized the Governor so harshly that his supporters felt duty bound to punish the Boston representative. Tyng was compelled to apologize to the chair (*ibid.*, 127-28).

60. *Shirley Correspondence*, II, 563-76; *The Boston Evening-Post*, Oct. 4, 1756; *Boston Gazette*, Sept. 20 and 27, 1756. Robert Hale's power during these transition months between the Shirley and Pownall administrations was so considerable that he was selected to join Pepperrell and Hutchinson in welcoming Lord Loudoun to Boston. Hale, however, refused the honor, probably out of respect for Shirley. See *Mass. House Journals*, XXXIII, pt. 1, 196, 228.

twenty-four years in office, had resigned his post, and most of the Newcastle Whigs opposed the new government headed by the Duke of Devonshire and dominated by William Pitt. These shifts in leadership resulted from the staggering losses of war in America and Europe, of which Braddock's defeat in 1755 and the seizure of Minorca in 1756 were the most crucial.

Shirley was cordially received by Newcastle's friends—Holderness, Barrington, Cumberland, Hardwicke, and Halifax—but their control of patronage was limited. Besides, they were committed to the support of Lord Loudoun, their appointee and client, and were not ready to see Shirley returned to any North American governorship. Shirley found himself in the peculiar position of having many friends who were restrained from helping him by consideration of larger political issues.

In addition, he had to counteract the influence of Pownall, whose energetic opposition to his command had a strong effect. Pownall, however, discovered that Newcastle and Cumberland were not going to court-martial the former governor. They were embarrassed by British military defeats and not sympathetic to further exposure of dubious military decisions. Pownall was surprised to find that Henry Fox would not even receive him and that his commission as governor of Massachusetts had not been signed.[61] He was unable to turn Newcastle against Shirley. Time and again he was irritated to meet the Governor at the same levees.[62]

Shirley persisted in rebutting Loudoun's arguments; he was especially determined to answer the complaint that he had abused his power of appointment. In January and February 1757, he put before Lord Barrington, the secretary at war, voluminous papers that showed the dates of commissions, the persons he had commissioned, and the power under which he had acted. He claimed that he had power to appoint officers until he was superseded by Abercromby, the acting military commander for Loudoun, in June 1756. To support his position he provided statements from Thomas Gage and William Alexander and offered this explanation:

61. Pownall to Loudoun, Jan. 3, 1757, Loudoun Papers, 2629.
62. Shirley to Pitt, Jan. 7, 1757, C. O. 30/8, 56.

Some vacant posts, which I understand have been filled up from the war office, were filled up likewise with commissions from me, particularly the post of Mr. Bristow, first apothecary of the hospital, and an ensigncy in the 40th regiment, which I gave to one Mr. Stevens, a volunteer who behaved remarkably well, and was much wounded at the Monongahela, which are the only instances, that I remember to have heard of. But as I had express power given me by the King's commission to fill them up and did not know that commissions would be made out for them here, I hope I shall not be blamed on that account.[63]

Shirley believed that he was on sound ground. To expect him to stop commissioning officers from January 1756 until he was superseded in June was unreasonable. Charges of misconduct based on such evidence appeared to him foolish, and the fact that they were made was a subject for military investigation. "Every person," he wrote Lord Barrington, "of common right is entitled to exculpate himself by his own assertion against the bare accusation of another without proof; and I can't but hope, that the rank, in which I have had the honor to serve his Majesty, and the character, I have maintained in it for many years, entitle me to that right in the present case."[64]

The Governor's dignified plea impressed Barrington, and he responded by ordering a court of inquiry. Before the court convened, Shirley was summoned as an expert witness before a parliamentary committee investigating Loudoun's contracting. The Baker-Kilby agreement was denounced by Charles Townshend, a member of Pitt's government, for its high schedule of charges, and in the course of the inquiry comparisons were made with the Livingston-Morris contract of 1755. Shirley welcomed the chance to defend himself, putting before the committee a selection of his personal records. In doing this, he placed himself in a most delicate position, with an excellent opportunity to explain his conduct, but with an equal possibility of damaging his relations with Newcastle. He was discreet in his testimony and managed to avoid taking a danger-

63. Shirley to Barrington, Feb. 8, 1757, W.O. 1, 4, 397; List of Commissions, *ibid.*, 403-8.
64. Shirley to Barrington, Feb. 8, 1757, *ibid.*, 397.

ous stand. But Townshend read into the record one of Shirley's letters to Bollan criticizing the Baker-Kilby contract as too expensive.[65] (Shirley later claimed that the letter had fallen into Townshend's hands accidentally.) A vigorous debate followed on the rates of provisioning. Newcastle's forces were victorious, but resentful against Shirley because of the introduction of his letter as testimony, Newcastle abruptly withdrew his patronage.

Other events then moved to Shirley's disadvantage: Pownall succeeded him in the Massachusetts governorship, and Lord Barrington's investigation of Shirley was allowed to end without any positive results. Barrington admitted that "sufficient matter and proof could not be found" in Loudoun's charges to initiate a court of inquiry to investigate Shirley's conduct, but he rejected Shirley's contention that an announcement of the court's proceedings would clear the air.[66] Shirley was annoyed by Barrington's refusal to issue a public statement in his favor and continued to memorialize the government. In June, while trying to close the military accounts, he reviewed his grievances in a long letter to Barrington: "I look upon the postponing of an inquiry into my conduct to so removed and uncertain a time, as waiting for a return from the Earl of Loudoun would put it off to . . . [as] ruinous to all my interests; [it would be like] . . . deferring the inquiry 'till seven years after my death." He believed that if the matter were allowed to drop, it would be "fatal in the end, both to my honor and fortune."[67]

In September, after Newcastle had been restored to a position of authority in a reorganized Pitt government, Shirley petitioned the Duke for a reconsideration of his case.[68] Though Newcastle ignored his letter, Shirley won strong support from Alexander, Livingston, and Thomlinson, when they published a dramatic account of the military operations in

65. *Shirley Correspondence,* II, 584-86; Barrington to Pitt, Mar. 30, 1757, S.P. 41, 23, 71; War Office to Shirley, Apr. 22, 1757, W.O. 1, 4, 479-81; Wood to Barrington, Mar. 26, 1757, *ibid.,* 469.
66. Shirley to Barrington, Apr. 25 and 29, 1757, W.O. 1, 4, 455-56, 459-63.
67. Shirley to Barrington, June 3, 1757, *ibid.,* 443-45.
68. *Shirley Correspondence,* II, 587-88.

which he was hailed as a hero. His enemies were described as motivated by greed: "Mr. de Lancey, by blowing up the coals of contention, did the province more injury, than he will ever be able to repair."[69]

Shirley was also helped by a military catastrophe in 1757. Late in the summer, Fort William Henry on Lake George fell to the enemy, opening the very gates of Albany to invasion. The siege and massacre overshadowed the capitulation of Oswego, and Loudoun was called home.[70] The confusion in New York weakened Pownall's ability to manage the Massachusetts legislature, which refused to supply quarters for Loudoun's regiments. The contest between Loudoun and the legislature nearly brought a military occupation of Boston. Pownall admitted that he had no gift for governing colonials and applied for another position.

There was now new hope of clearing Shirley's name. With the help of William Bollan, at whose home he often stayed while in London, Shirley arranged to meet Lord Halifax. Their discussion turned to Loudoun, military policy, and contracting, and Shirley expressed his regret over Townshend's attack on Newcastle. Halifax quizzed him on the source of Townshend's information and then described Newcastle's concern over Shirley's apparent disloyalty. In closing their conversation, Halifax promised to write the Duke, and Shirley apparently agreed to supply proof of his innocence. The extent of Shirley's alienation from Newcastle can be seen in the letter Halifax wrote to the Duke: "I think it but common justice to him to acquaint your Grace that the General's behavior in that affair turns out very different from what your Grace and I imagined it."[71]

Within a few days Shirley was received by Newcastle. It had been many months since they had met, and the strain of affairs showed itself in Shirley's appearance. The Duke was sympathetic and promised his patronage, although he gave

69. "A Review of the Military Operations in North-America," Mass. Hist. Soc., *Collections*, 1st Ser., 7 (1801), 69-70.

70. Lawrence H. Gipson, *The British Empire Before the American Revolution*, VII, chaps. 3 and 4. Mr. Gipson is more sympathetic than I am.

71. Halifax to Newcastle, Feb. 15, 1758, Add. MSS, 32877, fol. 466.

Shirley no idea of what his new employment would be.[72] After their meeting, Shirley flooded the Duke's office with petitions in which he again outlined his needs and described his aspirations. The customary delay followed, the anxious weeks of anticipation; but Shirley was now assured of help in obtaining a position.[73]

72. *Shirley Correspondence,* II, 599-603.
73. Shirley to Newcastle, Mar. 16, 1758, Add. MSS, 32878, fol. 228.

XIII

Patronage Regained

THOUGH SHIRLEY had no new position, the restoration of Newcastle's favor enabled him to settle his military accounts. Ever since his return to London the accounts had been under audit and were no closer to passing in 1758 than they had been a year earlier. Nor would they have ever passed, it is safe to say, if the rules of the Treasury had been applied. Shirley and his contractors had been faced with unusual circumstances and had adopted unusual methods to solve their problems. Although most of their practices could be plausibly explained, an aura of suspicion lingered around unprecedented procedures. Only by the relaxation of its rules, which the Treasury had extended to other contractors, could these accounts be settled.[1]

It is clear that Shirley did not personally benefit from the military contracts. There is no way of checking every business transaction, but he did not accumulate any wealth. It is true that his sons-in-law, his friends, and his governmental supporters were amply remunerated. Shirley's agents had been well rewarded with a commission of 5 per cent, certain profits from the sale of subcontracted provisions, and benefits from managing the exchange of money; but such emoluments were incident to public service in the eighteenth century, and Shirley's appointees provided valuable services that demanded expert judgment and engaged their personal capital for months. In 1755 they had acted as Shirley's quartermaster corps, assuming duties that Braddock should have assigned to army officers.

1. John A. Schutz, "British Marine Accounting and Auditor Edmund Herbert," *Huntington Lib. Qtly.*, 20 (1956-57), 269-80; Amherst to Commissioners, Sept. 1, 1761, W.O. 34, 197, 82-83.

The most damaging critic of Shirley's agents was Oliver de Lancey, a rival of Livingston and Morris, who had himself turned a good profit assisting Loudoun's contractors. His evaluation of the Livingston-Morris accounts will not stand scrutiny, except for his general criticism of the brevity of the entries, which is justified. In defense of Shirley, however, it is well to emphasize that he presented part of the accounts to a competent panel of New York merchants, chosen by Governor Hardy in July 1756, who examined the vouchers and passed them. This procedure had been used to settle the accounts of the Louisbourg expedition of 1745, the campaigns of 1746 and 1747, and the Braddock campaign of 1755; indeed, this was the only mode Shirley had known to settle military contracts, and it had received the approval of Halifax and Bedford in 1749.[2] Undoubtedly, if Lord Loudoun had not been hostile to Shirley in 1756, the accounts would have been settled quickly and satisfactorily. Instead, they were used by the de Lanceys as a weapon in colonial politics.[3]

So muddled was the status of the accounts in 1758 that Newcastle urged the Treasury to adopt a new approach to the accounting. A relaxation of the rules, which had been extended to other military officers, was now given to Shirley. An authorization was sent to Jeffrey Amherst, the commander-in-chief since 1759, to appoint a committee of merchants who would review and adjust the accounts. Oliver de Lancey was a member of the committee, and his presence perhaps inspired another painful review of the contracts, but the books were finally closed in 1763, nine years after the payments were due.[4]

Long before this matter was concluded, Shirley lost contact with the negotiations. Though he offered his services and appointed agents to represent his interests, he was shielded from further embarrassment. Much of the odium of suspicion was removed when he was honored in late 1758 with the

2. Shirley to Treasury, July 27, 1757, W.O. 1, 4, 431-34.
3. These papers are in Treasury 1, 367, fol. 57, and 1, 372, fol. 165; W.O. 34, 197, 1, and 1, 4, 51-56; Board of Trade proceedings, Mar. 23, 1766, C. O. 24/3, 204; Shirley to Barrington, Sept. 26, 1758, W.O. 1, 1, 255-56.
4. Shirley to War Office, May 18, 1759, *ibid.*, 381; Amherst to Petitioners, *ibid.*, 34, 81, 197.

governorship of the Bahama Islands and in early 1759 with the distinguished military rank of lieutenant general.[5]   He could rejoice, too, in having his only living son, Thomas, commissioned a major in the British army.

His new civilian position, if isolated and unimportant, had the quiet of a country estate and financial advantages that rivaled those of Massachusetts.   Though it appears that Shirley would have preferred the governorship of Pennsylvania, his appointment was more suitable for his advanced age than any of the continental posts.[6]   He enjoyed a few happy months at Ote Hall in Sussex, then took the long passage via Charleston, South Carolina, to the Bahamas.

I

The ill fate, which attended my late services in America, seems to pursue me in my passage from Charlestown. . . .   Having sailed from thence in his Majesty's ship, *Mermaid,* with the advantages of a fair wind, moon light nights, a pilot on board, and the best sailing instructions besides, on the fifth morning [December 31, 1759] at daybreak, when we expected to have had a happy sight of New Providence, I found myself shipwrecked upon the coast of my own government—from which, being delivered contrary to all expectations, I arrived safe, after a most perilous passage over shoals and reefs of rocks and falls within the Bahama keys, in a small sloop.[7]

The rescue from a distant Bahamian reef took most of the day, and Shirley was nearing exhaustion on his arrival at Nassau.   Accompanying him was his devoted friend and former secretary, James Bradford, who was the newly appointed secretary of the colony.   As they rode from the water front to Government House, instead of hearing the familiar noises of Boston and London, they were refreshed by the quiet beauty of the Bahamas at the close of day.   On the green-blue water of the harbor were reflected the sails of a few ships, and less than a hundred business and residential buildings

5. *Gentleman's Magazine,* 28 (1758), 557 and 29 (1759), 95, 147.

6. Partridge to Pemberton, Feb. 1, 1759, Pemberton Papers, Pa. Hist. Soc.; *Shirley Correspondence,* II, 599-600.

7. Shirley to Townshend, July 18, 1761, W.O. 1, 1, 409-11; *The South Carolina Gazette* (Charleston), Nov. 17, 1759.

were leisurely spaced along the mile of water front on the
harbor's southside. Gray fortresses stood at either end of
the harbor, and the sky line was broken only by the half-
finished tower of Christ Church and the high roof of Government House.[8]

Though his unusual arrival surprised the town, the cannon
at Forts Montagu and Nassau were sounding the welcome by
the time he reached his official home. The governor's residence was a large house with open porches and a high roof
surrounded by ten acres planted in palms and citrus trees. It
stood on a rise of land that separated the blue harbor from
the luxuriant dark green of the island, and its windows commanded a view of the village of Nassau.

Among the Bahamians who gathered at Government House
to pay their respects to Shirley and Bradford were the members of the Council and Assembly. John Gambier, the president of the Council and Acting Governor since John Tinker's
death in 1758, introduced his Council colleagues, Jeremiah
Tinker, John Brown, and Robert Stewart, wealthy owners of
timber and plantation lands. Since the legislature was taking
its winter recess, Gambier made apologies for the small delegation and tendered his services to the Governor.

At the dinner celebrating his arrival and at other times during the next four weeks, Shirley received reports on local conditions. Accustomed to the mercantile life of New England,
he found the Bahamas strangely provincial and isolated. The
colony's resources were undeveloped, its trade off the main-
stream of empire. Its people were few and scattered over
hundreds of islands that dotted the seas off Georgia and
Florida for 750 miles. Many of the residents lived like no-
mads, moving frequently from island to island, exploiting the
land's fertility, cutting timber, or catching turtles; and most

8. *The Boston Weekly News-Letter,* Feb. 14, 1760; Shirley to the Board of
Trade, Aug. 1, 1760, Treasury 401, fol. 14; Carter to S.P.G., S.P.G. MSS,
London, B Ser., VI, 67-81 (All S.P.G. MSS used in this chap. are taken from
the Frank J. Klingberg film collection, Univ. of California, Los Angeles);
*Journal of the Lower House of Assembly of the Bahama Islands from 1729-
1776* (Nassau, 1910), 1760 session, 11-12; Shirley to Board of Trade, Oct. 23,
1760, C. O. 23/7, 9.

who had settled in the villages were struggling in their oc-
cupations and rarely traveled to the capital city. The wealthy
few who had leisure time often made extended visits to
England or the mainland of North America, where they sought
escape from the provincialism of Nassau and an opportunity
to regain their health.[9] A heavy diet of hard liquor and rich
food, prevalent enough in northern climates, was especially
tempting in the south. Shirley soon suffered the debilitating
effects of immoderation.

The hard labor was done by several thousand Negroes.
Though slaves were in the minority on other Bahamian islands,
almost every family on New Providence owned one or more,
and they were twice as numerous as the white inhabitants.
Shirley purchased a house servant named David, who was offered for sale by a thoughtful legislator, and had the services of
three or four Negroes as gardeners and footmen.

The simplicity of Bahamian life left little formal business
for the legislature. Daily problems were settled without need
of governmental action. There were few public officials and
almost no public buildings. Budgets were small. Token
salaries were paid to the Governor and the other officials, who
supplemented their income by holding more than one office
and operating a business or plantation during the greater part
of their time. Regulations were passed by the legislature
to govern the conduct of the slaves and to provide for defense
and education, but these laws had only an incidental effect
on the hundreds of white inhabitants who lived on the distant
islands.

Taking stock of the situation, Shirley was anxious to meet
the Assembly. A call had gone out for a session in January
1760, but representatives were slow to leave their businesses
and make the long journey to Nassau. By mid-February
fifteen of the twenty-four representatives had joined the four
or five councilors in the tiny legislative chamber to witness
the Governor's oath-taking and hear his address.[10] They saw

9. Shirley to S.P.G., Jan. 15, 1761, S.P.G. MSS, VI, 10-19; Carter to S.P.G.,
ibid., 21.
10. *Journal of the Lower House*, 1760 session, 15.

standing before them a man of sixty-six, taller than most of them, though slightly bent by age and using a cane. His reputation as former governor of Massachusetts and commander-in-chief of the British armies in North America had preceded him, and curiosity, if nothing else, must have intensified their interest in his address. The message was simple and brief—a contrast to his first address to the Massachusetts General Court. In old age, he was most concerned with obtaining the cooperation of the legislature, and he pledged: "I shall do everything in my power to cultivate a perfect harmony with you upon all occasions for the public good."[11] With the assistance of the Council and the colonial secretary, he promised the Assembly that he would study the needs of the islanders, perfect the administrative machinery, and offer his recommendations in future addresses. For the present he had little to suggest, except the renovation of Government House, which had been neglected since the preceding governor's death.

After he left the legislative halls, the Assembly sent a committee of four, headed by Francis Bonnatyne, to inspect the house. Its report was favorably received, and the Assembly used up the remaining time of the session in voting a salary for Shirley, exchanging good wishes with him, and drinking bumpers of rum to king and governor.[12]

Since time pressed on no one, Shirley took nearly three months to prepare his first reports for the British government. They reflect the same thorough regard for detail and the same spacious imperial view as his earlier findings in Massachusetts. The dispatches outlined his conclusions: he had detected some smuggling; he had found inadequacies in the proceedings of the admiralty court; he was concerned over the substandard defense of the islands. Most of the problems, with the exception of smuggling, were of minor consequence to the home government, which suspected him of trying to create patronage for local merchants.[13]

11. The South Carolina Gazette (Charleston), Apr. 7, 1760.

12. Journal of the Lower House, 1760 session, 12; Shirley to the Board of Trade, Oct. 23, 1760, C. O. 23/7, 9.

13. Shirley to Barrington, Sept. 1, 1760, W.O. 1, 1, 399-403; Shirley to Egremont, Apr. 1, 1762, Halifax to Shirley, Nov. 8, 1764, C. O. 23/16, no page.

Certainly, his recommendation to refortify the islands was an attempt to give him some patronage to distribute and thereby make office holding more profitable. He had difficulty keeping a sufficient number of men on the Council to conduct the business of government. Replacements were often necessary, for the toll of death and poor health was heavy. On Shirley's arrival at Nassau there were four vacancies in a Council of seven members, and one vacancy was two years old. Shirley believed that one solution was to increase the Council's size without altering the requirement for a quorum, but the home government responded by giving him power to make interim appointments. Even so, he never could count upon a group of qualified men to share the responsibilities of government. Bradford was often away; Gambier and a brother Samuel were frequently managing their businesses on the neighboring islands; and Shirley himself was forced to leave Nassau in May 1763 for a nine-month rest at Boston. When he returned, he brought back his twenty-one year old grandson William Hutchinson, whom he intended to appoint a councilor when the youth was more experienced in governmental affairs.[14]

Shirley's first appointment was most regrettable. In trying to attach John Gambier to his administration, he appointed his younger brother Samuel to the Council and the vice-admiralty judgeship. The Gambiers were men of property, like Wendell, Hale, and Choate of Massachusetts, but Samuel did not enjoy the advantages of a formal education nor the disadvantages of a sense of responsibility. Even before the appointments had been confirmed by the London authorities, Shirley was troubled by the complaints of the local merchants, who ac-

14. In 1760 the councilors were Jeremiah Tinker, John Gambier, Robert Stewart (died in Jan. 1760), Jeremiah Duncomber (died in 1758), John Brown, John Peyton, and James Bradford. Shirley added Samuel Gambier, Charles Marshall, and Isaac Cox; in 1761 he replaced Samuel Gambier with Robert Carter and made an additional appointment of John Goochin. In 1762 the deceased Marshall was succeeded by Daniel Laroche, and the absent James Bradford was replaced by his son William, the acting secretary and collector of customs. William Bradford, in his own right, served as councilor after 1764. In that year Samuel Gambier was reinstated. In 1766, John Brown was again on the Council, with William Hutchinson and Thomas Bunch as the other new appointees.

cused Samuel of being a smuggler and, worse, a bankrupt. An investigation supported these accusations. Shirley wanted to avoid a break with the family, but he loathed such conduct on the part of a public official, and when Samuel Gambier failed to mend his ways, the Governor suspended him from office and reported the matter to the ministry.[15] His brother John apparently sided with Shirley.

Of all Shirley's appointees he was most pleased with the Reverend Robert Carter, the rector of Christ Church and a missionary for the Society for the Propagation of the Gospel at Nassau. A graduate of Trinity College, Cambridge, Carter had come to the islands as a young man in 1750. He had married and was the father of a large family. Needing additional money to supplement his salary, he pressed Shirley for help and won a sympathetic hearing. He was a delightful companion in this land of cultural desolation, and the two men often dined together at Government House, spending the evenings deep in discussions of religion and philosophy. Whenever a vacancy occurred in the administration, Carter was first in Shirley's mind. In 1762, he held temporary appointments as councilor, jurist, and secretary.[16]

II

In the early years of his governorship Shirley collected facts about the islands. He toured Eleuthera, Andros, Grand Bahama, Harbour, and some of the lesser islands, accompanied in 1761 by the learned Carter, and in 1765 by his young grandson. He gained sufficient insights, he believed, to make valid recommendations to the Assembly and the home government on the needs of the people. Neither government expected him to study island problems, but he was by habit a good administrator, and he prepared his report just the same.

It was natural for him to look first to religious activities, for he had long believed that a flourishing religion was basic

15. Shirley to John Pownall, Oct. 5, 1760, C. O. 23/7, 27. When Samuel Gambier was reinstated in 1764, Shirley asserted that his conduct was better.

16. Venn, *Alumni Cantabrigienses*, I, pt. 1, 301; Shirley to S.P.G., Jan. 15, 1761, S.P.G. MSS, VI, 1-2; Carter to S.P.G., Oct. 9, 1761, *ibid.*, 43-57.

to a community's welfare. He was always ready to entrust this mission to the clergy of the Anglican Church, but the responsibilities of his new position as governor included duties as a sort of unmitered bishop, and he had a particular duty to help the clergy. The state of the church in the islands, he discovered, was miserable: "Upon my arrival here I found the inhabitants destitute of a minister, through the absence of the Reverend Mr. Carter, who was obliged, on account of his bad state of health, to retire . . . to Philadelphia. This occasioned a cessation of public worship . . . for six months, which intermission (and sometimes much longer) has . . . happened before; and must . . . frequently happen again, whilst there is but one minister resident." He recommended the appointment of a missionary who could minister to the needs of inhabitants on the outer islands and of a catechist who could serve as schoolmaster during his spare time.[17]

Shirley sent similar reports to the Assembly and the S.P.G., but the isolation of the Bahamas prevented any rapid accomplishment. When John Robertson, first schoolmaster of the church, arrived in 1762, the legislature responded to Shirley's request and supplemented his salary with £35 a year. Robertson attracted a dozen or more pupils into his school, and when he gave his charge over to John Bascome three years later, the school was well established.[18]

The school house was near Christ Church. Every time Shirley visited the school and the church he was irritated by their appearance, and finally he placed the matter of their upkeep before the legislature in an address which the reporter said was "warmly urg'd." Work on the church's tower was begun, but the scarcity of workmen and funds prevented its completion for many years. The Governor was more successful in refurnishing Carter's home and enclosing the yard with a fence. He also won a promise from the Assembly to replace the old ship's bell of the church with a more melodious one.[19]

Money for Carter's salary was difficult to obtain. Shirley's

17. Shirley to S.P.G., Jan. 15, 1761, *ibid.*, VI, 1.
18. Carter to S.P.G., Mar. 19, 1761, *ibid.*, VI, 20-24.
19. Carter to S.P.G., Sept. 25, 1764, *ibid.*, VI, 76-81.

letters to the S.P.G. and messages to the Assembly brought
little relief, and Carter threatened to resign his curacy. To relieve his situation, Shirley gave him interim appointments in
the administration, which doubled his income but gave him
less time to devote to his chosen work.

With such care from the Governor, religious affairs should
have been peaceful if not prosperous. Instead, to Shirley's
disgust, a foot-loose, roving missionary, the Reverend Mr. William Duncanson, arrived in Nassau in 1761. He apparently
expected to step into Carter's place as S.P.G. missionary. Carter had asked permission to leave the islands some months be-
for Shirley's arrival, but when the Governor learned of Carter's
plans, he urged the minister to stay and petitioned the S.P.G.
for more salary. Much against his will Carter agreed to put
off his departure. This change of plans obviously upset Duncanson, who fulminated against the authorities and took his
grievances to the people. His opposition convinced the un-
steady Carter that he should now stay in Nassau, at least long
enough to fight Duncanson and await the result of the Governor's petitions.[20]

Shirley felt responsible for the disturbance and tried to arrange a meeting of the two ministers. He suggested that the
missionary territory be divided between them, for it was far
too large for one man, and that the two ministers discontinue
public criticisms of each other immediately: "I would recommend it to you, to meet and settle that matter between you . . .
some time today: tomorrow being Sunday."[21] Peace did not
come on Sunday, or the next Sunday—not until Duncanson
withdrew to the North American mainland. Thereafter, Carter's labor in the vineyard of sinners was not half so exciting,
but certainly more dignified. With his many offices in the
government and more money from the S. P. G., he found con-
tentment in his work and remained at Nassau until 1765, when
ill health and the death of his wife forced him to take the
children home to England. His departure deprived the Ba-

20. Duncanson to S.P.G., 1761, *ibid.*, VI, 37-40. Duncanson also complained that Shirley thought of himself as a bishop in the Bahamas.
21. Shirley to Carter and Duncanson, Apr. 10, 1761, *ibid.*, VI, 26.

hamas of a devout minister and devoted public servant, but by that time Eleuthera and New Providence had a number of schoolmasters who were performing some ministerial duties and could take over Carter's work. The minister's last report as rector revealed a steady increase in conversions among the whites as well as the Negroes since 1760.

III

The miserable condition of the islanders, especially on Eleuthera and Harbour Islands, was described by John Bascome, one of the schoolmasters, in 1766: "A parcel of poor people, who from the fine, wholesome climate they live in and from the fish, turtles, and other sea diet they live on, breed children in great numbers . . . there are many families (as I am informed) that have 15 to 16 children and very often 2 at birth. These poor creatures are very little better (if any) as to manners, living, and education than the savage Indians."[22]

Although Shirley was also struck by the low standard of living and wanted to help the Bahamians, he was almost powerless to institute changes. He had little money at his disposal and few officials to do his bidding. Nevertheless, considering the resources at his command, he accomplished some important things. He began by recommending a survey of the more valuable islands so that land titles could be registered and unoccupied areas opened to settlers.[23] The Assembly rejected the project, but approved a partial survey of Nassau in 1766, which included widening the roads and extending many of them into the interior. He also encouraged experimentation in planting cotton and induced some farmers to try a crop

22. Bascome to S.P.G., Jan. 6, 1766, *ibid.*, VI, no page.
23. Montford Brown to Board of Trade, May 6, 1775, Shelburne MSS, Clements Lib.; Thomas Shirley to Board of Trade, 1773, *ibid.* Shirley reported the following trade with Britain: in 1771, £2450 and in 1772, £1750. The major part of the trade was with South Carolina and then to world ports. During these two years, the colony exported 1,000 tons of mahogany and Madeira plants, 625 tons of lignum vitae, 4,880 bushels of salt, 30,000 pounds of turtle, and 30,000 pounds of Seville oranges.

or two.[24] At the same time, he offered to assist those Bahamians who wanted to market local products in England.

These ideas on commerce Shirley placed before the Board of Trade, and in 1764 he suggested the possibility of establishing a free port at Nassau. He reminded the Board that illegal trade flourished between foreign islands of the Caribbean and the North American mainland, a trade that had involved four to five hundred ships during the Seven Years' War. Since much of this trade was centered at Monte Cristo on Hispaniola, he hoped that a free port at Nassau would attract traders to the Bahamas instead. The free port would put the Bahamas on the shipping lanes, increase the demand for their precious woods, and bring new settlers. Similar proposals had been made before, but Shirley's suggestion at this time had some weight at home. In 1765 Parliament passed an act which empowered the ministry to select certain colonies for free ports; Jamaica and Dominica won the first authorization.[25] In preparation for the institution of a free port (which the Bahamas did not receive during Shirley's administration), the Governor urged the Assembly to reform the trade laws, proposing new codes and courts modeled on Massachusetts practice and citing oddities in the Bahamian code that discouraged commerce.[26]

In promoting the common good, the Governor advocated, as he had always done, the creation of an efficient government, with an alert administration, appreciative of local problems and helpful in times of need. He had gradually formed an able staff which, though smaller than his Massachusetts staff, included men of superb qualifications: the Bradfords, father and son; William Hutchinson; Robert Carter; and John Brown. These advisors were university educated, and Brown, whose

24. Shirley to Board of Trade, Nov. 21, 1764, C. O. 23/7, 190; *The Bahama Gazette* (Nassau), Jan. 15, 1785. The cotton crop yield on New Providence, Exuma, Cat Island, and Long Island was reported to be "abundant."

25. Robert Livingston Schuyler, *The Fall of the Old Colonial System* (New York, 1945), 80-82; Assembly to Shirley, Jan. 23, 1767, C. O. 26/5. "[We] beg leave to return your Excellency our most grateful thanks for the warmth with which you espoused the interest of this government on every occasion."

26. Message of Mar. 29, 1763, C. O. 26/5.

judgment Shirley valued very much, had wide legal experience.[27]   Most served the crown at low wages.   Bradford had to pay office rent out of his small secretarial salary, and Brown, as chief justice after 1766, was paid no more than a clerk in Boston would receive.

Shirley's salary, the issue that had often disturbed peaceful government in Massachusetts, was most satisfactory in 1758. When he accepted the governorship of the Bahamas the salary was approximately £1,400, which included admiralty court fees, a military subvention as captain of the local garrison, and compensation voted by the Bahamian legislature.   When the war ended in 1763, the home government disbanded the garrison, and the number of seizures and condemnations of enemy ships was sharply reduced.   The Governor's salary for 1764 was about £530.   It remained low until 1767, when the ministry agreed to add £300 sterling yearly to his local salary.[28]   In 1764, when he returned from a nine-month absence at Boston, the Assembly showed its sympathy for his depressed finances by giving him a travel grant of £100.[29]   Its action was exceptional, for money for any purpose was scarce.   When Shirley tried to secure funds for rebuilding Forts Montagu and Nassau, which guarded Nassau harbor, the Assembly sent a committee to inspect the forts.   Although the committee confirmed the obvious fact that Fort Nassau was "greatly out of repair" and was "in danger of falling down," the Assembly was not disposed to rebuild it without a subvention from London.[30] When Shirley petitioned for help from the Board of Trade, Lord Halifax wrote a tart reply: "The idea of securing them [the islands] by forts and garrisons in every bay and creek, where it is possible an enemy may land, has at all times been considered as equally unnecessary and impracticable, and, in the present state of the finance of this country, such a plan

27. Shirley to Board of Trade, Mar. 9, 1767, *ibid.*, 23/7, 241.   Brown was appointed to the Council in 1756 by Governor Tinker and had previous service as attorney general.

28. Board of Trade proceedings, Mar. 23, 1766, *ibid.*, 24/3, 204; Shelburne to Shirley, June 20, 1767, *ibid.*, 23/16, 1; Shirley's memorial, May 1765, *ibid.*, 23/7, 170; Shirley to Board of Trade, Oct. 27, 1766, *ibid.*, 23/7, 228.

29. Assembly resolution, May 15, 1764, *ibid.*, 26/5.

30. *Journal of the Lower House*, 1764 session, May 19, 17-18.

of endless expense cannot but be rejected as peculiarly inadmissable."[31]

An incident of French aggression in 1764 was of more aid to Nassau's defenses than any petitions. French colonials from Hispaniola invaded the Turk Islands and the Great Inagua, burned a few buildings belonging to fishermen and salt diggers, and planted a monument to their king. Shirley issued a protest, dispatched a merchant vessel to warn the French, and then filed notes with the appropriate ministers in London. Halifax at first belittled the Governor's reports, but he changed his attitude when supporting evidence arrived from the Jamaican governor and West Indian merchants. At his suggestion the ministry lodged a strong protest with the French foreign office, which quickly apologized. The British ministry warmly congratulated Shirley on the efficient handling of the episode and apparently authorized him to re-establish a small defense corps at Nassau.[32] The incident also reminded the ministers of his petitions for financial aid, for shortly thereafter his salary subvention was granted. The government later granted money for rebuilding the crumbling fortresses.

IV

Three or four times a year Shirley met with his legislature. Because his advanced age and delicate health confined him more and more to his hillside home, he was increasingly dependent upon others for his personal contacts. His legislative program, therefore, was weakened because he could not always give sufficient attention to parliamentary detail. Nevertheless, the list of his sponsored bills that became law shows that he enjoyed remarkable prestige. Some of the laws reveal an acceptance of his pet ideas. In the 1762-63 session, for example, the Assembly passed bills prohibiting tedious lawsuits, appointing new schoolmasters, and providing money for an agent in London. On the other hand, no doubt because of poor health, Shirley was not able to anticipate problems and often

31. Halifax to Shirley, Nov. 8, 1764, C. O. 23/16.
32. Thomas Shirley to Hillsborough, Dec. 9, 1768, Shelburne MSS; Halifax to Shirley, Mar. 9, 1765, C. O. 23/16.

resorted to emergency measures. Sometimes his methods stretched the law—to the discomfort of his friends and the horror of the Assembly. In 1762, he temporarily appointed Carter to the supreme court bench and drew £15 from the treasury to pay his salary. When criticized for his action, Shirley justified the interim appointment by simply saying: "I acted upon the occasion as I thought was most agreeable to justice and the honor of the government."[33]

The Assembly did not press the issue, but the Stamp Act riot of September 1765 was another matter. The legislature was critical of Shirley's handling of the crisis and would not drop the subject. Almost everywhere in America the Stamp Act had inspired some form of resentment against parliamentary taxation and British interference in local affairs. The stamps for the Bahamas were entrusted to Shirley, and he selected a now nameless resident as distributor. Like many of his fellows on the mainland, that hapless official found himself in the center of an angry crowd that demanded his resignation. When he resisted, the crowd dragged him to the graveyard, dug a suitable hole, and an obliging islander provided the coffin. Forced to lie down in the coffin, he was held there until the cover was nailed down. Then, with the bell of Christ Church ringing, the coffin was lowered into the shallow grave. To the delight of the crowd, some enterprising fellows threw dirt on the coffin. The added touch of realism convinced the entombed agent, who begged to sign the letter of resignation.[34]

The noise of this gay event was heard at Government House, where the Governor decided to accept the crowd's mandate. The sale of stamps was stopped, the crowd disbanded, and quiet returned. But when the Assembly met, Shirley raised the question of the use of stamps on official documents, and the Assembly, like many New England legislatures, denounced mother country, governor, and stamps in such an "enflamatory" manner that Shirley was forced to disband it. This was a measure he had never before been compelled to use either in the Bahamas or in Massachusetts.[35]

33. *Journal of the Lower House*, 1762 session, Apr. 22, 56.
34. *The Pennsylvania Gazette* (Philadelphia), Oct. 31, 1765.
35. *Journal of the Lower House*, 1766 session, Aug. 8, 32-37.

By the time the new Assembly met in December 1766, the Stamp Act had been repealed, and though Parliament declared its power to pass tax measures, it had not done so. Leaders of the Assembly wanted to dismiss the controversy with as much dignity as possible. A special committee was sent to the Governor with an address pledging the loyalty of the Bahamian people to the crown: "We have no injuries to complain of, no damages to reimburse, nor can we on retrospection accuse ourselves of any votes or acts repugnant to the dignity of his Majesty's government."[36]

One wonders who wrote that address. It was so typical of Shirley to play down controversy that he may have had a hand in composing it. In replying to the Assembly, moreover, he told the members that a letter had been sent home to "his Majesty's ministers" representing that "during the late tumults and riots which prevailed in most of our neighboring colonies, this government remained in a perfectly undisturbed state and that from its past behavior I had the greatest reason to assure them that the people of this colony will always show a ready and cheerful obedience to the laws of Great Britain and avoid every act that may tend to destroy the constitutional dependency of the colonies upon the Mother Country."[37]

After these sugar-coated messages, Shirley had a right to expect cooperation from the Assembly, and he probably received it in some degree, but not all legislators were ready to suppress their criticism of the British government. John Green, an intemperate politician, was so censorious that Shirley had him imprisoned, and the Assembly expunged the record of Green's words. After a year in jail, Green begged the Assembly to let him explain his conduct. Some of the members were curious; others were concerned about the violation of Green's rights as a legislator. Since Shirley had Green in his custody and stoutly refused to release him, the Assembly petitioned the Governor to allow it to hear Green's explanation. Shirley, in replying to the petition, insisted that Green

36. *Ibid.*, Dec. 3, 1766, 8-10.
37. Message to Assembly, Dec. 1, 1766, C. O. 23/5; Grey Cooper to Shirley, Oct. 10, 1765, Bundle 209, House of Lords MSS.

deserved his punishment and that the case was closed: "But Gentlemen," he added, "if not withstanding what I have said, you are still desirous Mr. Green should personally be heard. . . , I shall always . . . oblige you in everything, so far as it is in my power consistently with my duty to the King."[38]

Taking Shirley at his word, the Assembly asked to have Green released into its custody. Though the Governor protested, there was nothing that he could do after pledging his word. Green met with the Assembly, apologized for his conduct, and won reinstatement as a member. In the next session, his ready wit got the better of him, and this time the Assembly expelled him. Again his words were expunged from the record.[39]

V

During these years in the islands, Shirley never enjoyed robust health. His advanced age, his diet of rich food and drink, and his habit of working harder than his strength would permit wore his health to the breaking point. Though his long Boston vacation in 1763 benefited him greatly, his energy was taxed by the return trip to Nassau. After 1765 he had most of his addresses read to the Assembly, and he conducted legislative business through his staff. His hand became shaky and his voice so hesitant and quivering that he refrained from speaking in public.

Shirley would not consider resigning. His finances were better than they had been for years and would have allowed him to retire, but he wanted some mark of royal favor that would benefit his family. His son Thomas applied to the Board of Trade—perhaps even to Newcastle, who was living in retirement—for patronage, and Shirley was undoubtedly pleased by the recognition Lord Shelburne of the Board gave the family in November 1767. Shirley was retired on the half pay of a British colonel, and Thomas was named his successor as governor of the Bahamas.[40]

38. *Journal of the Lower House,* 1767-68 session, Jan. 19, 1768, 11-16.
39. *Ibid.,* 1768-69 session, 63.
40. Shelburne to Shirley, Nov. 14, 1767, Shelburne MSS; Shelburne to Board of Trade, Oct. 17, 1767, C. O. 23/7, 250c. Thomas Shirley relieved his father on Oct. 25, 1768.

Another year passed before the arrival of Thomas and his bride Anna Maria, daughter of Thomas Weston of Rivenhall, a distant cousin of the Shirleys.[41] The happy reunion of father and son after nine years was further heightened by Shirley's decision to stay in Nassau until the spring. With his private affairs settled, including the manumission of his Negro slave David by a special act of the legislature, he boarded a merchant vessel for Boston. He planned to live in Roxbury with Eliakim and Elizabeth Hutchinson, in the house built long ago by Frances and himself.

In the quiet of his old county seat, with his many grandchildren about him, Shirley was happy. Looking out from the upstairs windows of the mansion, he saw the trees and gardens of his son-in-law's estate, and at a distance the harbor of Boston. At his bedroom desk, he studied the newspaper reports of violence in Boston and the debate between Governor Thomas Hutchinson and the General Court. Life had changed, and he was bewildered by the names of its many actors. Once he explained to a visitor: "Where the devil this brace of Adamses came from, I know not."[42]

Shirley died on March 24, 1771. His body was carried from Roxbury to the home of his son-in-law John Erving, Jr., in Boston, where it lay in state until the afternoon of April 1. After a solemn service at King's Chapel, in which three surviving daughters were present, it was entombed beside the bodies of his wife and daughter. In the harbor Castle William fired its final salute for Shirley, and a detachment of the militia sounded three volleys. Governor Hutchinson joined the lieutenant governor, the councilors, and the representatives in paying their respects.[43]

The Shirley family, like other families responsible for British rule of the colonies, suffered during the American Revo-

41. The Westons were distantly related to the Shirleys through Anne Shirley, the daughter of Sir Robert Shirley. Sir Robert's father and William Shirley's grandfather were brothers.

42. James K. Hosmer, *The Life of Thomas Hutchinson* (Boston, 1896), 181-82; *The Massachusetts Gazette* (Boston), June 29, 1769.

43. Samuel Adams Drake, *Old Landmarks and Historic Personages of Boston* (Boston, 1876), 267.

lution.   The old Governor's daughters and sons-in-law, the Hutchinsons, Ervings, and Temples, left Boston with their children when the British army evacuated the town.   Elizabeth and Eliakim Hutchinson, penniless and heartbroken, abandoned their property and businesses, and the once beautiful mansion in Roxbury became an officers' quarters and later a barracks.   John Erving took his wife Catharina Maria to England, and, after a decade of litigation and petitioning in a hopeless attempt to recover their property, accepted a modest pension from the crown.   Their sons, John and Shirley, returned to Boston after the Revolution, where they engaged in business and politics.   Like the Ervings, Robert and Harriet Temple left all their possessions in America; Robert died soon after his departure.   Harriet survived her husband by nearly two decades, long enough to see their daughter Mehetable married to Hans Blackwood, the Baron Dufferin and Claneboynes, and the mother of a son named Robert Temple.[44]

Thomas Shirley remained at his post in the Bahamas until 1774, when he was rewarded with the governorship of Dominica and, in 1781, with that of the Leeward Islands.   Though he suffered some misadventures during the Revolution—both he and his family were prisoners of war for a time—he rose rapidly in the British army.   He was commissioned colonel of the 91st foot in 1781, lieutenant general of the army in 1793, and general of the army in 1798.   Long before that, moreover, he had achieved what his father always coveted—the distinction of being named a baronet.   Sir Thomas Shirley died in 1800.   His second son, William Warden Shirley, succeeded to the title.[45]

Shirley in his day was applauded by good men, and he was mourned with a state funeral at his death.   Yet in King's Chapel, which was built under his patronage, not even a marker is to be found, although there are memorials on the

44. George Erving to Robert C. Winthrop, Aug. 30, 1843, Mass. Hist. Soc., Proceedings, 2nd Ser., 5 (1889-90), 11-13; James H. Stark, The Loyalists of Massachusetts (Boston, 1910), 137, 142; E. Alfred Jones, The Loyalists of Massachusetts (London, 1930), 133.

45. Lorenzo Sabine, Biographical Sketches of Loyalists of the American Revolution (Boston, 1864), II, 350.

side wall in honor of his wife and daughter. His old home in
Roxbury, now on Shirley Street, is crowded with apartment
houses and marred by the years of weather and neglect. The
public memory of his life was cut short by the Revolution—
an era had passed.

For most Americans of his time who had wealth, position,
or education, London was the center of the universe, the
fount of trade, the arbiter of style and standards of conduct,
and the source of governmental authority. Citizenship was
a blend of local and imperial attachment. Although the issues that brought about the Revolution were in some degree
present during Shirley's administration, he like many of his
friends would have been shocked by the idea that the colonies
could revolt against the mother country. True, he worried
about maintaining a proper "spirit of dependency," and he
realized that some higher order of governmental organization
was needed in America. No doubt he would later have stood
with Joseph Galloway in advocating the establishment of an
American parliament; but his own ideas never advanced so
far. The most he visualized was an organization of American
governors who with their councils would come together from
time to time to consider problems no single colony was capable of handling. If a structural union was necessary, membership in Parliament seemed to him the only solution. But
whatever form the empire should take, he assumed that the
interests of colony and mother country were basically com-
patable. As it manifested itself to Shirley, the empire was a
working system of business and political alliances which were
mutually beneficial. Rival interests existed, to be sure, but he
made it his task in Massachusetts to harmonize them, or at
least to accommodate them within the scope of imperial
policy. His greatest accomplishment of this kind was to link
the aspirations of the New England people for territorial expansion, land speculation, and the exploitation of timber resources to the British war against France and Spain, which
was essentially European in its origins and objectives. When
Britain failed to support the conquest of Canada and took
war-making in America out of New England hands, she sacri-

ficed the cooperation of Shirley's friends and started a train of events that led to James Otis and the Writs of Assistance.

As a career administrator, Shirley conceived of the problems of government primarily in terms of the manipulation of patronage; indeed his success as a colonial executive was grounded in his astute distribution of political rewards and favors. He owed his own career to an affiliation with the Duke of Newcastle, which, except for one brief interruption, endured for nearly forty years, and he pursued his career by cultivating alliances that were primarily personal: ties of family, business, and locality. His personal phalanx included business and political acquaintances in London, as well as relatives, friends, and neighbors in New England. By propitiating their interests, he tied merchants on both sides of the Atlantic to his administration. He employed patronage to raise support for British policies in the colonies; over the years, in fact, his spoilsman approach to public affairs rose to the level of a philosophy of imperial administration. To attain political ends of great significance he used official appointments, the letting of government contracts, and the disposal of rewards and punishments. His projects for expanding the empire, unifying the colonies and reforming the currency system were statesmanlike conceptions of the highest order. Ironically, his failure to carry them through arose, at least in part, from his inability to command sufficient patronage. At the critical point, when his military and political authority were at their zenith, he lacked the power to control the patronage of New York, Pennsylvania, and Virginia. It is distinctly possible that if he had been made the leader of all the northern colonies in 1756, he could have aided Lord Loudoun sufficiently to have turned that year of indecision and turmoil into a year of victory.

In all his activities, Shirley had a strong sense of political reality. His coalition, which unseated Belcher in 1741, may have been an accidental combination of discontented elements, but the coalition that backed his administration after 1741 was maintained by the genius of his personality and ability.

It was basically an assortment of individuals driven together by circumstances, sometimes representing economic and political alignments like those arising from the banking crisis of 1740. During the remainder of his term of office Shirley could count on a solid core of supporters and a shifting number of auxiliaries. Before 1748, Apthorp, Hale, Choate, Bollan, and Eliakim Hutchinson were joined by Waldo, Kilby, and their friends in London and Boston. After 1748, the core group was associated with Thomas Hutchinson, Andrew and Peter Oliver, and certain rich Boston merchants, including the Ervings and Bowdoins. Shirley also relied upon office holders like Auchmuty and Russell and members of the Anglican churches of Boston. For most years of his administration, Pepperrell, Wendell, and Hancock gave it their support. Shirley used the French war, land and timber speculation, expanding trade, and the advantages of office to keep his friends together. Somehow he had the capacity in these matters to transform petty issues of rewards into imperial policies of importance. The coalition, therefore, was fed a rich diet of profits and was challenged at the same time to noble purpose.

While personal politics certainly set political patterns, there were nevertheless substantial public issues which had to be confronted. The Governor was ever ready to espouse causes to win support. His strength in most country areas was gained early and fluctuated very little during the years of his administration. Much the same could be said of the towns, with the exception of Boston, which gave him some trouble. The riot of 1747, the disturbances over currency reform in 1749, and the belligerence of James Allen in 1754 were critical examples of an adverse public reaction. Even so, Boston's opposition never seriously threatened the life of the administration, and Shirley, personally, never experienced any sustained hostility.

Shirley's accomplishments would have been less than they were if his talents as a spoilsman had not been joined to rare skill and integrity as an administrator. He believed government to be a trust, in which the talented and wealthy citizen should guide the general public towards goals that would promote the welfare of the colony and, of course, the empire. In his own execution of this honorable task, however, he never lost sight of the necessity for sound techniques. He took care to study the needs of the colonies, and he personally attended to many administrative details, thus gaining for his government the benefit of his knowledge of law and his personal insight into the motives of the people with whom he dealt. His gift for tactful behavior took the heat out of many a controversy, and he was a natural-born compromiser who never failed to take public opinion into account. Again and again he was content to accept merely the best bill he could get from the legislature, trusting that the future would provide better opportunities. He planned his moves with the utmost care, and in the support of essential measures he rallied his forces to his side.

Shirley's sense of duty included standards of honesty that were rarely attained by his fellow governors. His son Jack once observed to Governor Robert Hunter Morris that Shirley refused to appoint family members to military staff duties because he deemed it a violation of public responsibility. There was a line of morality which he drew for himself and never violated. He left both governorships with little more than what he saved from salary and fees. It is true that his friends Apthorp and Hancock made fortunes and his sons-in-law benefited greatly. He used the distribution of spoils to manage others, but he himself sought position and honor rather than wealth. His sense of honesty also extended broadly to his conduct of office. He worked hard and he compelled his associates to do the same, and he was never accused of holding office as a sinecure. Indeed, he was criticized for his desire to do more than was required of him: of exerting too much influence, of speaking out on issues that were only indirectly the business of Massachusetts, of stretching his military powers to accomplish worthwhile tasks for the empire.

After Shirley left Massachusetts in 1756, the position of the British governor in the colony was never the same. His

successors, Pownall and Bernard, did not have the war contracts, the opportunities for military glory, or the popular
issue of Canadian conquest to hold their supporters; nor did
they take the same delight as Shirley in manipulating patronage in behalf of policy and power. After 1756, the British
governors became less and less popular as public figures, and
when the threads of mutual advantage that bound the empire
were cut in the next decade, ideals of independence overshadowed the ideals of empire. Politics were divided by the
ocean, and the importance of the governor as a colonial leader
declined. Few Revolutionaries cared to recall that in earlier
days it was possible to live and prosper under a British king
and governor; few liked to remember the day in 1756 when
the Massachusetts General Court paid tribute to British Governor Shirley in these affectionate words, which may also
stand as his epitaph: "The affairs of this Province have been
so wisely conducted by your Excellency that your name ought
to be ever dear to the inhabitants."[46]

46. Lawrence H. Gipson, *The British Empire Before the American Revolution*, VI, 211.

Bibliographical Essay

When George Arthur Wood published *William Shirley: Governor of Massachusetts, 1741-1756* (New York, 1920), he had planned a second volume to complete the account of Shirley's governorship. A heavy teaching schedule and an early death frustrated these plans. Wood had, however, drawn from an enormous collection of political and economic materials, and he set the pattern of his entire study in the first volume. Like many historians, I have regretted that Wood could not finish his study; especially when I was working on my biography of Thomas Pownall I needed a bibliographical guide as trustworthy as Wood's notes. In consulting them later for other purposes, I was impressed that he had investigated almost all the sources then available. Though he did not consult many judicial records in the Suffolk County Court House and the published collections of the Sussex Archaelogical Society, he used manuscripts in the Massachusetts Archives, the British Public Record Office, and the Library of Congress and examined most published pamphlets and printed materials. He was apparently not interested in colonial newspapers and manuscripts in private hands.

Since the publication of his history, many vast collections now at the Massachusetts Historical Society and the Huntington Library have been opened to scholars. Most of these documents are invaluable to an evaluation of Shirley's motives, the influence of his family and friends, and the weight of patronage in governmental decisions. The most useful of these newer manuscript collections are the Shirley Papers in the Massachusetts Historical Society, particularly the correspondence between Shirley and Waldo and Shirley and Thomlinson, and the Loudoun Papers in the Huntington Library. Both have sufficient personal material to illuminate the hundreds of official papers in public depositories. They are good on politics, merchant affairs, and Shirley's relations with the Whig politicians. The vast assortment of Hancock Papers in the Baker Library at the Harvard Business School is undoubtedly the best collection of merchant papers for Shirley's administration.

Hancock was unusually outspoken in his personal letters, and his correspondence with Kilby, in particular, gives a running account of business and political developments for Massachusetts from the 1730's until his death in 1764. These papers, with Hancock Papers at the Massachusetts Historical Society and the Boston Public Library, form the core of W. T. Baxter's *The House of Hancock: Business in Boston, 1724-1775* (Cambridge, 1945). Baxter was more interested in Hancock's business methods and successes than in his politics and personal life, and there is, therefore, comparatively little on political dealings with Shirley. Although the Baker Library has other merchant collections for this period, most are incomplete. The majority of the Erving papers, for example, have been destroyed, and the few at the Baker Library, the Massachusetts Historical Society, and in possession of the Erving family are inadequate to the enormous importance of the family's ventures.

There are some items relating to business in the Wendell and Pepperrell collections at the Massachusetts Historical Society and in the smaller manuscript collections at the Boston Public Library. The best use of the Pepperrell Papers was made by Byron Fairchild in his *Messrs. William Pepperrell: Merchants at Piscataqua* (Ithaca, 1954), the story of the Pepperrell family to 1759. The Hutchinson business papers apparently have been scattered, though the Massachusetts Historical Society has several small collections. Malcolm Freiberg has published an excellent article on "Thomas Hutchinson: The First Fifty Years (1711-1761)" in the *William and Mary Quarterly*, 15 (1958), 35-55, in which he evaluates this and other evidence.

Some important military collections were unavailable to George Wood. The Clinton Manuscripts at the Clements Library contain a correspondence between Clinton and Shirley that ranges in topics from military policy to family matters and is most illuminating for the years 1748 and 1749. The Livingston Papers at the Museum of the City of New York give excellent descriptions of merchant opinion. Probably the best military collections are the Belknap, Pepperrell, and Williams papers at the Massachusetts Historical Society. The Parkman Transcripts, which Wood used as a basic collection, contain an excellent selection of Shirley's correspondence with the Duke of Newcastle and Sir Thomas Robinson. The Huntington Library has a small collection of the Pelham Manuscripts. The Admiralty Records are located at the Public Record Office (480), British Museum (3817-18), and the Library of Congress (Court Records of Massachusetts).

For Shirley's life after 1749, I had no guide such as Wood's bibliography. Shirley's career as a diplomat was described by Max Savelle in *The Diplomatic History of the Canadian Boundary, 1749-63* (New Haven, 1940) and Lawrence H. Gipson in volume five of *The British Empire Before the American Revolution*, 9 vols. (Caldwell, Idaho and New York, 1936-56). Both are less concerned with Shirley personally than with his actions as a commissioner, but they list the major sources of material. Mildmay's letter books are owned by the Clements Library. Much of the diplomatic correspondence is contained in series 323 at the Public Record Office. Important personal letters are in the Shirley-Willard correspondence at the Massachusetts Archives in the State House.

The vast collections of the Society for the Propagation of the Gospel contain approximately one hundred letters by Shirley and the ministers of the Church. William Stevens Perry has a selection of these documents in his *Papers Relating to the History of the Church of Massachusetts* (Privately Printed, 1873), and Henry Wilder Foote, *Annals of King's Chapel: From the Puritan Age to the Present Day*, 3 vols. (Boston, 1882-1940), has much useful information on church and state relations.. Of the more recent accounts of religion in Massachusetts, those of Joseph Haroutunian, *Piety Versus Moralism* (New York, 1932), and Ola Elizabeth Winslow, *Jonathan Edwards, 1703-1758* (New York, 1940) and *Meetinghouse Hill, 1630-1783* (New York, 1952), are valuable in understanding religious developments. Edwin Scott Gaustad's *The Great Awakenin New England* (New York, 1957) has a most penetrating discussion of religious opinions, but does not relate religious developments to the political and economic events of the day.

For Shirley's later years as governor, from 1753 to 1756, the *Journals of the House of Representatives of Massachusetts* (Boston, 1919—in progress) and the unpublished Council Records at the Massachusetts Archives are the best day-to-day accounts. The Maine Historical Society *Collections*, 3rd Ser. (Portland, 1831-1947) and the Baxter Manuscripts in the *Documentary History of the State of Maine: The Baxter Manuscripts*, ed. James Phinney Baxter (Maine Hist. Soc., *Collections*, 2nd Ser., vols. 4-24 [Portland, 1889-1916]) give good evidence of imperial expansion and the popular uneasiness over the undefended frontier. These vast published collections should be supplemented by the Parkman Transcripts at the Massachusetts Historical Society and the military papers at the Massachusetts Archives. The debates in the General Court for colonial union are not in existence, but there are some references to committee actions and legislative votes, particularly in volume four of the Massachusetts Archives. Lawrence H. Gipson has used these papers in his "Thomas Hutchinson and the Framing of the Albany Plan of Union, 1754," *Pennsylvania Magazine of History and Biography*, 74 (1950), 5-35.

The military side of Shirley's career for the years after 1753 is exceedingly well documented. The best single source is volume forty-six in series five at the Public Record Office, but the British Museum's Newcastle and Hardwicke papers are nearly as valuable for the correspondence of Robinson and Fox with Shirley. The Sterling Papers at the New-York Historical Society and the Loudoun Papers at the Huntington Library have an enormous body of information on contracting, military policy, and colonial relations. The Loudoun Papers have an abundance of Shirley letters, some duplicating collections in the Public Record Office and British Museum, but they are particularly important for the years 1756 and 1757. Stanley Pargellis used these Loudoun Papers extensively in writing *Lord Loudoun in North America* (New Haven, 1933). His account of Shirley's career is hostile and has been partly corrected by Gipson in volume six of *The British Empire Before the American Revolution*.

The best published sources for these years of military combat are James Sullivan and A. C. Flick, eds., *The Papers of Sir William Johnson*, 10 vols.(Albany, 1921-51). John Shirley's descriptive letters to Governor Robert Hunter Morris are printed in series one, volume two, of the *Pennsylvania Archives*, which includes a mine of other information on politics and military affairs. Both the *Proceedings* and the *Collections* of the Massachusetts Historical Society, together with the *Publications* of the Colonial Society of Massachusetts, are invaluable sources. E. B. O'Callaghan and Berthold Fernolds, eds., *Documents Relative to the Colonial History of the State of New York*, 15 vols. (Albany, 1856-87) holds an enormity of material basic to any study of the period.

For Shirley's later career in England and the Bahamas, the manuscripts of the Public Record Office are essential. The Amherst Papers (W.O. 34, 71-73) contain the military records on Shirley's contracting, and some correspondence on their settlement. Shirley's activities in the Bahamas can be followed in Colonial Office 23 (volumes 16, 18, and 21) and 24 (volume 33), which are the official proceedings of the legislature. The Shelburne Papers at the Clements Library supplement this material.

Shirley's correspondence was unusually heavy during most years of his life. Selections from it have been published in Henry Lincoln, ed., *The Correspondence of William Shirley*, 2 vols. (New York, 1912). No letters from Shirley's boyhood until his arrival in America and from 1761 until his death were uncovered by

Lincoln; nor have I, after years of searching, been able to find more than a half dozen, and these are for the period after 1761. Very few Shirley letters and papers are privately held. I have a few unimportant items on the Governor's military and financial affairs. Justin Turner of Westwood, California, owns a letter or two; Joseph W. P. Frost of Kittery Point, Maine, has some documents on Shirley and the Louisbourg campaign; and Gordon T. Banks of Shirley, Massachusetts, has collected Shirley materials for many years. James Gore King of New York City is the only member of the Erving-Shirley family that presently retains an interest in the Governor. He has some Erving letters and part of Frances Shirley's household account book.

Descendants of John and Maria Erving own some very fine portraits of the Shirley family. Mr. King has portraits of Frances Shirley and Maria Shirley (by Smibert); Mrs. Norman J. Marsh of Mount Kisco, New York, owns the Hudson portrait of William Shirley now hanging in the Wadsworth Athenaeum at Hartford, Connecticut; and Mr. Erving Pruyn of Colebrook, Connecticut, has a portrait of Frances Shirley and of John and Maria Erving. John Erving Cooper of Los Gatos, California, has paintings of Governor Shirley and Thomas Shirley.

Newspaper coverage in eighteenth-century America was particularly good in Boston. *The Boston Weekly News-Letter* and *The Boston Evening-Post* give excellent accounts of week-to-week happenings. Probably *The Independent Advertiser* (Boston) is the most interesting, because it was hostile to the Governor, and thus revealed some reactions to his policies. Unfortunately, it had a short life of two years.

Turning from primary materials for Shirley's later years, I want to mention first those invaluable and delightfully written volumes of *Sibley's Harvard Graduates*, 8 vols. (Boston, 1873-1951) by Clifford K. Shipton. His essays on Eliakim Hutchinson, Jonathan Belcher, and Robert Hale were most helpful in discovering both personalities and manuscripts. Robert E. Brown's *Middle-Class Democracy and the Revolution in Massachusetts, 1691-1780* (Ithaca, 1955), was most useful as was Carl Bridenbaugh's *Cities in Revolt: Urban Life in America 1743-1776* (New York, 1955). For the bank crisis in Massachusetts I relied upon the works of Andrew McFarland Davis, particularly his "Provincial Banks: Land and Silver," in the Colonial Society of Massachusetts, *Publications,* 3 (1900), 2-40. I also used George Athan Billias's recent essay on *The Massachusetts Land Bankers of 1740* (Orono, Me., 1959).

One cannot pass by the extraordinary work of Lawrence H. Gipson, whose *The British Empire Before the American Revolution* has already been noticed. In volume six he gives an eloquent defense of Shirley's conduct as military commander, in the best published analysis of the military situation for the years 1755-57. A different interpretation of Shirley's position in British politics is found in my "Imperialism in Massachusetts during the Governorship of William Shirley, 1741-1756," in *The Huntington Library Quarterly*, 23 (1960), 217-36, and "Cold War Diplomacy and the Seven Years' War," in the *World Affairs Quarterly*, 26 (1956), 323-37. My "Succession Politics in Massachusetts, 1730-1741," in *The William and Mary Quarterly*, 15 (1958), 508-20, extends the story into Shirley's early career. My *Thomas Pownall: British Defender of American Liberty* (Glendale, Calif., 1951) reveals the part Shirley's critics had in undermining the Governor's reputation. The best published essay on Shirley's Niagara campaign is by Theodore Thayer in *The William and Mary Quarterly*, 14 (1957), 31-46.

Many other published and documentary collections could be cited to illustrate the extensive materials available on Shirley's life, but it is enough to indicate the variety of these documents and the important places where they can be found. No particular reference was made to the Library of Congress and the Canadian Archives, but their extensive transcript collections were frequently consulted. The film resources of the University of California at Los Angeles were also used for the S.P.G. and Fulham Palace Manuscripts. Collections at the American Antiquarian Society, the Connecticut Archives, Essex Institute, and the University of Nottingham were important for general information, though not always cited in this biography. Since 1920, when Arthur Wood's *William Shirley* was published, new manuscripts have been constantly turning up. It would be a welcome addition to our knowledge if materials on Shirley's early life are located.

APPENDIX A

JUDGES OF THE SUPERIOR COURT, 1740-1756

Benjamin Lynde, 1712-28, chief: 1728-45
Paul Dudley, 1718-45, chief: 1745-51
Jonathan Remington, 1733-45
Richard Saltonstall, 1736-56
Stephen Sewall, 1739-52, chief: 1752-60
Nathaniel Hubbard, 1745-47
Benjamin Lynde, Jr., 1745-71, chief: 1771-72
John Cushing, 1747-71
Chambers Russell, 1752-66
Peter Oliver, 1756-72, chief: 1772-Revolution

JUDGES OF THE COMMON PLEAS, 1740-1756

Note: Lists of judges for Barnstable, Dukes, Nantucket, and York counties cannot be provided because information is incomplete and inaccurate. The tenure of the chief justice of Bristol County is approximate.

BRISTOL COUNTY
George Leonard, 1725-30, 1733-40, 1746-60, chief: 1760-75
Seth Williams, 1724-29, chief: 1730-60
Nathaniel Hubbard, 1728-45
Thomas Church, 1729-45
Job Almy, 1740-47
Stephen Paine, 1746-49
Ephraim Leonard, 1747-75
Stephen Leonard, 1747-?
Samuel Willis, 1749-60

ESSEX COUNTY
Timothy Lindall, 1729-32, chief: 1732-54
Thomas Berry, 1733-54, chief: 1754-56
Benjamin Marston, 1737-54
Benjamin Lynde, Jr., 1739-46
John Choate, 1746-56, chief: 1756-66
Henry Gibbs, 1754-59

John Tasker, 1755-61
Benjamin Pickman, 1756-61

HAMPSHIRE COUNTY

Samuel Partridge, 1692-1740
John Stoddard, 1748-?
Ebenezer Pomeroy, 1735-53
Eleazer Porter, 1737-57
William Pynchon, Sr., 1738-42
Timothy Dwight, 1737-41, 1748-57
Joseph Pynchon, 1741-52
Ephraim Williams, 1741-49
Josiah Dwight, 1750-68
Joseph Dwight, 1753-61

MIDDLESEX COUNTY

Jonathan Dowse, 1719-33, chief: 1733-41
Francis Fullam, 1719-41, chief: 1741-55
Francis Foxcroft, 1737-64
Thomas Greaves, 1733-38, 1739-47
Samuel Danforth, 1741-55, chief: 1755-76
Chambers Russell, 1747-52
Andrew Boardman, 1752-69
William Lawrence, 1755-63

PLYMOUTH COUNTY

Isaac Lothrop, 1721-31, chief: 1739-43
Josiah Cotton, 1729-47
Nicholas Sever, 1731-43, chief: 1743-62
John Cushing, 1738-47
Thomas Clapp, 1743-70
Peter Oliver, 1748-56
Isaac Lothrop, 1748-49
Elijah Cushing, 1751-62
Thomas Foster, 1756-75

SUFFOLK COUNTY

Adam Winthrop, 1715-41
Edward Hutchinson, 1723-31, chief: 1740-52
William Dudley, 1728-31, 1733-43
Anthony Stoddard, 1733-48
Eliakim Hutchinson, 1741-52, chief: 1752-75
Edward Winslow, 1743-53
Samuel Watts, 1748-70

Thomas Hutchinson, 1752-58
Samuel Welles, 1755-70

WORCESTER COUNTY

John Chandler, chief: 1731-43
Joseph Wilder, 1731-43, chief: 1743-57
William Ward, 1731-45
William Jenison, 1731-43
Joseph Dwight, 1743-53
Samuel Willard, 1743-53
Nahum Ward, 1745-62
Edward Hartwell, 1752-62
Jonas Rice, 1753-?
John Chandler, Jr., 1754-62
Thomas Steele, 1756-75

APPENDIX B

MEMBERS OF THE MASSACHUSETTS COUNCIL, 1738-1759

Name	Years of service	Expelled by Governor Belcher (B) or by the Legislature (L)
Bill, Richard	1738-42	
Berry, Thomas	1738-41, 1743-51	L
Bourne, Melatiah	1738-40	
Burrill, Ebenezer	1738-41, 1742-44, 1746	L
Came, Samuel	1738-42	
Cushing, John	1738-?	
Dudley, William	1738-41, 1742-44	L
Dummer, William	1738-40	
*Foxcroft, Francis	1738-58	
Hubbard, Nathaniel	1738-41, 1742-46	L
Hutchinson, Edward	1738-41	L
Hutchinson, Thomas	1738-40	
Jeffries, John	1738-45	
Lewis, Ezekiel	1738-41, 1742, 1747-53	L
Lynde, Benjamin, Jr.	1738-41, 1743-?	L
Moulton, Jeremiah	1738-52	
Osborn, John	1738-41, 1742-?	L
Pepperrell, William	1738-?	
Remington, Jonathan	1738-41	L
Russell, Daniel	1738-41, 1742, 1744-57	L
*Stoddard, Anthony	1738-43	
Stoddard, John	1738-?	
Turner, John	1738-41	L
Welles, Samuel	1738-41, 1747-49	L
Wendell, Jacob	1738-?	
Wilder, Joseph	1738-41, 1742-53	L
Willard, Josiah	1738-56	
Williams, Seth	1738-40	
Danforth, Samuel	1739-?	
Dudley, Paul	1739, 1740	B
Brown, William	1740-41, 1744-46	L
Gorham, Shubal	1740-44	

Name	Years of service	Expelled by Governor Belcher (B) or by the Legislature (L)
Little, Isaac	1740, 1743	B(1740)
Adams, Samuel	1741	B
Burchstead, Henry	1741	B
Clark, John	1741	B
Epes, Daniel	1741	B
Foye, William	1741-52	
Goddard, Edward	1741	B
Greenleaf, John	1741-57	
Hatch, Estes	1741	B
Minot, James	1741, 1746-59	
Norton, Thomas	1741	B
Otis, John	1741, 1747-57	B
Read, John	1741-43	
Stoddard, William	1741	B
White, Samuel	1741	B
Wilder, Ephraim	1741	B
Allen, James	1742	
Dwight, Joseph	1742-47	
Hill, John	1742-?	
Leonard, George	1742-?	
Quincy, John	1742, 1747-54	
Waldo, Samuel	1742-46, 1758	
Watts, Samuel	1742-?	
Bourne, Sylvanus	1743-?	
Chandler, John	1743-?	
Cheever, Ezekiel	1743-?	
Saltonstall, Richard	1743-46	
Bowdoin, James	1744-47	
**Hutchinson, Eliakim	1744-47	L
Wheelwright, John	1745-55	
Bradford, Perez	1746	
*Oliver, Andrew	1746-?	
Pynchon, Joseph	1747-?	
Hutchinson, Thomas	1749-?	
Royal, Isaac	1751-?	
Sewall, Stephen	1751-?	
Fox, Jabez	1752-55	
Lincoln, Benjamin	1753-?	
Porter, Eleazer	1753-58	
**Erving, John	1754-?	
Brattle, William	1755-?	

Name	Years of service	Expelled by Governor Belcher (B) or by the Legislature (L)
Cutt, Richard	1755-59	
Pickman, Benjamin	1756-59	
**Bowdoin, James, Jr.	1757-?	
Bradford, Gamaliel	1757-?	
Hooper, Robert	1757-59	
Hancock, Thomas	1758	
Hubbard, Thomas	1759-?	
*Oliver, Peter	1759-?	
Plaisted, Icabod	1759-?	
Russell, Chambers	1759-?	

* Related to Governor Belcher.
** Related to Governor Shirley.

Index

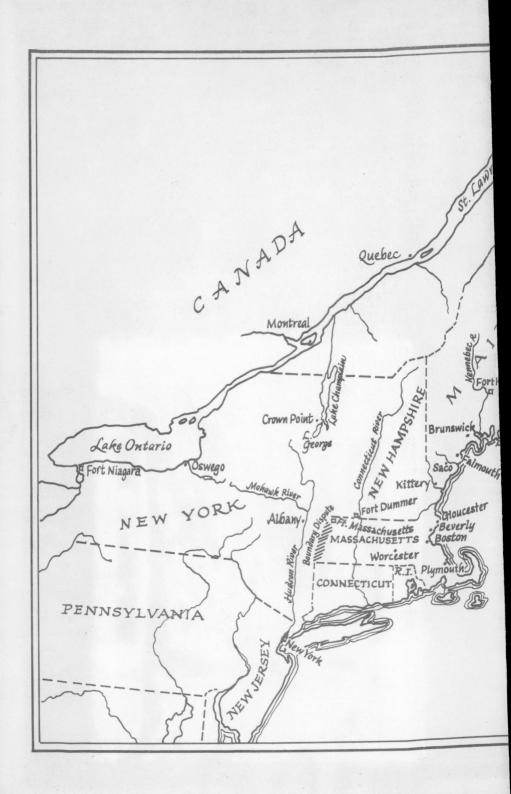